Microsoft®
Access 2000
At a Glance

D1370977

Microsoft Press

Microsoft Access 2000 At a Glance

PUBLISHED by **Microsoft Press**
A Division of Microsoft Corporation
One Microsoft Way
Redmond, Washington 98052-6399

Library of Congress Cataloging-in-Publication Data
Microsoft Access 2000 At a Glance. Perspection, Inc.
        p.   cm.
    Includes index.
    ISBN 1-57231-946-1
    1. Microsoft Access.   2. Database management.   I. Perspection, Inc.
  QA76.9.D3M5568   1999
  005.75'65—dc21
                                                    98-48183
                                                      CIP

Printed and bound in the United States of America.

2 3 4 5 6 7 8 9   QEQE   4 3 2 1 0 9

Distributed in Canada by ITP Nelson, a division of Thomson Canada limited.

A CIP catalog record for this book is available from the British Library.

Microsoft Press books are available through booksellers and distributors worldwide. For further information about international editions, contact your local Microsoft Corporation office. Or contact Microsoft Press International directly at fax (425) 936-7329. Visit our Web site at mspress.microsoft.com.

For Perspection, Inc.
Writers: Joan and Patrick Carey
Managing Editor: Steven M. Johnson
Series Editor: Jane E. Pedicini
Production Editor: David W. Beskeen
Developmental Editor: Joan Carey
Technical Editor: Maria Pinto

For Microsoft Press
Acquisitions Editors: Kim Fryer; Susanne Forderer
Project Editor: Jenny Moss Benson

Contents

Start Access.
See page 8

Work with database objects.
See page 22

Create a database.
See page 30

Detect and repair problems.
See page 35

Create tables with the
Table Wizard.
See page 42

*"How do I create
input masks?"*

See page 62

"How do I use filters to view records?"

See page 92

Create a query using the
Query Wizard.
See page 98

Find unmatched records.
See page 109

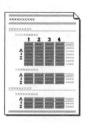

Create a report using the
Report Wizard.
See page 120

Create mailing labels.
See page 130

Work with form controls.
See page 141

"How do I group controls?"

See page 162

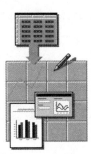

Insert a chart.
See page 176

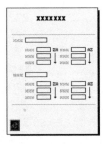

Create data access pages.
See page 198

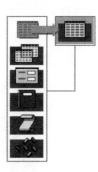

Split a database.
See page 221

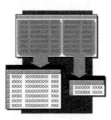

Analyze a database.
See page 222

"How do I learn to customize the menu bar?"

See page 232

"How do I assign a macro to a button?"

See page 242

"How do I create a custom function?"

See page 254

Acknowledgments

The task of creating any book requires the talents of many hardworking people pulling together to meet almost impossible demands. For their effort and commitment, we'd like to thank the outstanding team responsible for making this book possible: the writers, Joan and Patrick Carey; the series editor, Jane Pedicini; the developmental editor, Joan Carey; the technical editor, Maria Pinto; the production team, Gary Bellig and Tracy Teyler; and the indexer, Michael Brackney.

At Microsoft Press, we'd like to thank Kim Fryer and Susanne Forderer for the opportunity to undertake this project, and Jenny Benson for project editing and overall help when needed most.

Perspection

Perspection

Perspection, Inc., is a software training company committed to providing information to help people communicate, make decisions, and solve problems. Perspection writes and produces software training books, and develops interactive multimedia applications for Windows-based and Macintosh personal computers.

Microsoft Access 2000 At a Glance incorporates Perspection's training expertise to ensure that you'll receive the maximum return on your time. With this straightforward, easy-to-read reference tool, you'll get the information you need when you need it. You'll focus on the skills that increase productivity while working at your own pace and convenience.

We invite you to visit the Perspection World Wide Web site. You can visit us at:

http://www.perspection.com

You'll find descriptions of all of our books, additional content for our books, information about Perspection, and much more.

About This Book

Microsoft Access 2000 At a Glance is for anyone who wants to get the most from their software with the least amount of time and effort. We think you'll find this book to be a straightforward, easy-to-read, and easy-to-use reference tool. With the premise that your computer should work for you, not you for it, this book's purpose is to help you get your work done quickly and efficiently so that you take advantage of Microsoft Access 2000 while using your computer and its software to the max.

No Computerese!

Let's face it—when there's a task you don't know how to do but you need to get it done in a hurry, or when you're stuck in the middle of a task and can't figure out what to do next, there's nothing more frustrating than having to read page after page of technical background material. You want the information you need—nothing more, nothing less—and you want it now! And the information should be easy to find and understand.

That's what this book is all about. It's written in plain English—no technical jargon and no computerese. There's no single task in the book that takes more than two pages. Just look up the task in the index or the table of contents, turn to the page, and there it is. Each task introduction gives you information that is essential to performing the task, suggesting situations in which you can use the task, or providing examples of the benefit you gain from completing the procedure. The task itself is laid out step by step and accompanied by a graphic that adds visual clarity. Just read the introduction, follow the steps, look at the illustrations, and get your work done with a minimum of hassle.

You may want to turn to another task if the one you're working on has a "See Also" in the left column. Because there's a lot of overlap among tasks, we didn't want to keep repeating ourselves; you might find more elementary or more advanced tasks laid out on the pages referenced. We wanted to bring you through the tasks in such a way that they would make sense to you. We've also added some useful tips here and there and offered a "Try This" once in a while to give you a context in which to use the task. But, by and large, we've tried to remain true to the heart and soul of the book, which is that information you need should be available to you *at a glance*.

What's New

If you're looking for what's new in Access 2000, just look for our new icon: **New** 2000. We've inserted it throughout this book. You will find the new icon in the table of contents so you can quickly and easily identify new or improved features in Access. You will also find the new icon on the first page of each section. There it will serve as a handy reminder of the latest improvements in Access as you move from one task to another.

Useful Tasks...

Whether you use Access for work, play, or some of each, we've tried to pack this book with procedures for everything we could think of that you might want to do, from the simplest tasks to some of the more esoteric ones.

...And the Easiest Way to Do Them

Another thing we've tried to do in *Microsoft Access 2000 At a Glance* is to find and document the easiest way to accomplish a task. Access often provides many ways to accomplish a single result, which can be daunting or delightful, depending on the way you like to work. If you tend to stick with one favorite and familiar approach, we think the methods described in this book are the way to go. If you prefer to try out alternative techniques, go ahead! The intuitiveness of Access invites exploration, and you're likely to discover ways of doing things that you think are easier or that you like better. If you do, that's great! It's exactly what the creators of Access had in mind when they provided so many alternatives.

A Quick Overview

You don't have to read this book in any particular order. The book is designed so that you can jump in, get the information you need, and then close the book, keeping it near your computer until the next time you need it. But that doesn't mean we scattered the information about with wild abandon. If you were to read the book from front to back, you'd find a logical progression from the simple tasks to the more complex ones. Here's a quick overview.

First, we assume that Access is already installed on your computer. If it's not, the Setup Wizard makes installation so simple that you won't need our help anyway. So, unlike most computer books, this one doesn't start out with installation instructions and a list of system requirements. You've already got that under control.

Section 2 covers the basics: starting Access; opening a database; working with menus, toolbars, and dialog boxes; and using a variety of ways to get the help you need when you need it.

Section 3 describes how to create a database the easy way using a wizard and how to work with the database objects you find in the database you created.

Sections 4 and 5 introduce creating a custom database from scratch: how you plan the structure of your database and how you design tables and fields so they store your data most efficiently.

Section 6 describes how to work with the tables that store your data: how to locate data; how to enter and edit it accurately; and how to display the columns and rows that contain your data.

Section 7 describes how to locate and display only the records you need using queries. The section also describes specific queries that allow you to add records, create tables, update records, and delete records.

Sections 8 through 10 introduce you to forms and reports. These tasks include creating forms and reports with wizards or from scratch, creating mailing labels, and enhancing the appearance of forms and reports with color, graphics, lines, borders, and other special effects.

Section 11 describes how to use objects from other programs, such as pictures, charts, and maps, in your database; how to move data in and out of an Access database in a variety of formats; and how to work with data in other programs such as Microsoft Word or Microsoft Excel.

Section 12 describes how you can take advantage of the Internet and the World Wide Web to make Web resources available from your database and to make the data in your database accessible to the Web.

Section 13 describes how to use database analysis and management tools; how to make a database available to multiple users and ensuring database security; database reduction, replication, and repair techniques; and additional tools that extend your control over your database.

Sections 14 and 15 describe techniques that help you maximize the usefulness and efficiency of your database by customizing the Access environment and creating macros and modules that extend the power of Access beyond its existing set of commands.

A Final Word (or Two)

We had three goals in writing this book. We want our book to help you:

◆ Do all the things you want to do with Access 2000.

◆ Discover how to do things you didn't know you wanted to do with Access 2000.

◆ Enjoy doing your work with Access 2000.

Our "thank you" for buying this book is the achievement of those goals. We hope you'll have as much fun using *Microsoft Access 2000 At a Glance* as we've had writing it. The best way to learn is by doing, and that's what we hope you'll get from this book.

Jump right in!

Getting Started with Microsoft Access 2000

Microsoft Access 2000 is a database program that allows you to:

◆ Store an almost limitless amount of information.

◆ Organize information in a way that makes sense for how you work.

◆ Retrieve information based on selection criteria you specify.

◆ Create forms that make it easier to enter information.

◆ Generate meaningful and insightful reports that can combine data, text, graphics, and other objects.

◆ Share information easily over the Web.

What Is a Database?

Database is a rather technical word for a collection of information that is organized as a list. This definition might be oversimplified, but whenever you use or make a list of information—names, addresses, products, customers, or invoices—you are using a database. A database that you store on your computer, however, is much more flexible and powerful than a simple list you keep on paper, in your card file, or in your address book.

Understanding How Databases Store Data

Storing Data on a Computer

Some lists can serve a much more useful purpose when stored on a computer. For example, the names, addresses, and phone numbers you jot down on cards or in a paper address book can only be used when you have the paper list in your hand. Suppose you currently store names and addresses on cards. All the information about a particular person is stored in one place.

This information is shared by all people on the card.

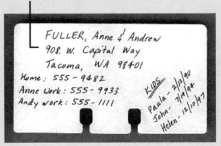

```
FULLER, Anne & Andrew
908 W. Capital Way
Tacoma, WA 98401
Home: 555-9482
Anne Work: 555-9933
Andy work: 555-1111

KIDS:
Paula - 2/3/90
John - 7/19/94
Helen - 12/10/97
```

If you store that list on a computer, however, you can do much more with it than just refer to it. For example, you can generate lists of your most important phone numbers to put next to every phone in the house, you

can print mailing labels for greeting cards, you can generate lists of this month's birthdays, and so on.

There are a number of ways to store lists on a computer. For example, you can store a list in a Microsoft Word table or on a Microsoft Excel worksheet.

Duplicate information

Last Name	First Name	Address	City	State	Zip	Phone Work	Phone Home	Birthday
Fuller	Anne	908 W. Capital Way	Tacoma	WA	98401	555-9933	555-9482	
Fuller	Andrew	908 W. Capital Way	Tacoma	WA	98401	555-1111	555-9482	
Fuller	Paula	908 W. Capital Way	Tacoma	WA	98401		555-9482	12/13/90
Fuller	John	908 W. Capital Way	Tacoma	WA	98401		555-9482	7/19/94
Fuller	Helen	908 W. Capital Way	Tacoma	WA	98401		555-9482	12/10/97

If you place this information in a Word table or on an Excel spreadsheet, you are faced with a problem: you end up repeating some of the information. Consider what happens if a family moves or a last name is changed. You have to ensure that information is updated everywhere it's stored. For a small list that might not matter, but for a large list with information that requires constant updating (such as an address list), it is a huge task to keep data up-to-date in this way.

Storing Data in a Database

If, on the other hand, you save address information in an Access database, you can ensure that each piece of information is entered only once.

You assign each piece of information a unique identification number, and any time you want to include or change that information again, you refer to the number.

Address information for the entire family appears only once, with Address ID 2.

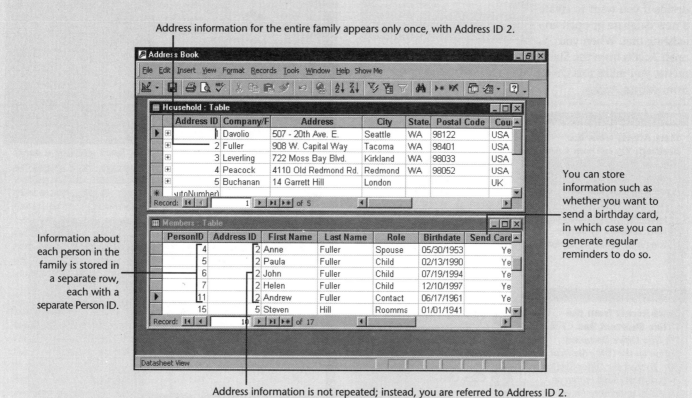

Information about each person in the family is stored in a separate row, each with a separate Person ID.

You can store information such as whether you want to send a birthday card, in which case you can generate regular reminders to do so.

Address information is not repeated; instead, you are referred to Address ID 2.

Viewing the Access Window

When you open a database, the Access program window opens and displays either the Database window or a switchboard. The *Database window* displays the database objects. A *switchboard* is a window that gives easy access to the most common actions a database user might need to take.

TIP

View the Database window. *All the databases that come with Access 2000 open with a switchboard. You can open the Database window by clicking the Window menu and then clicking the name of the database.*

SEE ALSO

See "Customizing Access Startup" on page 235 for information on hiding or displaying the Database window.

Parts of the Access Window

◆ The *title bar* displays the name of the open database.

◆ The *menu bar* contains menus that represent groups of related commands.

◆ The *Database toolbar* contains buttons that you can click to carry out commands.

◆ The *status bar* displays information about the items you click or the actions you take.

Title bar   Menu bar   Database toolbar

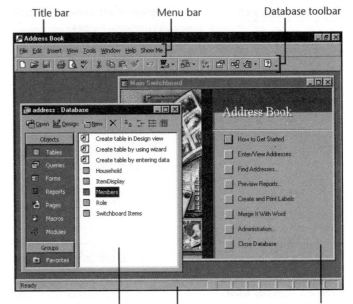

Database window for the Address Book database that comes with Access 2000   Status bar   Switchboard for the Address Book database

Viewing Objects in the Database Window

Access databases can contain seven database object types. The table on this page identifies the database objects that you use when creating a database

TIP

Create a shortcut to a database object. *You can create a shortcut to a database object from a folder or the desktop by dragging the object icon from the Database window to the folder or desktop. Make sure the Access window is not maximized before you attempt to drag the object icon.*

TIP

Show or hide the Objects or Groups bar. *When you click the Objects or Groups bar, the database objects associated with it appear underneath. When you show one, the other is hidden.*

View a List of Database Objects

1 Open the database whose objects you want to view.

2 If necessary, click the Window menu, and then click the name of the database.

3 Click Tables, Queries, Forms, Reports, Pages, Macros, or Modules on the Objects bar.

- ◆ The *Database window toolbar* contains buttons for commands that allow you to create, open, and manage database objects.

- ◆ The *Objects bar* lists the types of objects in a database.

- ◆ The *Groups bar* allows you to group database objects the way you want them, creating shortcuts to objects of different types.

Objects bar   Database window toolbar

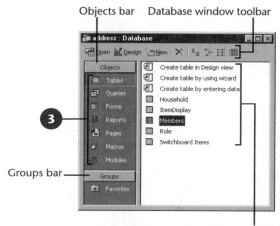

Groups bar

List of objects for the selected type (in this case, Tables)

2

DATABASE OBJECTS	
Database Object	**Description**
Tables	Grids that store related information, such as a list of customer addresses
Queries	A question you ask a database to help locate specific information
Forms	A window that is designed to help you enter information easily and accurately
Reports	Summaries of information that are designed to be readable and accessible
Pages	Separate files outside the Access database in HTML format that can be placed on the Web to facilitate sharing data with the World Wide Web community
Macros	Stored series of commands that carry out an action
Modules	Programs you can write using Microsoft Visual Basic

Working with Menus and Toolbars

You can perform most Access functions by choosing menu commands and clicking toolbar buttons. A toolbar contains buttons you can click to carry out commands you use most frequently. When you place the mouse pointer over a toolbar button, the name of the button appears in a small box called a *ScreenTip*.

Access 2000 features a personalized interface in which toolbars and menus are automatically customized to show only the commands that you use most often.

TIP

View more buttons. *When you click a button in the More Buttons drop-down arrow, it appears on the toolbar with the buttons you've used most recently.*

Select a Menu Command

1. Click a menu name on the menu bar.

2. If necessary, point to the double arrows at the bottom of the menu to show all its commands. (Commands that you don't use often might be hidden.)

3. If necessary, point to a command followed by an arrow to see a submenu of related options.

4. Click the command you want.

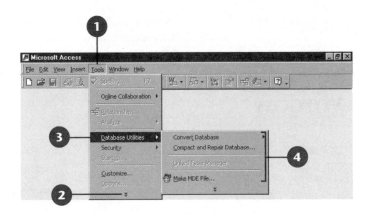

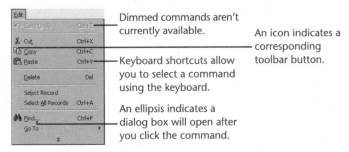

Dimmed commands aren't currently available.

Keyboard shortcuts allow you to select a command using the keyboard.

An ellipsis indicates a dialog box will open after you click the command.

An icon indicates a corresponding toolbar button.

Select a Toolbar Command

◆ Click a toolbar button to perform the command.

◆ Click the arrow next to the button to open a list of additional options, and then click the option you want.

ScreenTip

Single arrow indicates a drop-down list will open.

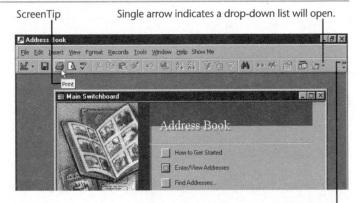

Double arrow indicates there are more buttons available.

Working with Dialog Boxes

Commands that are followed by an ellipsis (...) on a menu display a dialog box. A *dialog box* is a special window in which you can specify additional options for carrying out a command. You make your choices by typing in text boxes, clicking option buttons and check boxes, or clicking options from a drop-down list.

TRY THIS

Test your dialog box changes. *If a dialog box contains an Apply button, you can click this button to apply the changes without closing the dialog box. You can see the results of your changes and make additional changes as needed with the dialog box open.*

Select Dialog Box Options

1 Choose a command that opens a dialog box.

2 Choose the dialog box options you want.

3 Click OK to carry out the command or Cancel to cancel the command.

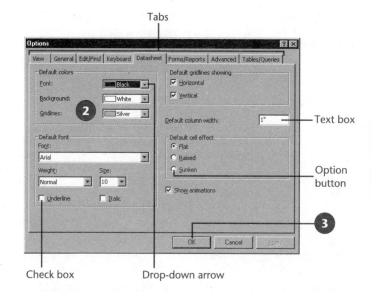

Tabs

Text box

Option button

Check box   Drop-down arrow

DIALOG BOX OPTIONS	
Option	**Description**
Tabs	Click different tabs to choose options for Access features.
Option buttons	Click one out of a mutually exclusive group to activate the feature you want.
Drop-down arrows	Click to display a list of related options.
Text boxes	Type the value you want to use, or choose it from a drop-down list.
Check boxes	Click to turn on or off a feature; unlike option buttons, you can choose as many check box options as you want.

Getting Office Assistant Help

The Access Help system provides much of the information you would expect to find in a manual or book, right on your computer screen. The *Office Assistant*, an animated helper, appears unless you have disabled it. When you click the Office Assistant, it displays topics that help you use the open window, or you can enter specific questions and it suggests topics.

Once you have selected the topic you want, the Microsoft Access Help window opens with the information you requested. You can access the Contents, Answer Wizard, and Index tabs, which guide you to find specific information.

> **TIP**
>
> **Hide the Office Assistant.**
> *Right-click the Office Assistant and then click Hide.*

Get Help with the Office Assistant

1. Click the Microsoft Access Help button on the Database toolbar.

2. Click the Office Assistant.

3. Type what you would like to do in the space provided.

4. Click Search.

5. Click a topic.

   You can click any underlined words or phrases within the topic to display a definition or more information.

6. Click the Close button.

Change Office Assistant Options

1. Right-click the Office Assistant, and then click the Options tab.

2. Click to select or clear the check boxes for the Office Assistant features you want to activate or deactivate.

3. Click the Gallery tab if you want to select a different character as the Office Assistant.

4. Click OK.

List of topics that might apply to the current window

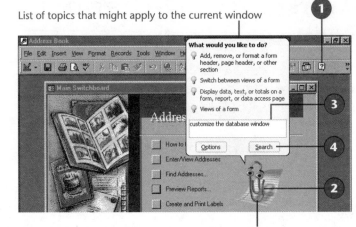

This Office Assistant's name is Clippit.

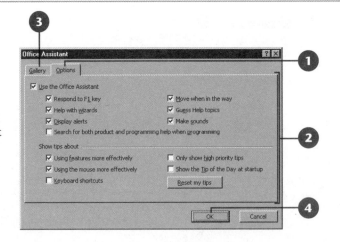

Locate Topics Using the Contents List

1. Click the Microsoft Access Help button on the Database toolbar.

2. In the Help window, click the Show button if necessary.

3. Click the Contents tab.

4. Double-click applicable folders until you locate the topic you want.

5. Click the topic you want.

6. Click the Close button.

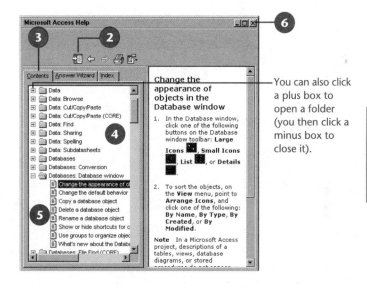

You can also click a plus box to open a folder (you then click a minus box to close it).

Search for Help Topics

1. Click the Microsoft Access Help button on the Database toolbar.

2. In the Help window, click the Show button if necessary.

3. Click the Index tab.

4. Type a keyword.

5. Click Search.

6. Click the topic you want to view.

7. Click the Close button.

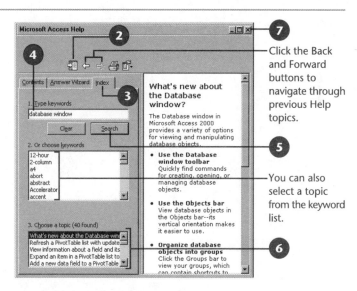

Click the Back and Forward buttons to navigate through previous Help topics.

You can also select a topic from the keyword list.

2

Getting Task-Oriented Help

A quick way to learn about Access features is to use the What's This? command on the Help menu. When you choose this command, the pointer changes to the *Help pointer*. With the Help pointer you can click different features and items to get information about them. Some dialog boxes contain a Help button. Clicking the Help button in a dialog box works the same way as clicking the What's This? command on the Help menu.

TIP

Find tips in the status bar. *Look on the status bar to find information about whatever field or window the mouse pointer is in.*

TRY THIS

Obtain topical Help. *Press F1 to display Help on the current window or action.*

Get Help with the Help Pointer

1. Click the Help menu, and then click What's This?

2. Click the item about which you want more information.

3. Click anywhere on the screen to close Help.

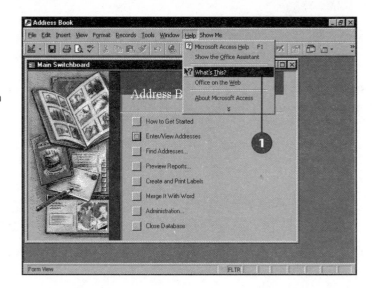

Get Help in a Dialog Box

1. Open a dialog box.

2. Click the Help button.

3. Click the item in the dialog box about which you want more information.

4. Click anywhere on the screen to close Help.

Help appears when you click with the Help pointer.

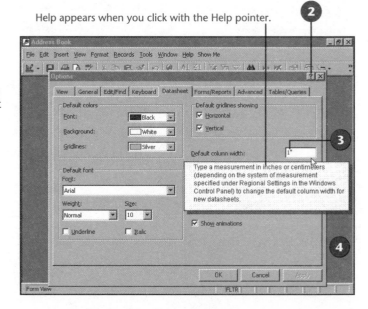

Getting Help on the Web

Because technology—not to mention people's needs—change so quickly, Microsoft provides a Web site, Office on the Web, that features the most up-to-date information on its products. Access users will find helpful information, as well as the latest templates and wizards.

When you select the Office On The Web command on the Help menu, your browser starts and displays the Office Update page. From the Office Update page you can download product updates, patches, templates, and utilities. You can also search for information, receive assistance, or connect to newsgroups on helpful topics.

Get Help from Microsoft's Web Site

1 Make sure you are connected to the Internet.

2 Click the Help menu, and then click Office On The Web.

3 Click the link for the information you want.

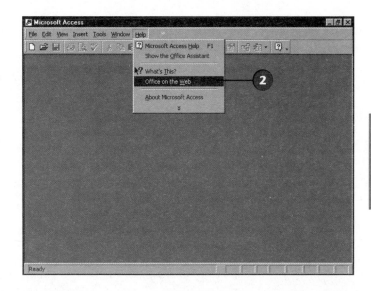

Search for Help on the Web

1 Click the Help menu, and then click Office On The Web.

2 Click Search.

3 Enter a question.

4 Click the Search button.

5 Click the link for the information you want.

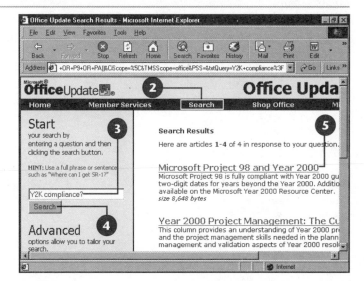

Closing a Database and Quitting Access

After you finish working in a database, you can close it. You can then choose to open another database or quit Access. If you made any changes to the structure of the database—for example, if you changed the size of any rows or columns in a table— Access prompts you to save your changes. Any changes you make to the data in a table are saved automatically as you make them. When you close a database or when you quit Access, any objects that are still open, such as tables or queries, will also be closed.

> **TIP**
>
> **Access compacts on close.**
> *Access automatically compresses a database when the file is closed. Click the Tools menu, click Options, click the General tab, click to select the Compact On Close check box, and then click OK.*

Close a Database

1 Click the Close button on the Database window.

2 If necessary, click Yes to save any changes you made or No to ignore any changes.

Quit Access

1 Click the Close button on the Access window title bar.

2 If necessary, click Yes to save any changes you made or No to ignore any changes.

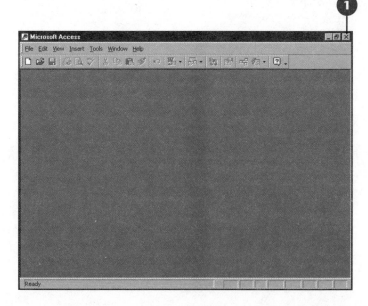

Touring Access Databases

Microsoft Access 200 helps you get started working with databases right away by providing sample database applications that you can use to store your own personal or business data. Access also offers a set of database wizards that aid you in creating common business databases. You can study these sample databases and wizards to get ideas for the databases you might want to design for other types of data that aren't covered by the existing samples and wizards.

When you are working with an existing database, however, you don't need to worry about the complexities of database design. You just need to know how to get around the database you are using. The tasks you are likely to perform with an existing database include entering and viewing data or subsets of data, creating and printing reports, and working efficiently with all the windows in front of you.

When you use Access 2000, you might find that some of the features you expect don't seem to be where you need them. Access saves space on your hard disk by initially installing only a minimum of features. If necessary, Access will prompt you to install additional features from the CD-ROM.

Opening a Sample Database

Access provides several sample database applications for you to explore and use with your own data.

If you have specialized database needs, you can study the structure of the sample databases and use them as models for your own.

Open button

SEE ALSO

See "Installing Additional Features" on page 36 for information on installing Access features on first use.

TRY THIS

Use switchboard Help.
Access sample databases include their own online Help. Click the How To Get Started button on the sample database switchboard.

Open a Sample Database

1. Click the Open button on the Database toolbar.

2. Click the Look In drop-down arrow.

3. Open the Samples folder, located in C:/Program Files/Microsoft Office/Office.

4. Click the sample database you want to open.

5. Click the Open button.

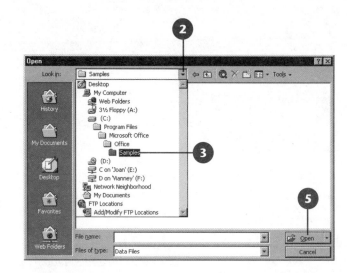

SAMPLE DATABASES	
Databases	**Description**
Northwind Traders	The Northwind Traders contains sample data and database objects for a specialty foods company. NorthwindCS allows you to set up an Access project.
Address Book	The Address Book database helps you save address and phone information, print address labels, and create reminders about special occasions.
Contact Management	The Contact Management database allows you to manage business contact information, such as addresses, records of calls, and reminders.
Household Inventory	The Household Inventory database helps you save information about possessions, serial numbers, purchase information, and charitable donations.

Using a Switchboard

The sample databases that come with Access all employ switchboards. A switchboard is a customized window that makes many features of a specific database available at the click of a button. The Address Book switchboard, for example, offers immediate access to printing mailing labels, merging addresses with a Word document, or locating an address quickly.

Often, switchboard options open forms that allow you to view or enter data, reports that allow you to see summaries of data, or queries that allow you to view subsets of data.

SEE ALSO

See "Creating a Database Switchboard" on page 226 and "Managing a Switchboard" on page 227 for information on creating and managing a switchboard for a database.

Open a Switchboard

1. Open the database. If the database contains a switchboard, it usually appears automatically when the database is opened.

2. If necessary, click the Window menu, and then click Main Switchboard to view the switchboard.

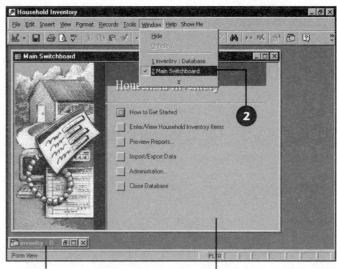

The database window appears minimized at the bottom of the program window.

The switchboard appears when you first open a sample database.

Select Switchboard Options

1. Read the descriptions on the switchboard to find the task you need to perform.

2. Click the button that corresponds to the task you want to perform.

   Access opens or starts whatever database object will help you perform that task.

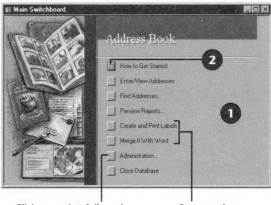

Click an option followed by an ellipsis to see additional options.

Some options run programs.

Working with Database Objects

When you open an existing database, the first thing you usually see is the Database window. However, if the database was created with a switchboard, you must close the switchboard before you can view the Database window. The *Database window* is the container for all the objects in a database, including tables, forms, reports, queries, pages, macros, and modules. These database objects work together to help you store and manage your data.

Objects are organized by object type on the *Objects bar*. You can open, rename, and delete database objects from the Database window.

SEE ALSO

See "Repair Renaming Errors" on page 86 for information on setting Name AutoCorrect options.

View the Database Window

1. Open the database.

   If no special startup options are specified, the Database window opens automatically.

2. If necessary, click the Window menu, and then click the name of the database to open the Database window.

   Databases with multiple users might have security measures in effect that prevent some users from accessing the Database window.

Database window

Open a Database Object

1. If necessary, click the Objects bar.

2. Click the object type icon on the Objects bar.

3. Click the object you want to open.

4. Click the Open button on the Database Window toolbar to view the object's data, or click the Design button to work with the object's design.

TIP

Switch to the Database window. *You can press F11 to switch to the Database window from a switchboard or any other window.*

TIP

Handle renamed objects. *When you rename a database object, you don't have to worry about confusing other Access objects that use the object you just renamed. The* Name AutoCorrect *feature automatically fixes common side effects that occur when a user makes name changes. Click the Tools menu, click Options, click the General tab, and then work with the Name AutoCorrect settings to enable this feature.*

SEE ALSO

See "Customizing Access Startup" on page 235 for information on determining what object opens first when a user opens a database.

Manage Database Objects

◆ To create a new object, click the type of object you want to create on the Objects bar, and then click the New button on the Database window toolbar.

◆ To delete an object, right-click it in the Object list and then click Delete.

◆ To rename a database object, right-click the object in the Object list, click Rename, and then type a

Click to create a new database object.

The menu opens when you right-click an object.

Click to delete the selected object.

Click to rename the selected object.

Close a Database Object

◆ To close an open database object, click its Close button.

Close button

Touring a Table

A database is made up of groups of fields organized into tables. A *field* is a specific category of information, such as a name or a product. Related fields are grouped in tables. All the fields dealing with customers might be grouped in a Customer table, while fields dealing with products might be grouped in a Products table.

You usually enter data into fields one entity at a time (one customer at a time, one product at a time, and so on). Access stores all the data for a single entity in a *record*. You can view a table in Datasheet or Design view. Design view allows you to work with your table's fields. Datasheet view shows a grid of fields and records. The fields appear as columns and the records as rows.

Open and View a Table

1 In the Database window, click Tables on the Objects bar.

2 Click the table.

3 Click Open. The table opens in Datasheet view.

♦ Drag the horizontal scroll box to scroll through the fields in a table.

♦ Drag the vertical scroll box to scroll through the records in a table.

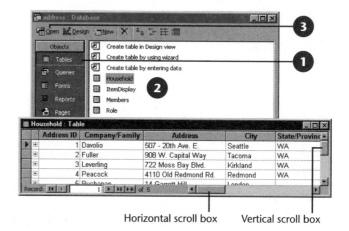

Horizontal scroll box   Vertical scroll box

Select a Column or Row

♦ Click the column selector to select a column.

♦ Click the row selector to select a row.

Each record has a unique identification number, which appears in the Specific Record box when that record is selected.

Row selector   Column selector

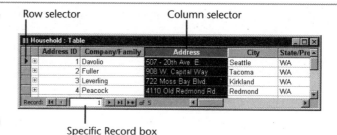

Specific Record box

Resize a Column or Row

♦ Drag the border between column selectors left or right to resize a column.

♦ Drag the border between two row selectors up or down to change the height of all rows in the table.

Pointer when you change row height   Column border

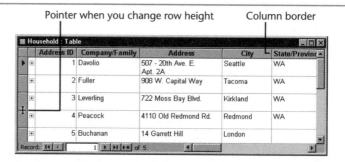

SEE ALSO

See "Moving to a Specific Record in a Table" on page 87 for information on table navigation.

TIP

AutoNumber fields. *The first field in a table is often an AutoNumber field, which Access uses to assign a unique number to each record. You can't select or change this value.*

TIP

Delete a database. *To delete a database you must open the My Computer window or Windows Explorer. Open the folder that contains the database. Right-click the database and then click Delete. Click Yes if you are asked if you are sure.*

TIP

Delete related data. *When you delete a record, such as a supplier, you might want to delete the products the supplier supplies.*

SEE ALSO

See "Ensuring Referential Integrity" on page 52 to see how Access ensures referential integrity automatically.

Enter a New Record in a Table

1 Open the table in Datasheet view from a switchboard or from the Objects bar in the Database window.

2 Click the New Record button.

3 Press Tab to accept the AutoNumber entry.

4 Enter the data for the first field. If you make a typing mistake, press Backspace.

5 Press Tab to move to the next field or Shift+Tab to move to the previous field.

6 When you reach the end of the record, click the New Record button or press Tab to go to the next record. Access saves your changes when you move to the next record.

Delete a Record from a Table

1 Right-click the row selector.

2 Click Delete Record.

3 Click Yes to confirm the deletion.

Touring a Form

Database designers often display data in forms that mimic the paper forms used to record data. Forms facilitate data entry and record viewing. They can also contain buttons that allow you to perform other actions, such as running macros, printing, or creating labels. The options that appear on a form depend on what features the database designer included.

A form directs you to enter the correct information and can automatically check your entries for errors. Access places the data you've entered in the form into the proper table or tables.

You can open a form in Form view or Design view. Form view allows you to view all the information associated with a record; Design view allows you to modify the form's design.

Enter a New Record in a Form

1 In the Database window, click Forms on the Objects bar, click the form you want to use, and then click the Open button.

2 Click the New Record button.

3 Enter the data for the first field.

4 Press Tab to move to the next field or Shift+Tab to move to the previous field.

5 When you have finished entering the data, you can close the form, click the New Record button to enter another record, or view a different record.

The View button allows you to switch between Design view and Form view.

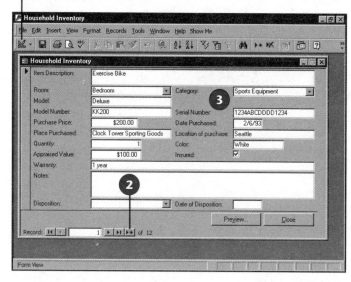

Delete a Record from a Form

1 Display the record you want to delete.

2 Click the Delete Record button on the Form View toolbar.

3 Click Yes.

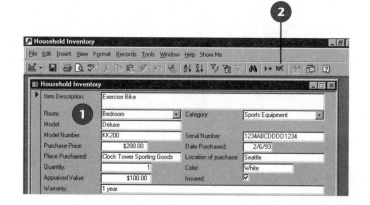

Entering Data

Normally you enter data into a form, because forms are specifically designed to facilitate data entry. You can, however, enter data into a table or a query. The methods are similar.

How you enter data in a field depends on how the database designer created the field. Some fields accept only certain kinds of information, such as numbers or text. Some fields appear as check boxes or groups of option buttons; others appear as text boxes. Some text boxes only allow dates; others only allow certain predefined entries, such as a state or country.

When you enter data, you don't have to click a Save button to save the data. Access automatically saves the data as you enter it.

Enter Data into a Field

1 Open the query, table, page, or form into which you want to enter data.

2 Activate the field into which you want to enter data.

◆ Click a field to activate it.

◆ Press Tab to move to the next field or Shift+Tab to move to the previous field.

3 Enter data in the active field.

◆ Click a drop-down arrow and click one of the available choices (such as a category).

◆ Click a check box or option button.

◆ Type text in a box. When you click a box, a blinking *insertion point* appears, indicating where the text will appear when you type.

◆ Enter dates in the required format (such as month/day/year).

4 When you're done, click the Close button.

Some forms have tabs that you click to enter different types of information.

This date field requires dates to be entered in 8 digits.

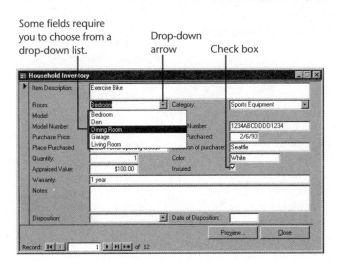

Some fields require you to choose from a drop-down list.

Drop-down arrow

Check box

Touring a Query

To locate and retrieve information in a table (or in multiple tables), you create a query. A *query* is simply a question that you ask a database to help you locate specific information. For example, if you want to know which customers placed orders in the last six months, you can create a query to examine the contents of the Order Date field and to find all the records in which the purchase date is less than six months ago.

Access retrieves the data that meets the specifications in your query and displays that data in table format. You can sort that information or retrieve just a subset of its contents with still more specific criteria, so that you can focus on exactly the information you need—no more or less.

Open and Run a Query

1 In the Database window, click Queries on the Objects bar.

2 Click the query you want to run.

3 Click the Open button.

The query opens in a table called a *dynaset*. The dynaset displays the records that meet the specifications set forth in the query.

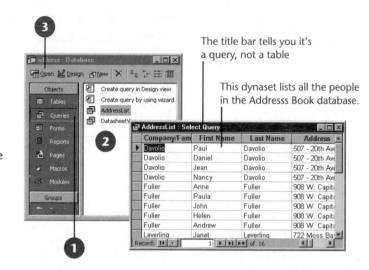

The title bar tells you it's a query, not a table

This dynaset lists all the people in the Addresss Book database.

View a Query in Design View

1 In the Database window, click Queries on the Objects bar.

2 Click the query you want to run.

3 Click the Design button.

In Design view, you can see the criteria that specify what records to include in the dynaset.

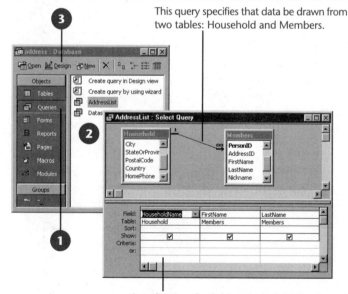

This query specifies that data be drawn from two tables: Household and Members.

Specifications for fields to include in the dynaset

Touring a Report

After you have retrieved and organized only the specific information you want, you can display and print this information as a *report*. In Access you can create a simple report that displays each record's information, or you can customize a report to include calculations, charts, graphics, and other features to go beyond the numbers and really emphasize the information in the report.

You can print a report, a table, a query, or any data in a single step using the Print button, in which case Access automatically prints a single copy of all pages in the report. If you want to print only selected pages or if you want to specify other printing options, use the Print command on the File menu.

Create a Report

① In the Database window, click Reports on the Objects bar.

② Click the report you want to view.

③ Click the Preview button.

Print button

A preview of the report will appear.

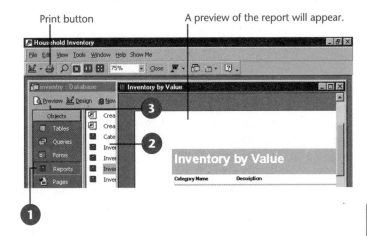

Print Data

① Click the File menu, and then click Print.

② If necessary, click the Name drop-down arrow, and then select the printer you want to use.

③ To print selected pages in the report, click the Pages option button, and then type the first page in the From box and the ending page in the To box.

④ To print more than one copy, click the Number of Copies spin arrows to choose the number you want.

⑤ Click OK.

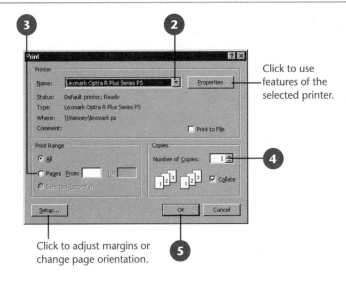

Click to use features of the selected printer.

Click to adjust margins or change page orientation.

Creating a Database

If the sample databases that come with Access don't meet your needs, you can use a wizard to create a database, or you can create a custom database from scratch.

The Access database wizards help you create databases suited to specific needs. Each wizard guides you through the process of selecting and creating fields, tables, queries, reports, and forms that will make it easier to use the database.

When you create a database with a wizard or from scratch, you need to assign a name and location to your database.

SEE ALSO

See Section 4, "Planning and Creating a Custom Database," on page 37 for information on creating a database from scratch.

Create and Save a New Database Using a Wizard

1 Choose one of the following options.

◆ Start Access, click the Access Database Wizards, Pages, And Projects option button, and then click OK.

◆ In Access, click the New button on the Database toolbar.

2 Click the Databases tab.

3 Double-click the icon of database you want to create.

4 Click the Save In drop-down arrow, and then select the folder in which you want to store your database file.

5 Type a filename for the database, or use the default filename.

6 Click Create.

7 Click Next and follow the instructions that appear.

8 Click Finish.

Access builds the database according to your specifications.

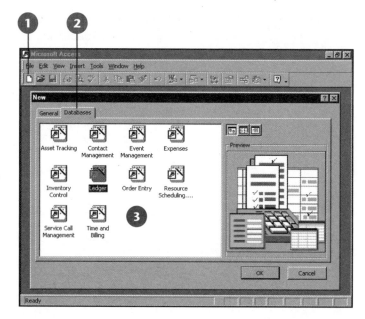

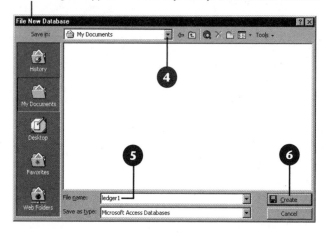

This dialog box appears automatically when you create a new database.

Stepping Through a Database Wizard

The choices that appear as you progress through a database wizard depend on the kind of information the database is designed to manage. All the wizards, however, share certain features.

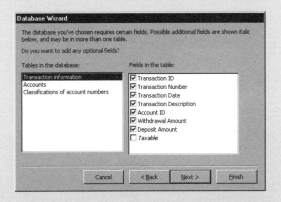

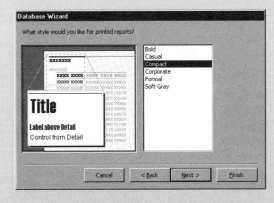

DATABASE WIZARD CHOICES	
Wizard Choice	**Description**
Field selection	The wizard presents a list of tables it will include in the database. Each table requires certain fields. You can click a table to see which fields it includes. Required fields are checked; optional fields appear in italics. To include an optional field in your database, click its check box.
Report style	You can choose from a set of report styles, such as Bold, Casual, or Corporate. Report styles give printed reports a professional look.
Screen style	Access offers a set of visual styles for on-screen database objects that use a variety of color, font, and background enhancements. Click the style you want to see a sample of it.
Name and picture	Access provides a default name for its wizard databases, but you can enter your own. You can also include a picture with your database.

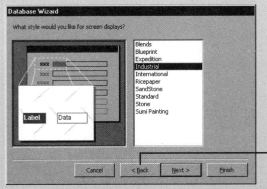

Click to return to previous options.

Sizing and Arranging Windows

You can adjust the size of each open window to fit your needs. Each window's title bar has three buttons: Minimize, Maximize, and Close. The Minimize button shrinks a window so that only its title bar appears. The Maximize button expands the window so it fills the Access window or the entire screen. When you maximize or minimize a window, the Maximize or Minimize buttons are replaced by the Restore button, which you click to restore a window to its original size.

You can also drag window borders to resize them, move windows, or arrange them using the Tile and Cascade commands.

Resize or Move Windows

◆ Click the Minimize button to reduce the window to a title bar.

◆ Click the Maximize button to enlarge the window so it fills the entire program window or screen.

◆ Click the Restore button to restore the window to its original size.

◆ Drag a top or bottom border to change a window's height or a side border to change a window's width.

◆ Drag a corner to change window width and height simultaneously.

◆ Drag a window's title bar to move the window.

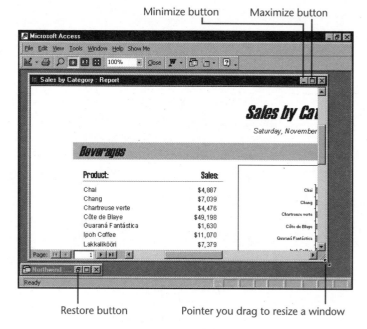

Minimize button   Maximize button

Restore button   Pointer you drag to resize a window

Quickly switch between restored or minimized and maximized windows. *Double-click a window title bar to quickly switch between window sizes.*

Hide and unhide a window. *Display the window you want to hide, click the Window menu, and then click Hide. To unhide a window, click the Window menu, click Unhide, click the window you want to unhide, and then click OK.*

Arrange Open Windows

1. Click the Window menu.

   ◆ Click Tile Horizontally to display windows one above the other or Tile Vertically to arrange them side by side.

   ◆ Click Cascade to stagger window title bars.

2. Click any part of a window to make it active.

Tiled windows

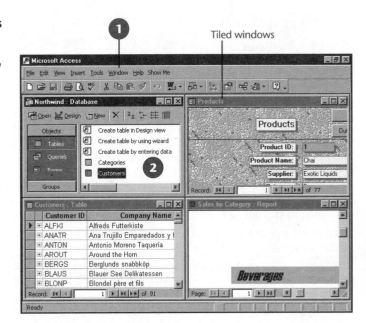

Cascaded windows

Grouping Database Objects

You can group shortcuts to related objects of different types together using the *Groups bar*. When you first create a group, it is empty until you populate it with shortcuts to the related objects. When you add an object to a group, you do not change the object's original location, nor are you creating a new object. Instead, you are simply creating a shortcut to an object that already exists.

TIP

Delete or rename a group. *In the Database window, click the Groups bar, right-click anywhere under the Groups bar, click Delete Group or Rename Group. When you rename a group, type a new name, and then click OK.*

TIP

Resize the Groups bar. *If the Groups bar is too small, you can drag the Groups button up to display more groups.*

Create a Group

1 In the Database window, click the Groups bar.

2 Right-click anywhere under the Groups bar.

3 Click New Group.

4 Type a name for your group, and then click OK.

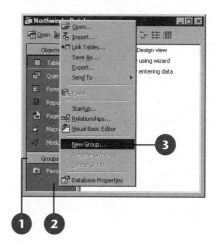

Add or Remove a Group Shortcut

1 In the Database window, display the database object you want to add to a group.

2 Drag an object from the Object list to the group.

Click to delete a group shortcut

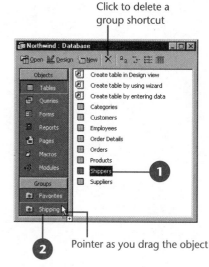

Pointer as you drag the object

Detecting and Repairing Problems

At times you may determine that Access is not working as efficiently as it once did. This sometimes happens when you install new software or move files into new folders. Use the *Detect And Repair* command to improve performance by repairing problems such as missing files from setup and registry settings. Note that this feature does not repair personal files such as your database. If you try to access a feature or file, such as a template, not currently installed, Access will install the feature or file on first use.

SEE ALSO

See "Installing Additional Features" on page 36 for information on installing features and files on first use.

Detect and Repair Problems

1. Click the Help menu, and then click Detect And Repair.

2. Click Start.

   Insert the Office CD in your CD-ROM drive.

3. If necessary, click Repair Office, and then click the Reinstall Office or Repair Errors In Your Office Installation option button.

4. Click Finish.

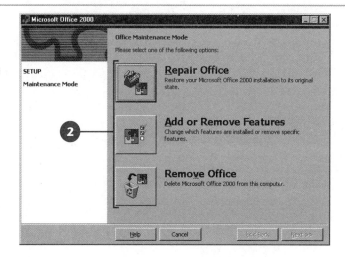

Click to restore shortcuts to the Start menu.

Perform Maintenance on Office Programs

1. In Windows Explorer, double-click the Setup icon on the Office CD.

2. Click one of the following maintenance buttons.

   ◆ Repair Office to repair or reinstall Office

   ◆ Add Or Remove Features to determine which and when features are installed or removed

   ◆ Remove Office to uninstall the Office program

3. Follow the wizard instructions to complete the maintenance.

Installing Additional Features

When you first install Microsoft Access 2000, the installation program typically does not install every Access feature. Many users don't require features such as international language support and specialized application tools. To minimize wasted hard disk space, the installation program installs only the most common features.

Additional features are installed on "first use"—that is, when you try to use the feature, Office 2000 automatically installs it from the CD-ROM. You must install less common features yourself, using the Setup program. The Setup program lists the Office components in a hierarchy; you navigate the hierarchy to locate the components you want. You can designate a component to run from your computer, from the CD, or to be installed on first use.

Install Individual Components

1. Close all open programs.

2. Click the Start button, point to Settings, and then click Control Panel.

3. Double-click the Add/ Remove Programs icon.

4. Click Microsoft Access or Microsoft Office.

5. Click the Add/Remove button.

6. Click the Add or Remove Features button.

7. Click the plus sign next to Microsoft Access For Windows and any other necessary plus signs.

8. Click the drive icon for the component you want to install.

9. Click the installation option you want to use.

10. Click Update Now and follow the instructions that appear on the screen.

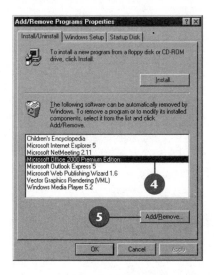

The plus sign changes to a minus sign when you click it.

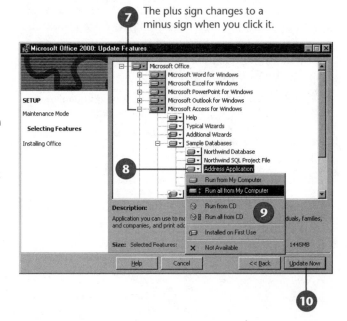

Planning and Creating a Custom Database

The Access database wizards make creating databases easy, but you may need to create a database that does not fit any of the wizard's predefined choices. In that situation, you may need to create the database "from scratch."

Creating a database from scratch involves careful planning. You must:

◆ Determine the purpose and scope of your database.

◆ Decide what tables your database will contain and what the content of those tables will be.

◆ Define how data in one table is related to data in another table.

When you create a database from scratch, you can take advantage of the tools that Microsoft Access 2000 provides. If you don't plan to create a database from scratch but instead plan to use only existing Access databases, you might not need the information in this chapter. Understanding database design concepts, however, will help you better understand how to create effective queries later on.

Planning Tables
and Table Relationships

Although you can always make changes to your database when necessary, a little planning before you begin can save time later on. When you plan a database, consider how you will use the data. What kind of data are you collecting? What kind of data are you entering? How are data values related to one another? Can your data be organized into separate, smaller groups? What kinds of safeguards can you create to ensure that errors do not creep into your data? As you consider these questions, you should apply the answers as you structure your database.

Planning Tables

Tables are one of the fundamental building blocks of a database. Database planning begins with deciding how many and what kinds of tables your database will contain. Consider organizing your database information into several tables—each one containing fields related to a specific topic—rather than one large table containing fields for a large variety of topics. For example, you could create a Customers table that contains only customer information and an Orders table that contains only customer order information. By focusing each table on a single task, you greatly simplify the structure of those tables and make them easier to modify later on.

Choosing Data Types

When you create a table, you must decide what fields to include and the appropriate format for those fields. Access allows you to assign a *data type* to a field, a format that defines the kind of data the field can accept. Access provides a wide variety of data types, ranging from text and number formats to object-based formats for images, sound, and video clips. Choosing the correct data type helps you manage your data and reduces the possibility of data-entry errors. For example, a data type that allows only positive integers for an individual's age removes a source of data-entry error.

Specifying a Primary Key

You should also identify which field or fields are the table's primary keys. *Primary keys* are those fields whose values uniquely identify each record in the table. A social security number field in a personnel table could be used as a primary key since each employee has a unique social security number. A table with time-ordered data might have two primary keys—a date field and a time field (hours and minutes)—which together uniquely identify an exact moment in time. Although primary keys are not required, their use is one way of removing the possibility of duplicate records existing within your tables.

Establishing Table Relationships

When you place data into separate tables, you need some way of merging this data together for forms and reports. You can do this by establishing table relationships that indicate how data in one table relates to data in another.

Specifying Common Fields

Data from several different tables are related through the use of common fields. A *common field* is a field existing in two or more tables, allowing you to match records from one table with records in the other tables.

For example, the Customers table and the Orders table might both contain a Customer ID field, which functions as a primary key that identifies a specific customer. Using Customer ID as a common field allows you to generate reports containing information on both the customer and the orders the customer made. When you use a primary key as a common field, it is called a *foreign key* in the second table.

Building Table Relationships

Once you have a way of relating two tables with a common field, your next task is to express the nature of that relationship. There are three types of relationships: one-to-one, one-to-many, and many-to-many.

TABLE RELATIONSHIPS	
Type	**Description**
One-to-one	Each record in one table is matched to only one record in a second table, and vice versa.
One-to-many	Each record in one table is matched to one or more records in a second table, but each record in the second table is matched to only one record in the first table.
Many-to-many	Each record in one table is matched to multiple records in a second table, and vice versa.

A table containing customer names and a second table containing customer addresses exist in a one-to-one relationship if each customer is limited to only one address. Similarly, a one-to-many relationship exists between the Customers table and the Orders table because a single customer could place several orders. In a one-to-many relationship like this, the "one" table is called the *primary table*, and the "many" table is called the *related table*.

Finally, if you allow several customers to be recorded on a single order (as in the case of group purchases), a many-to-many relationship exists between the Customers and Orders tables.

Maintaining Referential Integrity

Table relationships must obey standards of *referential integrity*, a set of rules that control how you can delete or modify data between related tables. Referential integrity protects you from erroneously changing data in a primary table required by a related table. You can apply referential integrity when:

◆ The common field is the primary table's primary key.

◆ The related fields have the same format.

◆ Both tables belong to the same database.

Referential integrity forces you to do the following:

◆ Before adding a record to a related table, a matching record must already exist in the primary table.

◆ The value of the primary key in the primary table cannot be changed if matching records exist in a related table.

◆ A record in the primary table cannot be deleted if matching records exist in a related table.

Access can enforce these rules by cascading any changes across the related tables. For example, Access can automatically copy any changes to the common field across the related tables. Similarly, if a record is deleted in the primary table, Access can automatically delete related records in all other tables.

As you work through these issues of tables, fields, and table relationships, you will create a structure for your database that will be easier to manage and less prone to data entry error.

4

Creating a New Database

A database created without using one of the database wizards is empty; it doesn't contain any tables, forms, or reports. Unlike new documents created with other Microsoft Office 2000 programs, a blank Access database must be saved to a hard disk or floppy disk before you can work with it. Once you save the database, you can add the elements and features your database requires.

TIP

Start Access with a new database. *When you start Access, you will be prompted to create a new blank database, to create one with a wizard, or to open an existing database file. To create a blank database, click the Blank Access Database option button, click OK, and then enter a filename and location for the new database.*

Create a New Database

1. Close any open databases.

2. Click the New button on the Database toolbar.

3. Double-click the Database icon.

4. Select the drive and folder in which you want to save your database, and then enter a filename for your database.

5. Click Create.

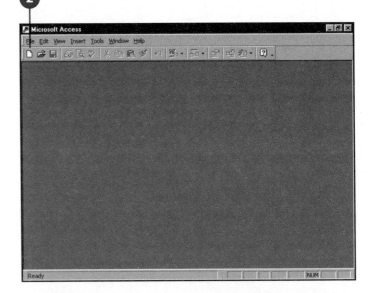

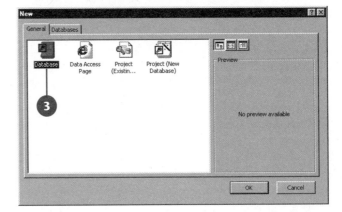

Creating Tables in a Database

After creating a database file, you need to create the tables that will store the data. There are several ways to create a new table: in Design view, in Datasheet view, with a Table Wizard, or by importing a table from another Access database. Depending on the method you choose, creating a table can involve one or more of the following:

♦ Specifying the fields for the table

♦ Determining the data type for each field

♦ Determining the field size (for text and number fields only)

♦ Assigning the primary key

♦ Saving and naming the table

METHODS FOR CREATING A TABLE	
Method	**Description**
Datasheet	When you create a table in Datasheet view, you can start viewing and entering data right away. Access automatically assigns a data type based on the kind of information you entered in the field, and it assigns a default field size for text and number fields. After you close and save the table, Access prompts you to identify a primary key or to allow Access to designate one for you.
Design	In Design view, you must specify the fields, specify the data type for each field, assign the size (for text and number fields), assign the primary key, and save the table yourself.
Table Wizard	Using a Table Wizard, you select fields from sample tables that are appropriate for the type of database you are creating. The data type and other field properties are already defined for each field.
Importing	If you want to use data from another Access database in the database you are creating, you can import it. When you import a table, all the field names and data types are retained with the imported data. However, you must name the new table and identify the primary key or have Access create a primary key for you. Also, you may need to change the field size and other properties after importing.
Linking	When you link a table, the data is retrieved from a table in another database. Linking a table saves disk space because there is only one table rather than multiple tables with the same data. Linking a table saves time because there is no need to update the same information in more than one table.

4

Creating a Table Using the Table Wizard

One of the easiest ways to create a table is to use the Table Wizard. The *Table Wizard* walks you through a series of dialog boxes that help you choose the types of tables your database will contain and the fields present in each table. You can change table names and field names and properties as you proceed through the wizard. The wizard also makes it easy to create a primary key for your table and to establish relationships between the new table and other tables in the database.

TIP

Select fields in the order you want them to appear in the table. *In the Sample Fields list, you can choose the fields you want to include in your table in any order. The fields you choose will appear in the table in the order you chose them.*

Start the Table Wizard

1. In the Database window, click Tables on the Objects bar, and then double-click the Create Table By Using Wizard icon.

2. Click the Business or Personal option button.

3. Click the table that best matches your needs.

4. Double-click each field you want to include in the table. Click Next to continue.

5. Type a new name for the table, or accept the suggested name.

6. Click the Yes option button to have the Table Wizard assign the primary key, or click the No option button to assign your own primary key. Click Next to continue.

7. If you chose to set the primary key, select the field and data type. Click Next to continue.

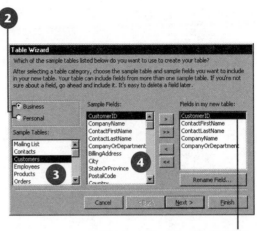

Click to rename the selected field.

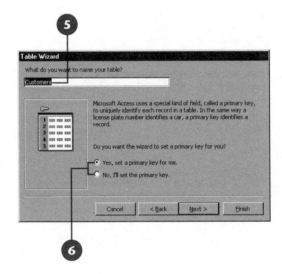

TIP

A database with at least one table. *The Table Wizard prompts you to define how the table you are creating will relate to other tables in the database. Review the relationships of this new table with the other tables in the database before making any changes.*

SEE ALSO

See "Setting a Primary Key Using the Table Wizard" on page 44 to learn how to create a primary key with the Table Wizard.

SEE ALSO

See "Defining Table Relationships" on page 50 for information on relating tables to one another.

8. If your database already contains at least one table and you want to make changes, select the relationship you want to change, click the Relationships button, specify the new table relationships, and click OK. Click Next to continue.

9. In the final wizard dialog box, click one of the option buttons, either to modify the table design (in Design view) before entering data, to enter data right away (in Datasheet view), or to enter data in a form that the wizard creates for you.

10. Click Finish to complete the wizard and create the table.

This dialog box appears only if your database already contains at least one table.

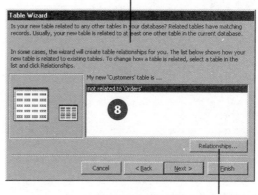

Click to specify table relationships.

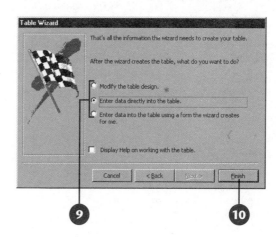

Setting a Primary Key Using the Table Wizard

When you create a table with the Table Wizard, you can choose either to set a primary key yourself or to have the wizard do it for you. If you set the primary key, a dialog box appears that allows you to select the primary key and define its data type. Access can generate primary key values automatically, or you can enter a unique value for each new record when you enter data.

SEE ALSO

See "Specifying a Primary Key in Design View" on page 49 for more information on creating and altering primary keys.

Set the Primary Key Yourself

1. When the Table Wizard prompts you to set the primary key, click the No, I'll Set The Primary Key button. Click Next to continue.

2. Click the drop-down arrow to select the field you want to use as the primary key.

3. Click the option button corresponding to the data type you want to use for your primary key.

4. Click Next to continue.

5. Click the option button corresponding to what you want to do after the wizard creates the table.

6. Click Finish.

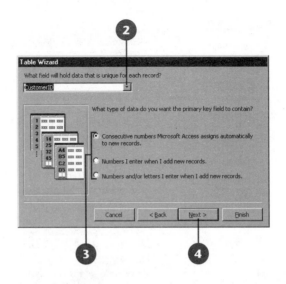

PRIMARY KEY OPTIONS	
Option	**Description**
Consecutive Numbers	Access assigns the primary key value for a new record that is automatically one more than the primary key value in the previous record.
Numbers I Enter When I Add New Records	You enter a unique number for the primary key of each new record.
Numbers And/Or Letters I Enter When I Add New Records	You enter a unique string of text for the primary key of each new record.

Assigning Table Relationships in the Table Wizard

When you create a table using the Table Wizard, you have the option to relate the new table to the other tables in the database. The Table Wizard displays a list of established tables. You can choose to create a relationship between the new table and any of the tables in the list.

TIP

Create a one-to-many relationship. *When you create a one-to-many relationship, the Table Wizard automatically adds new fields to the related table if necessary.*

SEE ALSO

See "Defining Table Relationships" on page 50 for more information about establishing table relationships.

Create a Relationship Between Tables

1 When the Table Wizard displays the dialog box listing related and unrelated tables, select the table whose relationship you want to change, and then click the Relationships button.

2 Click one of the three option buttons describing the relationship between the new table and the established table.

3 Click OK.

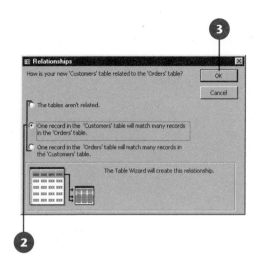

RELATIONSHIP OPTIONS	
Option	**Description**
The Tables Aren't Related	No relationship will exist between the new table and the established table.
One Record In The New Table Will Match Many Records In The Old Table	Create a one-to-many relationship. Access sets the new table as the primary table and the established table as the related table.
One Record In The Old Table Will Match Many Records In The New Table	Create a one-to-many relationship. Access sets the new table as the related table and the established table as the primary table.

4

Creating Tables by Entering Data

Access allows you to display many of its objects in multiple viewing modes. Datasheet view displays the data in your tables, queries, forms, and reports. Design view displays options for designing your Access objects. You can create a new table in both views. When you create a table in Datasheet view, you enter data and Access creates the table as you type. Access determines the data type of each field based on the data you enter. When you finish entering data, Access will prompt you for the name of the table you've just created.

Enter Data to Create a New Table

1 In the Database window, click Tables on the Objects bar.

2 Double-click the Create Table By Entering Data icon.

3 Enter the data.

4 Close the Table window.

5 Click Yes to save the table, enter a table name, and then click OK.

If no primary key is defined, a dialog box appears which allows you to automatically define one.

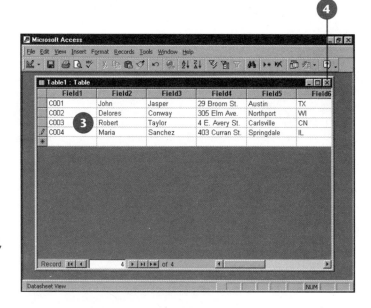

Getting Data from Other Access Tables

You can create new tables from other Access databases by importing and linking tables. When you *import* a table, you copy data from a table in one Access database and place it in a new table in your database. When you *link* a table, the data stays in its original location, but you can display and access that data from within your database. If data in the original database changes, the changes will appear in your database too.

TIP

Identify linked tables. *You can identify a linked table in the Database window by the arrow that appears to the left of its table icon.*

SEE ALSO

See "Getting Data from Other Programs" on page 178 for more on retrieving information from other sources.

Import a Table into Your Database

1. In the Database window, click the New button.

2. Double-click Import Table.

3. Locate and select the database file that contains the data you want to import, and then click Import.

4. Click the tables you want to import.

   To deselect a table, click the table again.

5. Click OK.

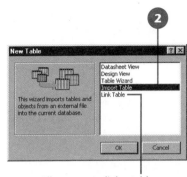

Allows you to link a table rather than import one

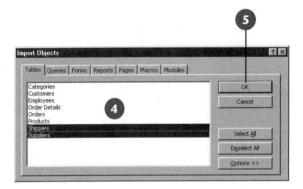

Creating Tables in Design View

Most Access objects can be displayed in Design view, which allows you to work with the underlying structure of your tables, queries, forms, and reports. To create a new table with Design view, you define the fields that will comprise the table before you enter any data. You can create any field you choose, but Access does not provide as much help in creating those fields as it does with its wizards.

SEE ALSO

See "Inserting, Deleting, and Reordering Fields" on page 54 for information on inserting and creating fields in Design view.

Create a New Table in Design View

1. In the Database window, click Tables on the Objects bar.

2. Double-click the Create Table In Design View icon.

3. Type a field name for the first column you want to create in the Field Name column.

4. Press Tab, click the Data Type drop-down arrow that appears, and then click the data type you want to assign to the field you just created

5. Press Tab and type a description of the field's properties and purpose.

6. Press Enter to go to the next row.

7. Repeat steps 3 through 6 as necessary to add new fields to the table.

8. Close the Table window.

9. Click Yes to save the table, enter a table name, and then click OK.

   If no primary key is defined, a dialog box appears which allows you to automatically define one.

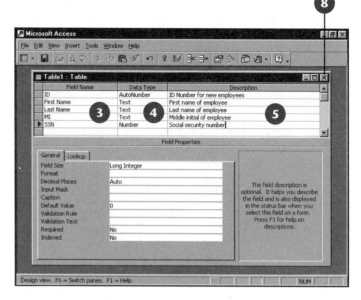

Specifying a Primary Key in Design View

In Design view, you can use the Primary Key button to assign or remove the primary key designation for the selected field or fields. When you create a table in Design view, you can specify more than one field as a primary key. However, since you are not using the Table Wizard, you are responsible for determining the data type of the primary key. Whatever data type you choose, values for the primary key must be unique for each table record.

TIP

Select more than one primary key. *To create more than one primary key, press and hold Ctrl and click the row selector for each field you want to designate as a primary key, and then click the Primary Key button.*

Specify a Primary Key

1 In Design view, create a field that will be that table's primary key and select an appropriate data type.

◆ If you choose the AutoNumber data type, Access assigns a value to the primary key for a new record that is one more than the primary key in the previous record.

◆ If you choose any other data type, such as Text, Number, or Date/Time, during data entry, you must enter a unique value in the appropriate format for the primary key of each new record.

2 Click the row selector of that field.

3 Click the Primary Key button on the Table Design toolbar.

3 Click to assign or remove a primary key.

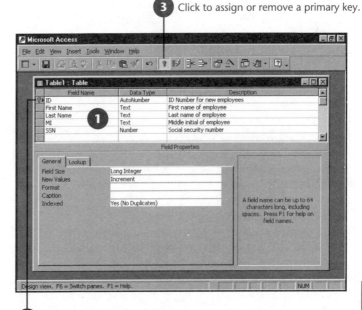

2 This symbol indicates the primary key field. Click to select a row.

4

Defining Table Relationships

You can define table relationships in several ways. When you first create tables in your database using the Table Wizard, the wizard gives you an opportunity to define table relationships. You can also define relationships in the Database window or in Design view. This last method gives you more control over your table relationships and also gives you a quick snapshot of all the relationships in your database.

Relationships button

Define Table Relationships

1 In the Database window, click the Relationships button on the Database toolbar.

If relationships are already established in your database, they appear in the Relationships window.

2 If necessary, click the Show Table button on the Relationship toolbar to display the Show Table dialog box.

3 Click the Tables tab.

4 Click the table you want.

5 Click Add.

The table or query you selected appears in the Relationships window.

6 Repeat steps 4 and 5 for each table you want to use in a relationship.

7 Click Close.

8 Click the common field in the first table and drag it to the common field in the second table. When you release the mouse button, a line appears between the two tables, signifying that they are related.

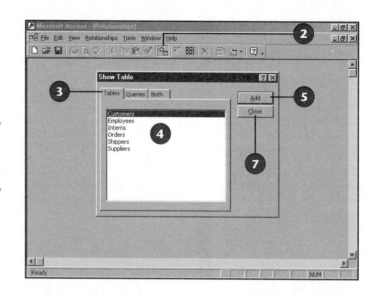

Show Direct Relationships button   Show All Relationships button

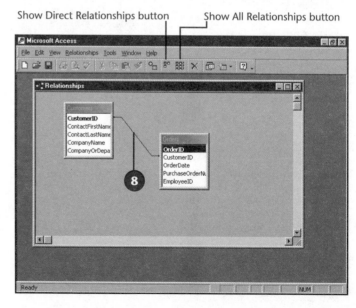

9 Click the Join Type button if you want to specify the join type. Click OK to return to the Edit Relationships dialog box.

10 Click Create to create the relationship.

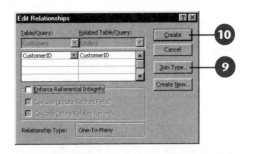

JOIN TYPES

Join Type	Description
Include rows only where the joined fields from both tables are equal	Choose this option if you want to see one record in the second table for every record that appears in the first table. The number of records you see in the two tables will be the same.
Include ALL records from "xxx" (the first table) and only those records from "yyy" (the second table) where the joined fields are equal	Choose this option if you want to see all the records in the first table (even if there is no corresponding record in the second table) as well as the records from the second table in which the joined fields are the same in both tables. The number of records you see in the first table might be greater than the number of records in the second table.
Include ALL records from "yyy" (the second table) and only those records from "xxx" (the first table) where the joined fields are equal	Choose this option if you want to see all the records in the second table (even if there is no corresponding record in the first table) as well as the records from the first table in which the joined fields are the same in both tables. The number of records you see in the second table might be greater than the number of records in the first table.

4

Ensuring Referential Integrity

Referential integrity in table relationships keeps users from accidentally deleting or changing related data.

If a primary table contains a list of employees and related tables contain additional information about those employees, and an employee quits, his record is removed from the primary table. His records should also be removed in all related tables.

Access allows you to change or delete related data, but only if these changes are then cascaded through the series of related tables. You can do this by selecting the Cascade Update Related Fields and Cascade Delete Related Records check boxes in the Edit Relationships dialog box.

Ensure Referential Integrity

1 In the Database window, click the Relationships button on the Database toolbar.

2 Double-click the join line for the relationship you want to work with.

3 Click to select the Enforce Referential Integrity check box to ensure that referential integrity always exists between related tables in the database.

4 If you want changes to the primary field of the primary table automatically copied to the related field of the related table, click to select the Cascade Update Related Fields check box.

5 If you want Access to automatically delete records in the related tables whenever records in the primary table are deleted, click to select the Cascade Delete Related Records check box.

6 Click OK.

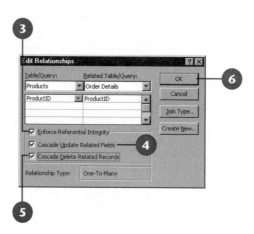

5

Working with Fields

An important part of creating your own database is field design. How you design your fields determines how accurately they will be able to store data. Microsoft Access 2000 provides flexibility and control in field design. You can design fields so that they allow you to:

- ◆ Assign a data type so the field accepts and displays the data in the appropriate format.

- ◆ Include input masks that guide users during data entry.

- ◆ Specify whether data must be entered into certain fields.

- ◆ Include a default value for a field.

- ◆ Include validation checks to ensure that correct data is entered.

- ◆ Accommodate data whose values are taken from lookup lists.

By taking advantage of these tools during the database design stage, you can save yourself and your database users a lot of trouble later on. By properly designing your fields, you can remove many sources of data-entry error and make your database simpler to manage.

Inserting, Deleting, and Reordering Fields

You can insert, delete, and edit fields in your database tables in Design view. In Design view for tables, each row corresponds to a field. You add a field by inserting a new row that contains the field name, data type, and other properties. You delete a field by removing a row. You can change field order by re-ordering the rows to better suit your data entry needs. Using Design view for tables makes these tasks easy.

TIP

Assign field names. *Field names can contain up to 64 characters and can include numbers and spaces.*

Insert a New Field

1. In the Database window, click Tables on the Objects bar, click the table in which you want to insert a new field, and then click the Design button.

2. Click the row selector for the field that will be below the new field you want to insert.

3. Click the Insert Rows button on the Table Design toolbar.

   A new blank row appears above the row you selected.

4. Click the Field Name cell for the row you inserted, type the name of the new field, and then press Tab.

5. Click the drop-down arrow in the Data Type column, click the data type you want to assign to the field, and then press Tab.

6. Type a brief description of the new field.

7. Set additional field properties in the property sheet if appropriate.

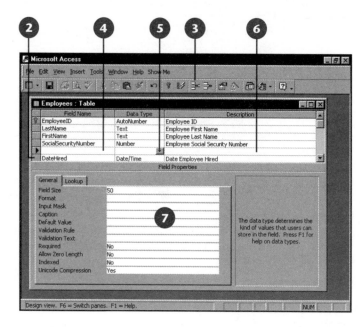

Delete a Field

① Display the table in Design view, and then click the row selector for the row you want to delete.

② Click the Delete Rows button on the Table Design toolbar.

If any records in the table contain data for this field, a message informs you that deleting this field will also delete any data in the field.

③ Click Yes to confirm you want to continue, or click No to cancel the deletion.

Change the Order of Fields in a Table

① Display the table in Design view, and then click to select the row selector for the field you want to move.

② Click the row selector again, and then press and hold the mouse button.

③ Drag the row to the new position where you want the field to appear, and then release the mouse button.

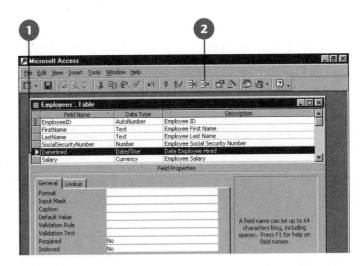

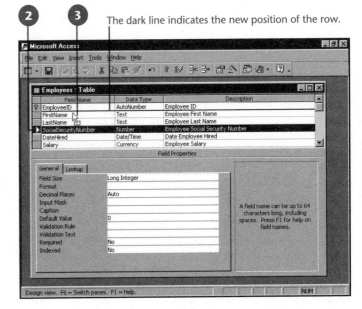

The dark line indicates the new position of the row.

Specifying Data Types and Field Properties

Access provides 10 different *data types*, field formats that define the kind of data the field can accept, which cover a wide variety of data. When you choose a data type for a field, Access will accept data entered only in the format specified by the data type. Selecting the appropriate data type makes it easier for users to enter and retrieve information in the database tables. It also acts as a check against incorrect data being entered. For example, a field formatted to accept only numbers removes the possibility that a user will erroneously enter text into the field.

You can change the data type for a field even after you have entered data in it. However, you might need to perform a potentially lengthy process of converting or retyping the field's data when you save the table. If the data type in a field conflicts with a new data type setting, you may lose some or all of the data in the field.

Once you've selected a data type, you can begin to work with field properties. A field *property* is an attribute that defines the field's appearance or behavior in the database. The number of decimal places displayed in a numeric field is an example of a property that defines the field's appearance. A property that forces the user to enter data into a field rather than leave it blank controls that field's behavior. In Design view for tables, Access provides a list of field properties, called the *property sheet*, for each data type.

DATA TYPES	
Data Type	**Description**
Text (default)	Text or combinations of text and numbers, as well as numbers that don't require calculations, such as phone numbers. Limited to 255 characters.
Memo	A lengthy text or combinations of text and numbers. Limited to 64,000 characters.
Number	Numeric data used in mathematical calculations.
Date/Time	Date and time values for the years 100 through 9999.
Currency	Currency values and numeric data used in mathematical calculations involving data with one to four decimal places. Values are accurate to 15 digits on the left side of the decimal separator.
AutoNumber	A unique sequential number (incremented by 1) or random number Access assigns whenever you add a new record to a table. AutoNumber fields can't be changed.
Yes/No	A field containing only one of two values (for example, Yes/No, True/False, On/Off).
OLE Object	An object (such as a Microsoft Excel spreadsheet) linked to or embedded in an Access table.
Hyperlink	A link that when clicked takes the user to another file, a location in a file, or a site on the World Wide Web.
Lookup Wizard	A wizard that helps you to create a field whose values are chosen from the values in another table, query, or list of values.

Viewing Field Properties

TEXT FIELD PROPERTIES	
Field	**Action**
Field Size	Specify the maximum number of characters (up to 255) that can be entered in the field.
Format	Specify how the data for the field will appear on the screen.
Input Mask	Specify a format or pattern in which data must be entered.
Caption	Enter a label for the field when used on a form. If you don't enter a caption, Access uses the field name as the label.
Default Value	Specify a value that Access enters automatically.
Validation Rule	Enter an expression that limits the values that can be entered in this field.
Validation Text	Enter an error message that appears when a value prohibited by the validation rule is entered.
Required	Indicate whether data entry is required.
Allow Zero Length	Specify if field allows zero length text strings.
Indexed	Indicate whether Access will keep an index of field values.
Unicode Compression	Indicate whether you want Access to save space if only plain text is entered.

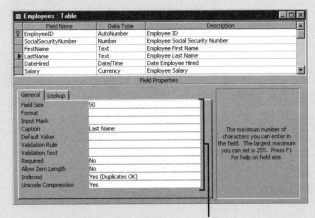

Properties list changes depending on the data type

5

Setting Field Size

For Text, Number, and AutoNumber data types, you can use the Field Size property to set the maximum size of data stored in the field. In the case of text data, this property specifies the number of characters allowed (from 0 to 255).

Numeric field sizes include Byte, Integer, and Long Integer options for integer values, and Single and Double options for decimals. The difference between these sizes lies in the amount of storage space they use and the range of possible values they cover. If your integers will cover only the range 0 to 255, you should use Byte, but for a larger range you should use Integer or Long Integer.

TIP

Use small field sizes. *You should use the appropriate field size that uses the smallest storage space because Access can process smaller data sizes faster, using less memory.*

Specify Field Size

1 Display the table in Design view, and then click the text or numeric field in the field list.

2 Click the Field Size box in the properties sheet, and either type the Field Size value (for text fields) or choose the value from the drop-down list (for numeric fields).

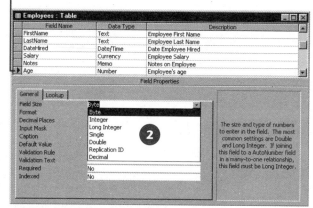

The size and type of numbers to enter in the field. The most common settings are Double and Long Integer. If joining this field to an AutoNumber field in a many-to-one relationship, this field must be Long Integer.

NUMERIC FIELD SIZES		
Field Size	**Range**	**Storage**
Byte	Integers from 0 to 255	1 byte
Integer	Integers from -32,768 to 32,767	2 bytes
Long Integer	Integers from -2,147,483,648 to 2,147,483,647	4 bytes
Single	from -3.402823E38 to -1.401298E-45 (negative values) and 1.401298E-45 to 3.402823E38 (positive values)	4 bytes
Double	from -1.797693E308 to -4.940656E-324 (negative values) and 1.797693E308 to 4.940656E324 (positive values)	8 bytes
Replication ID	Values used to establish unique identifiers	16 bytes

Formatting Text Values

A *format* is a property that determines how numbers, dates, times, and text are displayed and printed. Access provides custom formats for dates and times, but you can also create your own formats using formatting symbols.

Formatting symbols are symbols that Access uses to control how it displays data values. For example, the formatting symbol "<" forces Access to display text characters in lowercase, while the symbol ">" displays those same characters in uppercase.

Formatting may also include use of *literals*, which are text strings that are displayed exactly as they appear in format.

TIP

Field values. *Formatting only affects the way the data is displayed. It does not affect the data itself.*

Format Text Data

1 Display the table in Design view, and then click a text field for which you want to set formatting values.

2 Click the Format box, and then enter a text format for all data values in the text field.

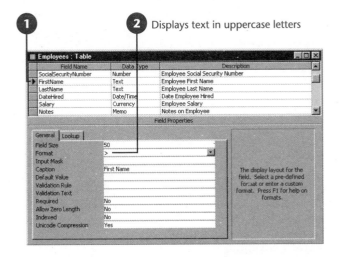

1

2 Displays text in uppercase letters

GENERAL AND TEXT FORMATTING SYMBOLS				
Symbol	**Description**	**Data**	**Format**	**Display**
!	Left align	321	!	321
<	Lowercase	Today	<	today
>	Uppercase	News	>	NEWS
"ABC"	Display quoted text as literal	20	&" lbs."	20 lbs.
(space)	Display blank space	16	& "oz."	16 oz.
\	Display next character as literal	10	&\k	10k
@	Character is required	5552115	@@@-@@@@	555-2115
&	Character not required	Mr	&\.	Mr.
*	Fill available space with next character	Hello	&*!	Hello!!!!!!!
[color]	Display values in color	Alert	[gray]	Alert

5

Formatting Number and Currency Values

If a field has a Number or Currency data type, Access provides a list of predefined formats to display the data values. You can also create your own format using formatting symbols applicable to numeric values and currency.

TIP

Using different formats for different values. *Access allows you to specify different formats for positive, negative, zero, and null values within a single field. Use online Help for more information.*

TIP

Setting the number of decimal places. *Another way to set the number of decimal places for numeric fields is to specify the number of decimal places in the Decimal Places box in the list of field properties.*

Choose a Predefined Numeric or Currency Format

1 Display the table in Design view, and then click a numeric or currency field.

2 Click the Format drop-down arrow.

3 Select a format from the predefined list of formats, or enter the appropriate formatting symbols.

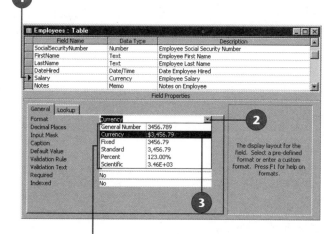

List of predefined number and currency formats

NUMERIC AND CURRENCY FORMATTING SYMBOLS				
Symbol	**Description**	**Data**	**Format**	**Display**
#	Display a digit or nothing	15	#	15
0	Display a digit or 0	20.1	#.00	20.10
.	Display a decimal separator	15	#.	15.
,	Display thousands separator	24829	#,###	24,829
$	Display the literal character, "$"	19.9	$#.00	$19.90
%	Multiple the value by 100 and append a percent symbol	0.95	#%	95%
E-,E+,e-,e+	Scientific notation	284121	#.00E+00	284E+05

Formatting Date and Time Values

Access provides formatting symbols and predefined formats for date and time values that allow you to display different combinations of the time, date, and day.

Access date values are *year 2000 compliant,* which means that Access correctly stores dates and date functions involving the year 2000 and beyond. Databases that are not 2000 databases store only the last two digits of a year and can incorrectly interpret "00" in the year 2000 to mean "1900."

Specify a Date and Time Format

1 Display the table in Design view, and then click a date and time field.

2 Click the Format drop-down arrow.

3 Select a format from the predefined list of formats, or enter the appropriate formatting symbols.

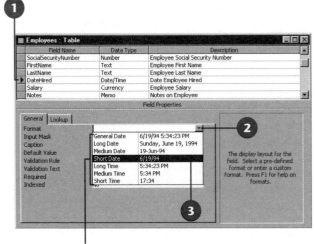

List of predefined date formats

PREDEFINED DATE FORMATS	
Format	**Display**
General Date	6/19/00 5:34:23 PM
Long Date	Sunday, June 19, 2000
Medium Date	19-Jun-00
Short Date	6/19/00
Long Time	5:34:23 PM
Medium Time	5:34 PM
Short Time	17:34

5

Creating Input Masks

An *input mask* allows you to control what values a database user can enter into a field. Input masks consist of literal characters, such as spaces, dots, parentheses, and placeholders. A *placeholder* is a text character, such as the underline symbol (_), that indicates where the user should insert values. An input mask for a phone number field might appear as follows:

$$(\_\,\_\,\_)\;\_\,\_\,\_\;-\;\_\,\_\,\_\,\_$$

The parenthesis and dash characters act as literal characters, and the underscore character acts as a placeholder for the phone number values.

Access provides several predefined input masks, which cover most situations, but you can create your own customized masks if necessary.

Specify an Input Mask

1 Display the table in Design view, and then click a field for which you want to specify an input mask.

2 Click the Input Mask box.

3 Click the Build button to start the Input Mask Wizard.

4 Select an input mask from the predefined list.

5 Type some sample values to see how the input mask affects your sample values.

6 Click Next to continue.

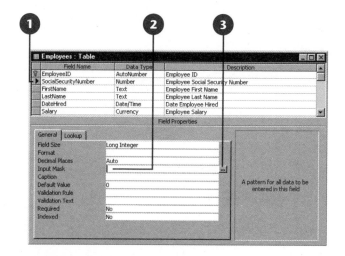

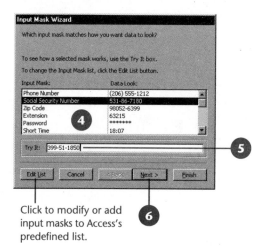

Click to modify or add input masks to Access's predefined list.

Using the Input Mask Wizard. *The Input Mask Wizard is available only for text and date fields. If you want to create an input mask for numeric fields, you must enter the formatting symbols yourself.*

Creating a password mask. *For sensitive data, choose the password input mask from the Input Mask Wizard. Any text the user types will be saved as the text, but displayed as an asterisk (*)*

7 If you change the input mask, type new formatting codes.

8 If you want to display a different placeholder, click the Placeholder drop-down arrow, and select the placeholder you want to use.

9 Enter values to test the final version of your input mask.

10 Click Next to continue.

11 Indicate whether you want to store the input mask symbols along with the data values.

12 Click Next, and then click Finish to complete the Input Mask Wizard.

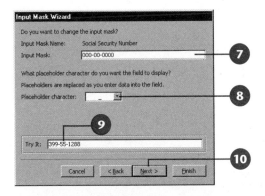

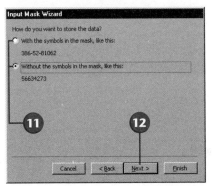

INPUT MASK SYMBOLS			
Symbol	Description	Symbol	Description
0	Digit 0 to 9 (required)	A	Letter or digit (required)
9	Digit 0 to 9 (optional)	A	Letter or digit (optional)
#	Digit or spaces	&	Any character or space (required)
L	Letter A–Z (required)	C	Any character or space (optional)
?	Letter A–Z (optional)	<	Make following characters lowercase
>	Make following characters uppercase		

5

Specifying Required Fields and Default Values

Some fields contain essential information. For example, social security numbers are required for employees in order to process payroll and other reports. You set fields like these as *required fields*, which means that Access refuses to accept a record until you enter an acceptable value for that field.

You can also set a *default value* for a field, a value Access uses unless a user enters a different one. If a field usually has the same value, such as a city or state if most contacts are local, you could assign that value as the default in order to speed up data entry.

Create a Required Field

1. Display the table in Design view, and then click a field that you want to be a required field.

2. Click the Required box.

3. Click the drop-down arrow, and then click Yes.

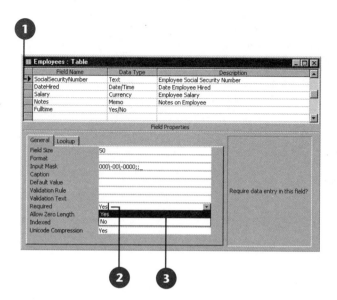

Specify a Default Value

1. Display the table in Design view, and then click a field for which you want to set a default value.

2. Click the Default Value box.

3. Enter the default value for the field in the box.

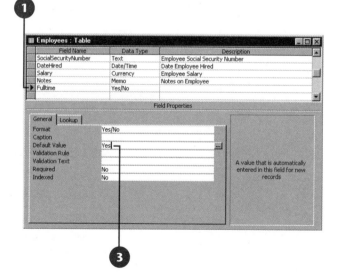

Adding a Caption to a Field

A field *caption* is text displayed alongside a field to better describe its purpose and content. You can add a caption to a field, and later when you create forms and reports that use this field, Access automatically displays the caption you specify.

Captions can contain up to 2,048 characters, including spaces. If you don't specify a caption, Access uses the field name as the field caption in any forms or reports you create.

TIP

Setting zero-length strings. *Text and Memo data type fields allow you to control whether or not a user can leave a field blank. To ensure that some text is entered, set the Required property to Yes.*

Set the Caption Property

1 Display the table in Design view, and then click a field for which you want to set a caption.

2 Click the Caption box.

3 Type text you want to appear as the field's caption.

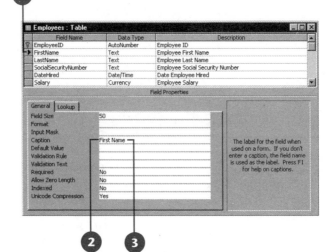

5

Creating Indexed Fields

Just like an index in a book, an index in Access helps you locate and sort information quickly, especially in a very large table. An *index* in Access is an invisible data structure that stores the sort order of a table based on the indexed field or fields. When you sort a large table by an indexed field, Access consults the index and is able to sort the table very quickly. It can be helpful to index fields you frequently search or sort or fields you join to fields in other tables in queries.

If a field contains many different values, rather than many values that are the same, indexing can significantly speed up queries. After indexing a field, you can view and then modify indexes as necessary.

Create a Field Index

1. Display the table in Design view, and then click a field you want as an index.

2. Click the Indexed box.

3. Click the drop-down arrow, and then select one of the following.

   ◆ Yes (Duplicates OK) if you want to allow multiple records to have the same data in this field

   ◆ Yes (No Duplicates) option if you want to ensure that no two records have the same data in this field

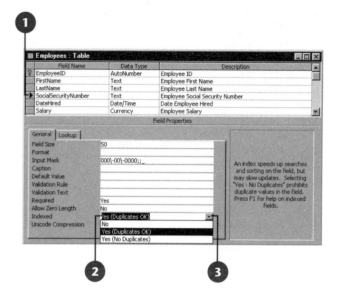

An index speeds up searches and sorting on the field, but may slow updates. Selecting "Yes - No Duplicates" prohibits duplicate values in the field. Press F1 for help on indexed fields.

Index data types. *You don't have to index all data types, and there are some data types you cannot index. For example, you do not need to index the primary key of a table, because it is automatically indexed. You can index a field only if the data type is Text, Number, Currency, or Date/Time. You cannot index a field whose data type is Memo or OLE Object.*

Create a multiple-field index. *If you think you'll often search or sort by two or more fields, create a multiple-field index by adding additional fields in the Field Name column for each index name.*

View or Edit Indexes

1. Display the table in Design view.

2. Click the Indexes button on the Table Design toolbar.

3. Type a name for the index.

4. Select a field to act as an index.

5. Indicate whether the field should be indexed in ascending or descending order.

6. Click the Close button.

Click to make the index the primary key.

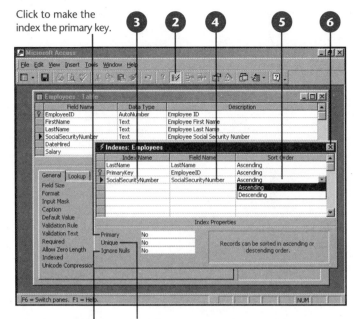

Click to remove null values from the index.

Click if every value in the index must be unique.

Validating Field Values

When you need explicit control over data entered in a field, such as a range of numbers or dates, you can enforce a *validation rule*, which causes Access to test values a user enters in a field. If the value doesn't satisfy the validation rule's criteria, Access refuses to enter the value and displays an error message. You can specify the text of the error message yourself.

You can use the Expression Builder to create a validation rule by selecting the functions, constants, and operators you need for your rule from a list of options.

SEE ALSO

See "Performing Calculations in Reports" on page 132 and "Performing Calculations in Queries" on page 106 for information on using the Expression Builder in reports and queries.

Create a Validation Rule

1. Display the table in Design view, and then click a field that you intend to validate.

2. Click the Validation Rule box, and then click the Build button to open the Expression Builder.

3. Create an expression by clicking the appropriate elements in the Expression Builder dialog box.

4. Click OK.

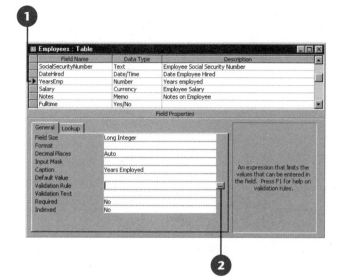

Specify Validation Text

1. Display the table in Design view, and then click a field.

2. Click the Validation Text box.

3. Type the text that Access will display when the user tries to enter incorrect data for the field.

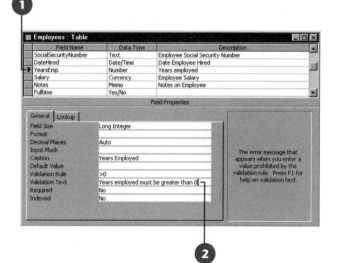

Using Expression Builder

Click a button to insert one of these frequently used functions, constants, and operators.

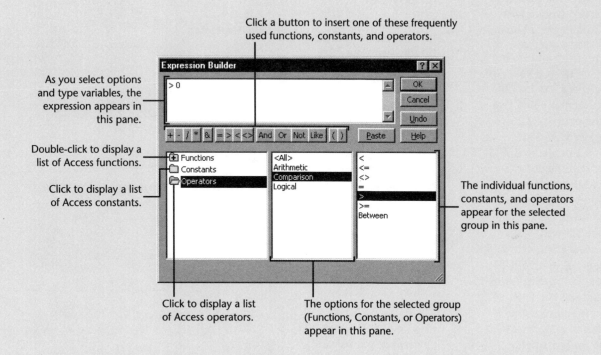

As you select options and type variables, the expression appears in this pane.

Double-click to display a list of Access functions.

Click to display a list of Access constants.

The individual functions, constants, and operators appear for the selected group in this pane.

Click to display a list of Access operators.

The options for the selected group (Functions, Constants, or Operators) appear in this pane.

5

Creating a Lookup Field

The *Lookup Wizard* helps you create a field that displays either of two kinds of lists during data entry: a Lookup list that displays values looked up from an existing table or query, or a Value list that displays a fixed set of values you enter when you create the field.

Because values are limited to a predefined list, using Lookup fields helps you avoid data entry errors in situations where only a limited number of possible values are allowed.

The lists are not limited to a single column. You can include additional columns that could include descriptive information for the various choices in the list. However, only a single column, called the *bound column*, contains the data that will be extracted from the list and placed into the Lookup field.

Create a Field Based on a Lookup List

1. Display the table in Design view, enter a new field, click the Data Type drop-down arrow, and then click Lookup Wizard.

2. Click the I Want The Lookup Column To Look Up The Values In A Table Or Query option button. Click Next to continue.

3. Select the table or query you want to use for the Lookup list. Click Next to continue.

4. Select the fields that you want to appear in the Lookup list. Click Next to continue.

5. Resize the column widths in the Lookup list, and indicate whether or not to include the primary key column. Click Next to continue.

   If the table or query lacks a primary key, you will be prompted for the column that will act as the bound column. Otherwise the primary key will be the bound column.

6. Enter a label for the Lookup column, and then click Finish.

Click to place the selected field in the Lookup list.

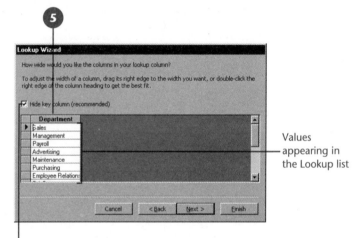

Click to place all fields in the Lookup list.

Values appearing in the Lookup list

When this option is selected, the primary key does not appear in the Lookup list.

Choosing the bound column. *The Lookup Wizard does not allow you to select the bound column in a Lookup list if the source table has a primary key. If you want to choose a different column, you will have to set the Bound Column property yourself.*

Create a Field Based on a Value List

1. Display the table in Design view, enter a new field, click the Data Type drop-down arrow, and then click Lookup Wizard.

2. Click the I Will Type In The Values That I Want option button. Click Next to continue.

3. Specify the number of columns you want in the Value list.

4. Enter the values in the list. Resize the column widths if necessary. Click Next to continue.

5. Choose which column will act as the bound column. Click Next to continue.

6. Enter a label for the Lookup column, and then click Finish.

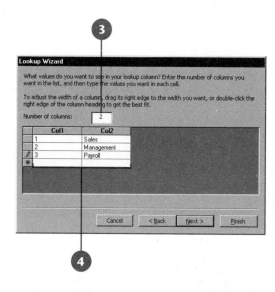

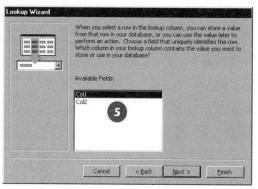

5

Setting Lookup Properties

If you want to create a Lookup field manually or to make changes to the field created by the wizard, you can do so by changing the values in the Lookup properties. These properties allow you to specify the type of drop-down box Access will display, the source of the values in the list, the appearance of the list, and the column that will act as the bound column. You can also indicate whether the user is limited to the choices in the list or can enter other values during data entry.

Click to choose the type of list box to display.

Specify the type of source for the Lookup data.

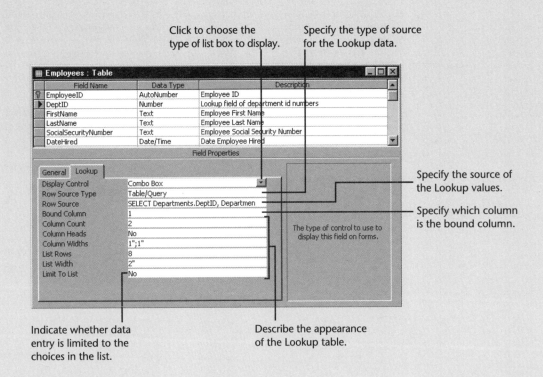

Specify the source of the Lookup values.

Specify which column is the bound column.

Describe the appearance of the Lookup table.

Indicate whether data entry is limited to the choices in the list.

6

Working with Tables

Tables are the storage containers of your data. To help you work effectively with tables, Microsoft Access 2000 provides features that assist you not only in entering and editing the data in your tables but also in locating the information you need.

◆ You can locate records based on the text they contain with the Find feature.

◆ You can enter and edit data more accurately with features like AutoCorrect, copy, collect, and paste, and language features.

◆ You can display records in either ascending or descending order based on the contents of a specific field.

◆ You can arrange records and columns so your information is listed in the order you want, and adjust the size of your rows and columns to show more or less of the information displayed in any of the fields. You can also view subdatasheets that show groups of data related to the records in your tables.

◆ To focus on certain records in a table, you can apply a filter to change which records are displayed. With a filter you describe characteristics or contents of the records you want to view.

Searching for and Replacing Text

To locate one or more records in which you expect to find specific text, you can use the Find feature. In the Find dialog box, you enter the text you want to find, and specify whether Access should search the current field or the entire table, and whether the text you enter should match part of the field or the whole field. You can also indicate whether Access should look for matching capitalization. When Access finds the first record that contains the specified text, it selects that record. You can then move to the next matching record or cancel the search. You can also use the Find and Replace feature to automatically replace specified text with new text. You can review and change each occurrence individually, or replace all occurrences at once.

Search for Text in the Current Field

1. Display the table in Datasheet view.

2. Click the insertion point anywhere in the field (column) where you expect to find the text for which you want to search.

3. Click the Find button on the Table Datasheet toolbar.

4. Type the text you want to find in either uppercase or lowercase letters.

5. Click the Look In drop-down arrow to specify whether Find should search the current field or the entire table.

6. Click the Match drop-down arrow, and indicate whether you want the text you typed to match the whole field or part of the field.

7. Click Find Next as many times as necessary to view all the records that contain the specified text.

8. When you're done, click the Close button.

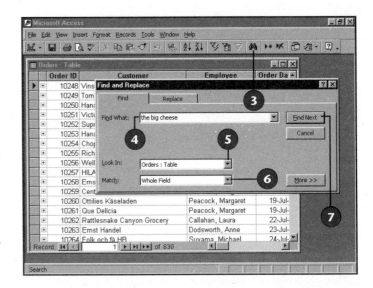

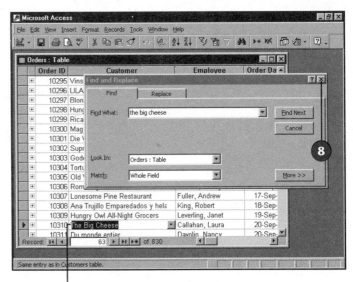

Find selects the first instance.

Search in either direction.
*By default, Access searches the
entire table. You can also search
backwards through a table,
ignoring any records following
the current record. Or you can
ignore the previous records and
search only those records that
appear after the current record.
Click the Search drop-down
arrow in the Find In Field
dialog box to specify the
direction of the search.*

**Search for records
matching case.** *To search for
records matching the case of the
text you typed, click the Match
Case check box.*

Search for formatted text.
*You might need to find
information that has been
assigned a specific data format,
such as a date format, without
entering the information in the
specified format. For example,
if dates are displayed in the
format 05-Jan-00, you can
locate that number by typing
1/5/00. Click the Search Fields
As Formatted check box. Be
aware that searching this way
can be slow.*

Refine a Search

1 In the Find And Replace
dialog box, click the
More button.

2 Specify the options you
want to use to refine your
search.

3 Click the Less button to
hide the additional
options.

Once you click the More button, it appears as the Less button.

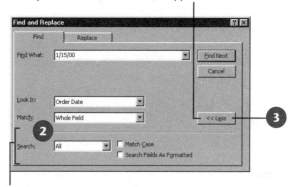

The bottom pane appears when
you click the More button.

Find and Replace Text

1 In the Find And Replace
dialog box, click the
Replace tab.

2 Type the text you want to
find, and then press Tab.

3 Type the replacement text.

4 Click Find Next.

5 Click Replace to replace
the first occurrence with
the replacement text, or
click Replace All to replace
all occurrences with the
replacement text, or click
Find Next to skip to the
next occurrence.

6 Click the Close button.

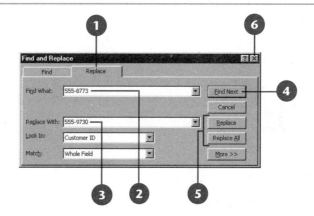

6

Entering Data Accurately with AutoCorrect

As you enter data in tables, you might occasionally make typing mistakes. For certain errors, Access will correct the errors as soon as you type them and then press the Spacebar or Enter. For example, if you type *comapny* when you meant to type *company*, the AutoCorrect feature will correct the error automatically.

You can easily customize the preset AutoCorrect options or add errors that you commonly make to the list of AutoCorrect entries.

SEE ALSO

See "Working with Language" on page 80 for more information about correcting spelling errors.

Enable AutoCorrect

1. Click the Tools menu, and then click AutoCorrect.

2. Click to select the Replace Text As You Type check box.

3. Click OK.

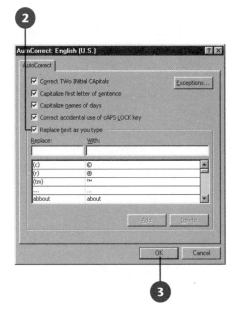

Correct Errors as You Type

◆ To correct incorrect capitalization or spelling errors automatically, simply continue to type and AutoCorrect will make the required correction.

EXAMPLES OF AUTOCORRECT CHANGES		
Type of Correction	If You Type	AutoCorrect Inserts
Capitalization	CAlifornia	California
Capitalization	thursday	Thursday
Common typos	accomodate	accommodate
Common typos	can;t	can't
Common typos	windoes	windows

Prevent AutoCorrect from correcting specific abbreviations or capitalized text. *To prevent AutoCorrect from correcting abbreviations or capitalized text in certain instances, click AutoCorrect on the Tools menu, click Exceptions, and then choose the exception you want to enforce, or add your own by clicking the Add button.*

Add an AutoCorrect Entry

1. Click the Tools menu, and then click AutoCorrect.

2. Type a word or phrase that you often mistype or misspell.

3. Type the correct spelling of the word.

4. Click Add.

5. Click OK.

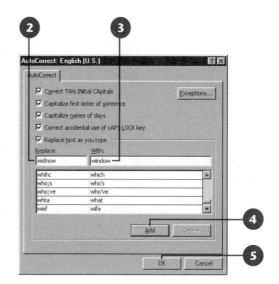

Add an AutoCorrect entry during a spelling check. *To add a misspelled word and its correct spelling during a spelling check, make sure you have selected or typed the correct spelling of the word in the Change To box, and then click AutoCorrect.*

Set AutoCorrect Options

1. Click the Tools menu, and then click AutoCorrect.

2. Click to select the check boxes you want to enforce.

   ◆ Correct two initial capital letters so that only the first letter is capitalized.

   ◆ Always capitalize the first word in a sentence.

   ◆ Capitalize the names of days.

   ◆ Disable the Caps Lock key.

3. Click OK.

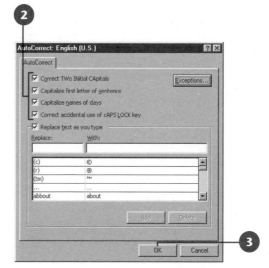

6

Editing Text

You can edit text you enter in a record by selecting the text you want to change and then performing an action. When you want to insert or delete text one character at a time, you point between two characters or words and then click to place the *insertion point*, a vertical cursor that indicates your location in a section of text.

You can also use the Cut, Copy, and Paste functions to cut or copy selected text to the Windows Clipboard and then paste it elsewhere. With *Collect and Paste*, you can cut or copy multiple selections to the Office Clipboard and then can paste them in a new location, all at once or singly. Unlike the Windows Clipboard, which only stores a single piece of information at a time, the Office Clipboard allows you to copy up to twelve pieces of text and pictures from one or more places.

Select Text

To modify text, you first select it.

◆ Double-click a word.

◆ Drag to select multiple words.

◆ Click the border of a table cell to select its entire contents in Datasheet view.

Pointer when you click a cell border to select all text in the cell

Delete Text

◆ Select the text you want to delete, and then type new text or press Delete to remove the selected text.

◆ Click next to the text you want to delete. Press Delete to delete text to the right of the insertion point, or press Backspace to delete text to the left of the insertion point.

Pressing Delete removes selected text.

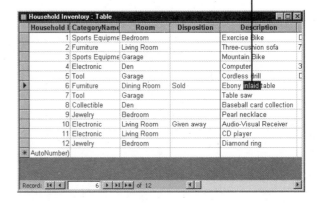

Insert Text

1️⃣ Position the insertion point where you want to insert text.

2️⃣ Type the text.

Insertion point

Use Cut, Copy, and Paste to Move or Copy Text

1 Select the text you want to move or copy.

2 Click the Cut button to move the text or the Copy button to copy the text.

3 Place the insertion point where you want to paste the text, and then click the Paste button.

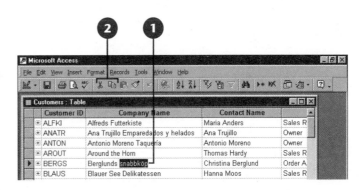

Collect and Paste Multiple Items

1 Select the text you want to collect.

2 Click the Copy button on the Database toolbar or the Clipboard toolbar.

3 Select the next item you want to copy.

You can repeat steps 2 and 3 to collect up to 12 items.

4 Click where you want the items to be pasted, and then click the Paste All button on the Clipboard toolbar.

5 Click the Close button on the Clipboard toolbar.

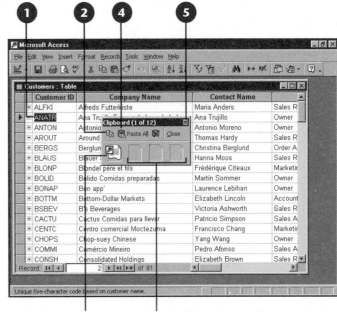

First collected item   Additional collected items will appear in place of the blank boxes.

6

Working with Language

The Spelling feature helps you proofread your document by identifying potentially misspelled words and suggesting possible spellings to use instead. You can correct the spelling, ignore the word, add the word to the dictionary, or create an AutoCorrect entry. In addition, you can control the kinds of spelling errors Access identifies by specifying the spelling options you want in effect.

If you work with documents that contain text in more than one language or if you share documents with those who use Microsoft Office in other languages, you can use the Office 2000 multilanguage features to edit in additional languages. You might need to modify your computer, including your keyboard layout, to do so.

Check the Spelling in a Table

1 Display the table in Datasheet view, click the row selector for the record or select the field you want to check. Drag to select additional rows.

2 Click the Spelling button on the Table Datasheet toolbar. If Access identifies any misspelled words, it opens the Spelling dialog box.

3 Correct or ignore the identified words, as appropriate.

- ◆ Click Ignore to ignore the word and retain its spelling. Click Ignore All to ignore all instances of the word.

- ◆ Click Add to add the word to the dictionary so the spelling checker won't identify it as a misspelled word.

- ◆ Click a word in the Suggestions list, and then click Change to spell the word with the selected spelling. Click Change All to change all instances of the word to the selected spelling.

- ◆ Click AutoCorrect to add the word to the AutoCorrect list.

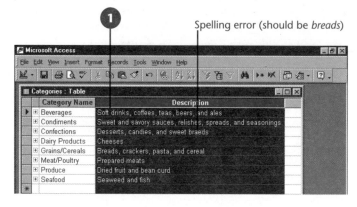

Spelling error (should be *breads*)

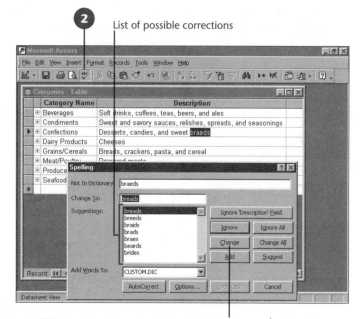

List of possible corrections

Click to replace the misspelled word with the selected word, which is spelled correctly.

Customize Spelling Options

1. In the Spelling dialog box, click Options.

2. Select the options you want to change.

   ◆ Clear the Suggest check boxes if you want to omit the list of suggested spellings or to check spelling from both the Custom and Main dictionaries.

   ◆ Clear the Ignore check boxes if you don't want to ignore words in uppercase or words with numbers.

3. Click OK.

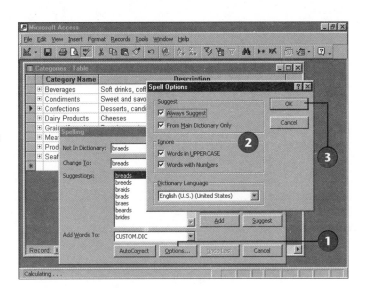

Enable Multiple Language Editing

1. Click the Start button, point to Programs, point to Microsoft Office Tools, and then click Microsoft Office Language Settings.

2. Click to select the languages you want.

3. Click OK.

4. Click Yes to make the change.

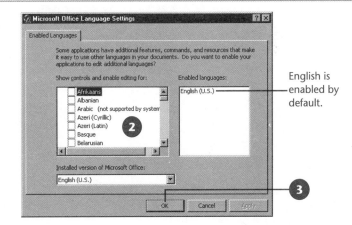

English is enabled by default.

6

Arranging Columns

The order in which columns appear in the Table window in Datasheet view is initially determined by the order established when you first designed the table. If you want to temporarily rearrange the order of the columns in a table, you can do so without changing the table design. You can arrange columns in the order you want by selecting and then dragging columns to a new location. You can also hide columns you do not want to view.

The *freeze column* feature allows you to "freeze" one or more of the columns on a datasheet so that they are visible regardless of where you scroll.

SEE ALSO

See "Changing the Size of Rows and Columns" on page 84 for more information about working with rows and columns.

Move a Column

1. In Datasheet view, click the column selector of the column you want to move.

2. Drag the selected column to its new location.

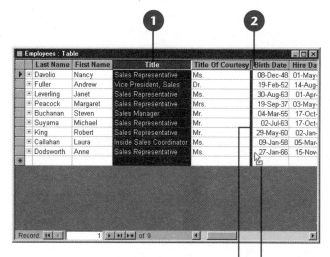

A vertical bar indicates where the column will appear.

Pointer when you drag a column

Hide a Column

1. In Datasheet view, right-click the column or columns you want to hide.

2. Click Hide Columns.

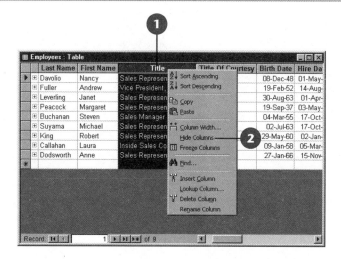

Display a Hidden Column

1 In Datasheet view, click the Format menu, and then click Unhide Columns.

2 Select the names of the columns that you want to show.

3 Click Close.

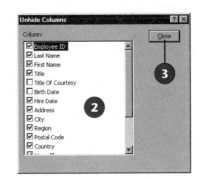

Freeze or Unfreeze Columns

1 In Datasheet view, select the column(s) you want to freeze or unfreeze. (To freeze just one column, skip step 1.)

2 Right-click the selected columns, and then click Freeze Columns or Unfreeze All Columns.

A vertical bar appears to the right of a frozen column.

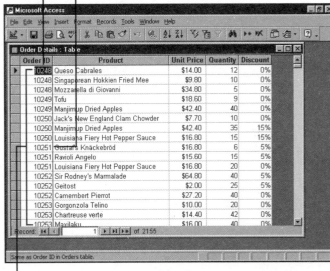

If you scroll through this table, the first column will remain frozen.

6

Changing the Size of Rows and Columns

If some of the text in a column is hidden because the column is too narrow, you can increase the width of the column. You can also change the height of the rows to provide more space for the text. Unlike changing the column width, which affects only the selected column or columns, changing the row height affects all the rows in the table. You can adjust the size of columns and rows by using commands or by dragging the borders between columns or rows.

TIP

Format columns in other Access objects. *These formatting steps also work for columns in queries, forms, views, or stored procedures.*

Change Column Width

◆ Point to the border between two field selectors, and then drag the border left or right.

◆ Right-click a field selector, and then click Column Width. Enter a new width, and then click OK.

Number of characters that can be displayed with current column width

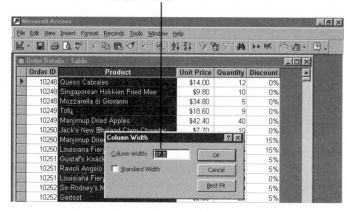

Change Row Height

◆ Point to the border between two row selectors, and then drag the border up or down to adjust the height of all the rows in the table.

◆ Right-click a row selector, and then click Row Height. Enter a new height, and then click OK.

Pointer when you change row height

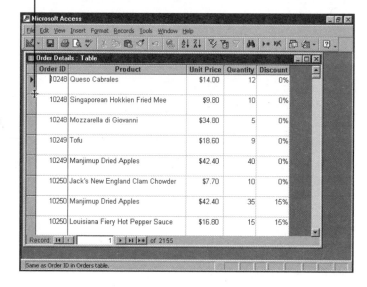

Managing Columns in Datasheet View

You can quickly add, remove, and rename columns from within Datasheet view. If you remove a column, Access deletes all the data it contains, so delete a column only if you are sure you no longer require its data.

If other database objects contain references to a deleted field, such as a query, Microsoft automatically updates those references.

TIP

Delete a column in a relationship. *You can't delete a column that's part of a relationship. You must delete the relationship first.*

TIP

Rename a column. *In Datasheet view, right-click the selector for the column you want to rename, click Rename, type the name you want, and then press Enter.*

Insert a Column

1 In Datasheet view, right-click the column selector to the right of where you want to add the new column.

2 Click Insert Column. The column is inserted with the name *Field1*, so you might want to rename it.

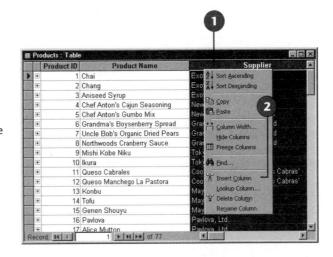

Delete a Column

1 In Datasheet view, right-click the column selector(s) for the column(s) you want to delete.

2 Click Delete Column.

3 Click Yes to confirm the deletion.

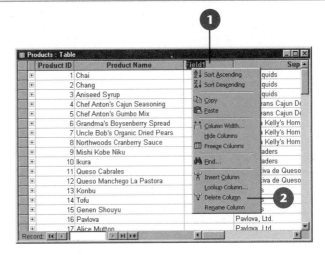

6

Repairing Renaming Errors

Access can correct errors that commonly occur when you rename forms, reports, tables, queries, text boxes, or other controls in a database. When Access detects a change in the name of one of these objects, it automatically corrects all the other objects that use that name. You can set Access to track renaming without taking action, to apply changes if you rename an object, and to log any changes it makes.

Enable Name AutoCorrect

1 Click the Tools menu, click Options, and then click the General tab.

2 Click to select the Track Name AutoCorrect Info check box to allow Access to maintain the information it needs to perform Name AutoCorrect but not take any action.

3 Click to select the Perform Name AutoCorrect check box to perform Name AutoCorrect as changes are applied to the database.

4 Click OK.

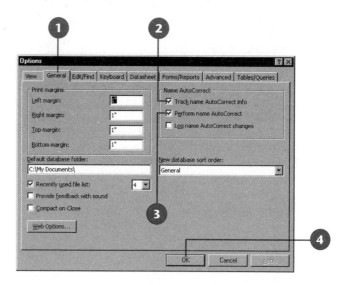

Log Name AutoCorrect Changes

1 Click the Tools menu, click Options, and then click the General tab.

2 Click to select the Track Name AutoCorrect Info, Perform Name AutoCorrect, and Log Name AutoCorrect Changes check boxes.

3 Click OK.

You can view the name changes in a table called AutoCorrect Log.

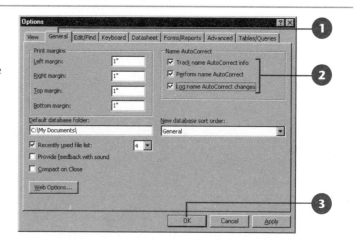

Moving to a Specific Record in a Table

When you scroll through a table in Datasheet view, you are simply viewing different parts of the table; the insertion point (cursor) stays in its original location in the first record. If you type any text, it appears in the first record, regardless of which record is currently visible. To move the insertion point to a specific record, you must click the record (or a field in the record). If the record you want to select is not visible, you can use the navigation buttons to move to the next, previous, first, or last record. Or you can type the number of the record (if you know it) in the Specific Record box to display that record.

TRY THIS

Go to a specific record. *For a quick way to display a specific record, click the Edit menu, point to Go To, and then click the record you want to go to.*

Move to a Record

◆ Current Record icon:

Indicates the current record.

◆ Specific Record box:

To move to a new record, select the current record number, type the new record number, and then press Enter.

◆ New Record button:

Click to create a new, blank row at the end of the table.

◆ Selection bar:

Click the row selector to the left of a record to select it.

◆ First Record button:

Click to move to the first record in the table.

◆ Previous Record button:

Click to move to the previous record in the table.

◆ Next Record button:

Click to move to the next record in the table.

◆ Last Record button:

Click to move to the last record in the table.

Current Record icon — Specific Record box — New Record button

First Record button

Previous Record button

Last Record button

Next Record button

Rearranging Records

You can change the order in which records appear in a table by *sorting* the records. You can select a field and then sort the records by the values in that field in either ascending or descending order. *Ascending* order means that records appear in alphabetical order (for text fields), from earliest to most recent (for date fields), or from smallest to largest (for numeric fields). In *Descending* order, the order is reversed.

You might also want to sort records by more than one field; this is referred to as a *secondary sort*. For example, in a table containing information about video programs, you might need to view information about specific types of programs and the date on which each program was recorded. You could sort the records first by program type and then, in records with the same program type, sort the records by recording date.

Sort Records Based on One Field

① In Datasheet view, right-click the column selector of the column that contains the values by which you want to sort the records.

② Click Sort Ascending to sort the records in ascending order, or click Sort Descending to sort the records in descending order.

Records currently sorted by Supplier ID column

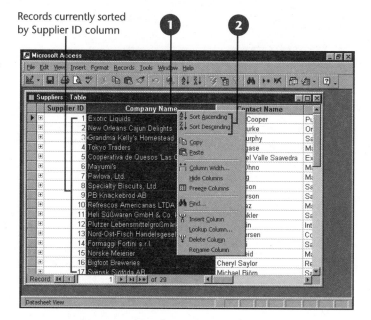

Records now sorted by Company Name column

TIP

Specify a sort order when designing a table. *Changing the order of records displayed in a table is not the same as specifying the sort order when you first design the table. Use the Sort feature when designing a table to display records in the order that you are likely to use most often, and then use the Sort Ascending and Sort Descending buttons to handle the exceptions when you display the table in Datasheet view.*

SEE ALSO

See "Using Filters to View Specific Records" on page 92 for more information about the sort order of records in a table.

Change the Order of Records Based on Multiple Fields

1 Display the table in Datasheet view.

2 Because multiple fields that you want to sort must be adjacent and in the order of sort priority, rearrange columns if necessary.

3 Click the column selector of the first column you want to sort, and before you release the mouse button, drag the mouse to the right to select the adjacent columns fields.

4 Click the Sort Ascending button on the Table Datasheet toolbar to sort the records in ascending order, or click the Sort Descending button on the Table Datasheet toolbar to sort the records in descending order.

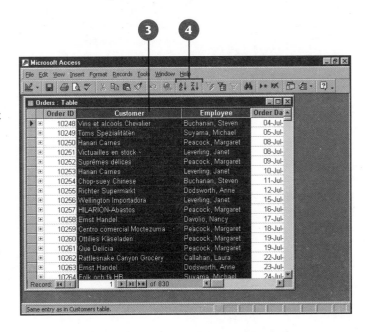

Column is first sorted by Customer

Within each customer, records are sorted by Employee.

Copying and Pasting Records

When you are entering a lot of records in Datasheet view that are nearly identical, you can use the Windows Clipboard to copy and paste existing records to create new records quickly. After copying and pasting, you can edit individual records to make a few changes. If only part of the record is similar, you can still use the Windows Clipboard to copy and paste the data in a single table cell.

TIP

Select data to copy. *When you select data to copy, you can select an entire row or a single cell, but not multiple cells within a single row.*

Copy and Paste a New Record

1. In Datasheet view, right-click the row selector for the row you want to copy.

2. Click Copy.

3. Right-click an empty row selector for the new record row.

4. Click Paste.

5. Edit the new record as required.

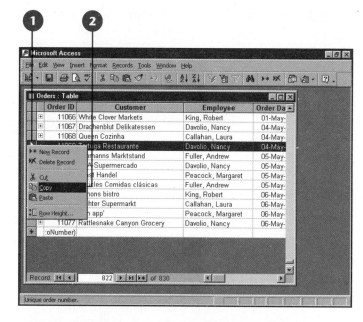

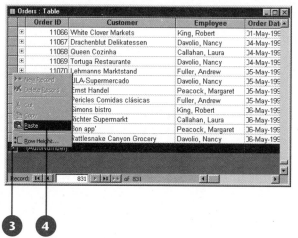

Viewing a Subdatasheet

In a table that has a one-to-many relationship with another table, a given record might have multiple related items. For example, a customer in a Customers table might have many products in a Products table. Access allows you to view the products related to that customer from the Customers table. You can open a *subdatasheet*, a list of the records from the "many" table that relate to a single record from the "one" table in a one-to-one or one-to-many relationship.

Subdatasheets help you browse related data in tables, queries, forms, and subform datasheets. For any related tables, Access automatically creates subdatasheets. You can also insert a subdatasheet in a table or query to view related data.

Display or Hide a Subdatasheet

1 In Datasheet view of the table, click the plus sign next to the record for which you want to see related information.

2 To hide the subdatasheet, click the minus sign next to the record whose subdatsheet you want to hide.

Insert a Subdatasheet in a Table

1 Display the table or query in Datasheet view.

2 Click the Insert menu, and then click Subdatasheet.

3 Click the tab corresponding to the object you want to insert as a subdatasheet.

4 Click a table or query in the list.

5 Click the field you want to use as a foreign key.

6 Click the field you want to use as a primary key.

7 Click OK.

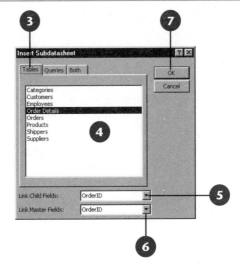

Using Filters to View Specific Records

Instead of displaying all the records in a table, you can use a *filter* to display only those records that you want to see. You can display records based on a specific value in one field or on multiple values in multiple fields. You can filter by selecting the field value on which to base the filter in Datasheet view, or by using the Filter By Form feature to help you create more complex filters involving multiple field values. After you apply a filter, Access displays only those records that match your specifications. You can remove a filter to return the datasheet to its original display. If you enter a series of criteria in a filter that you expect you might need again, or if you create a rather complex filter, consider saving the criteria as a query.

Filter a Table by Selection

1. Display the table in Datasheet view.

2. Right-click the field value on which you want to base the filter.

3. Click Filter By Selection.

Notice that the bottom of the Table window tells you the number of records matching your filter criteria. Also the notation *FLTR* in the status bar indicates that a filter is currently in effect.

Clear a Filter from a Table

1. Right-click the filtered table, and click Remove Filter.

Notice that the status bar removes the indication that the table is filtered.

You can also click the Remove Filter button to remove a filter.

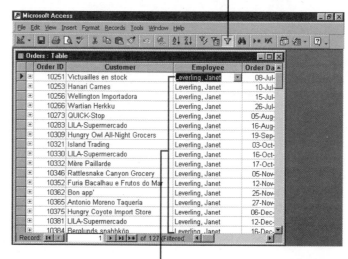

Only records matching filter criteria appear.

Save a Filter as a Query

1. Display the filtered table in Datasheet view.

2. Click the Records menu, point to Filter, and then click Advanced Filter/Sort.

   The details of the filter appear in Design view.

3. Click the Save As Query button on the Filter/Sort toolbar.

4. Type the name you want to assign to the query. If you enter the name of an existing query, Access will ask if you want to overwrite the existing query. Be sure to answer "No" if you want to retain the original query, so you can give the new query a different name.

5. Click OK to save the filter as a query.

   The query you have just saved appears in the Queries list in the Database window.

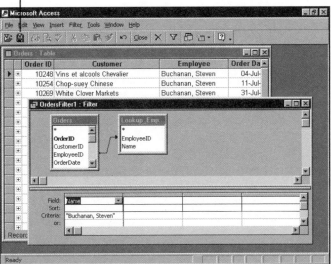

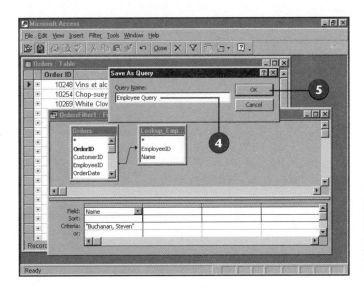

6

Creating Complex Filters Using a Form

The *Filter By Form* feature allows you to create a more complex filter. Adding criteria on a particular tab in the form restricts the filter so that records must match *all* the criteria on the form for the records to be displayed; this is called an *AND filter*. To expand the filter to include more records, you can create an *OR filter* by specifying criteria on the subsequent Or tab in the Filter By Form grid. To be displayed, a record needs to match only the criteria specified on the Look For tab or the criteria specified on any one of the Or tabs.

Create an AND or OR Filter

1. In Datasheet view, click the Filter By Form button on the Table Datasheet toolbar.

2. Click in the empty text box below the field you want to filter.

3. Click the drop-down arrow and then click the field value by which you want to filter the records.

4. For each field by which you want to filter, click the drop-down arrow and select the entry for your filter. Each new field in which you make a selection adds additional criteria that a record must match to be included.

5. If you want to establish Or criteria, click the Or tab at the bottom of the form to specify the additional criteria for the filter. If not, proceed to step 6.

6. Click the Apply Filter button on the Filter/Sort toolbar.

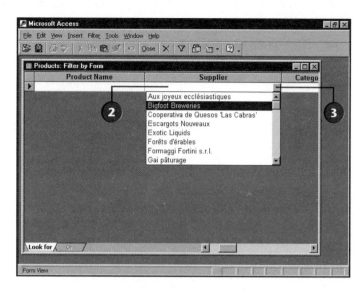

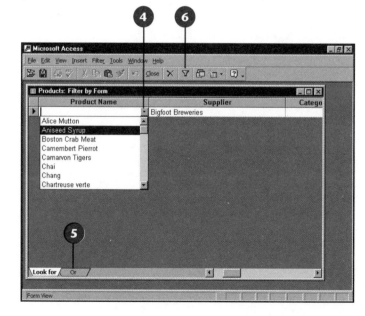

7

Querying a Database

A *query* is a description of the records you want to retrieve from a database. As the name implies, a query helps answer specific questions about the information in your database—for example, "Which customers have placed orders in the last six months?" or "Who sent us greeting cards over the holidays in the last two years?" The description of the records you want to retrieve identifies the names of the fields and the values they should contain; this description is called the *selection criteria*. With a Microsoft Access 2000 query you can:

◆ Focus on only the information you need by displaying only a few fields from a large table.

◆ Apply functions and other expressions to fields to arrive at calculated results.

◆ Add, update, or delete records in tables; or create entirely new tables.

◆ Summarize and group values from one table and display the result in a table.

◆ Save a query definition that Access will treat as a table for the purpose of creating forms and reports.

◆ Retrieve information stored in multiple tables, even if the tables are not open.

Understanding the Different Types of Queries

Access offers several types of queries that help you retrieve the information you need: select queries, crosstab queries, action queries, and parameter queries.

- ◆ A *select query* retrieves and displays records in the Table window in Datasheet view.

- ◆ A *crosstab query* displays summarized values (sums, counts, and averages) from one field in a table, and groups them by one set of fields listed down the left side of the datasheet and another set of fields listed across the top of the datasheet.

- ◆ An *action query* performs operations on the records that match your criteria. There are four kinds of action queries that you can perform on one or more tables: *delete queries* delete matching records; *update queries* make changes to matching records; *append queries* add new records to the end of a table; and *make-table* queries create new tables based on matching records.

- ◆ A *parameter query* allows you to prompt for a single piece of information to use as selection criteria in the query. For example, instead of creating separate queries to retrieve customer information for each state in which you do business, you could create a parameter query that prompts the user to enter the name of a state, and then continues to retrieve those specific records from that state.

Creating Queries in Access

As with most database objects you create in Access, there are several ways to create a query. You can create a query from scratch or use a wizard to guide you through the process of creating a query.

With the Query Wizard, Access helps you create a simple query to retrieve the records you want. All queries you create and save are listed on the Queries tab in the Database window. You can then double-click a query to run it and display the results. When you run a select query, the query results show only the selected fields for each record in the table that matches your selection criteria. Of course, once you have completed a query, you can further customize it in Design view. As always, you can begin creating your query in Design view without using the wizard at all. Queries are not limited to a single table. Your queries can encompass multiple tables as long as the database includes a field or fields that relate the tables to each other.

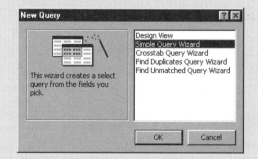

Creating a Query in Design View

Although a wizard can be a big help when you are first learning to create a query, you do not need to use a wizard. If you prefer, you can create a query without the help of a wizard. Instead of answering questions in a series of dialog boxes, you can start working in Design view right away.

TIP

Switch between Datasheet and Design view. *For many of the tasks you do in Access, you will switch back and forth between Design and Datasheet view. In Design view, you format and set controls for queries, reports, forms, or tables that you are creating from scratch or modifying from an original wizard design. In Datasheet view, you observe the result of the modifications you have made in Design view. To switch between the two, click the View button on the toolbar, and then select the appropriate view.*

Create a Query in Design View

1. In the Database window, click Queries on the Objects bar.

2. Click New, click Design View, and then click OK.

3. Select the table or query you'll use.

4. Click Add.

5. Repeat steps 3 and 4 for additional tables or queries, and then click Close.

6. Double-click each field you want to include in the query from the field list.

7. In the design grid, enter any desired search criteria in the Criteria box.

8. Click the drop-down arrow in the Sort box, and then specify a sort order.

9. Click the Save button, type a name for the query, and then click OK.

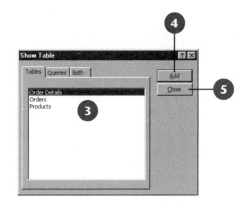

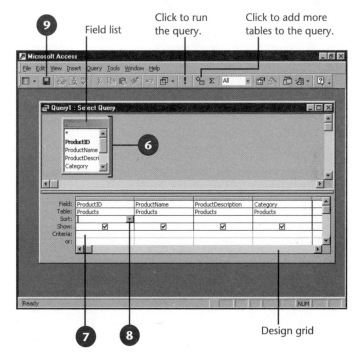

Field list

Click to run the query.

Click to add more tables to the query.

Design grid

Creating a Query Using the Query Wizard

When you create a query with a Query Wizard, you can specify the kind of query you want to create and type of records you want to retrieve. The Query Wizard guides you through each step; all you do is answer a series of questions, and Access creates a query with your data.

Create a Simple Query Using the Query Wizard

1 In the Database window., click Queries on the Objects bar, and then double-click the Create Query By Using Wizard icon.

2 Select a table or an existing query.

3 Click to select the fields that will be included in the query.

4 Click Next to continue.

5 If you have selected numeric or date fields in step 3, indicate whether you want to see detail or summary information. If you choose Summary:

◆ Click Summary Options to specify the calculation for each field.

◆ Select averages, counts, minimum and maximum values, and whether or not you want the records in the Query counted.

◆ Click OK.

6 Click Next to continue.

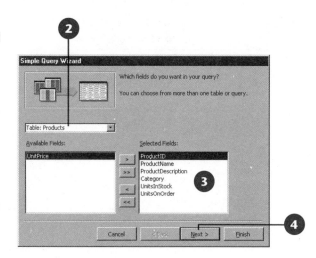

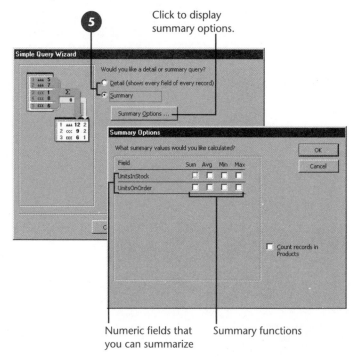

Click to display summary options.

Numeric fields that you can summarize   Summary functions

7

Use the New button to create a query. *In the Database window, click Queries on the Objects bar, click New, click the wizard you want to use, click OK, and then follow the wizard instruction.*

Include fields from another source. *Click the Tables/Queries drop-down arrow if you want to include a field from another source.*

Sort the retrieved records. *In Datasheet view, you can select a field and then click the Sort Ascending or Sort Descending button on the Table Datasheet toolbar to sort the query results in either ascending or descending order by the values in the selected field.*

7 In the final wizard dialog box, type the name of the query.

8 Choose whether you want to view the results of the query or modify the query design in Design view.

9 Click to select the Display Help On Working With The Query check box for more help on queries.

10 Click Finish.

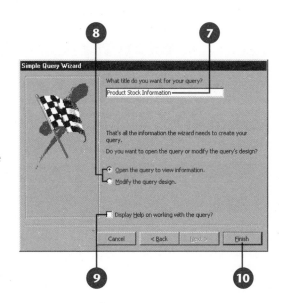

Name of query   Type of query

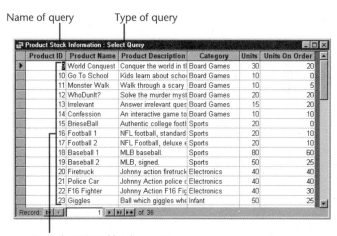

Records retrieved by the query

Changing the Query Fields

In Design view, you can add or remove fields in your query design to produce different results. You can also include fields from other tables in your database. In some cases you might want to hide a field from the query results while keeping it part of the query design for selection criteria purposes. For example, in a query showing the data for only the customers in California, you do not need to display the State field in the results.

TIP

Delete versus hide a query field. *When you remove a field from the query design grid, you're only removing it from the query specifications. You're not deleting the field and its data from the underlying table. When you hide a field by clearing the Show check box, the field remains part of the query; it just won't be displayed to the user.*

Add a Field to a Query

1 Display the query in Design view.

2 Double-click a field name from the field list to place the field in the next available column in the design grid, or drag a field to a specific column in the design grid.

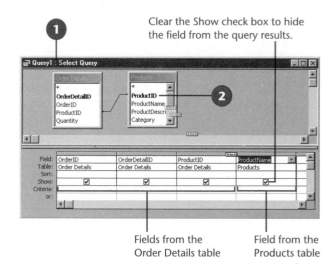

Clear the Show check box to hide the field from the query results.

Fields from the Order Details table

Field from the Products table

Remove a Field from a Query

1 Display the query in Design view.

2 Select the field you want to remove from the query.

3 Press Delete, or click the Edit menu, and then click Delete Columns.

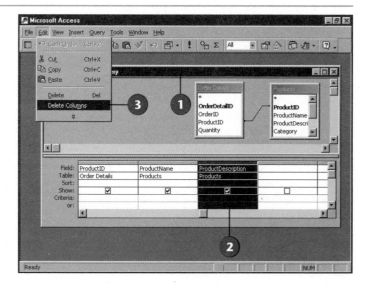

7

Remove a table from the Query design grid. *To remove a table, right-click its field list in the top portion of the Query Design View window, and then click Remove Table.*

Change the order of fields in a query. *In the design grid, point at the column selector for the column you want to move. (The column selector is the thin gray box at the top of a column.) When the pointer changes to a small black arrow, click to select the column. When the black arrow changes back, use the mouse pointer to drag the selected column to a new position.*

Format a query field. *To modify the appearance of a query field, click anywhere within the query field's column, and then click the Properties button on the toolbar. You can then specify the format, caption, input mask, and other features of the query field.*

Add a Field from Another Table to a Query

1 Display the query in Design view.

2 Click the Show Table button on the Query Design toolbar.

3 Select the table that contains the fields you want to include in the query.

4 Click Add.

5 Repeat steps 3 and 4 for each table you want to include.

6 Click Close.

7 Double-click or drag the fields you want to include to the design grid.

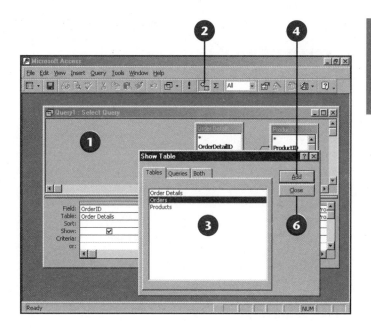

Specifying Criteria for a Single Field

For each field you include in a query, you can specify criteria that a record must match to be selected when you run the query. For example, you can create a query to retrieve toys of a certain type, such as infant toys, from a toys database. You do this by entering a criterion's value in the Query Design window.

Access allows you to add multiple criteria values for a single field so that the query retrieves records that meet either (or both) of the criteria you specify.

Specify Criteria for a Single Field in a Query

1. Display the query in Design view.

2. Click the field's Criteria box.

3. Enter a criterion value for the field.

4. If additional values of the field are allowed, enter them into the Or box listed below the Criteria box.

5. Click the Run button on the Query Design toolbar.

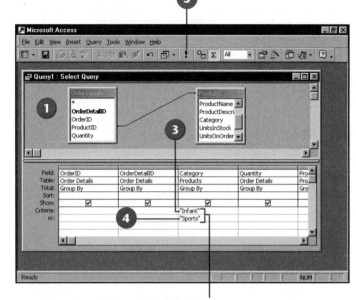

The query retrieves records whose Category field equals "Infant" or "Sports."

The query retrieves infant or sports toys.

Specifying Criteria for Multiple Fields

You can specify several query fields. If the criteria for the fields occupy the same row in the Query Design window, Access retrieves records for which *all* of the criteria are satisfied. For example, if you specify the toy type as "Infant" and the order quantity as "2," only orders containing 2 infant toys will be retrieved.

On the other hand, if the criteria are entered into different rows, Access retrieves records for which *any* of the criteria are satisfied. For example, placing "Infant" and "2" in different rows will cause Access to retrieve either infant toys or orders containing two toys.

Specify Criteria for Multiple Fields in a Query

1. Display the query in Design view.

2. Enter the criteria value or values for the first field.

3. Enter a criteria value or values for additional fields.

4. Click the Run button on the Query Design toolbar.

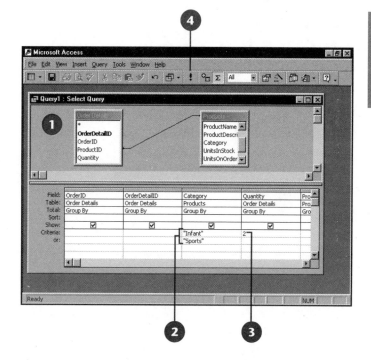

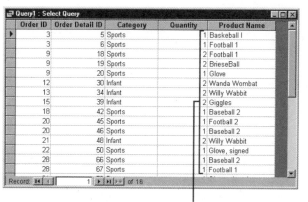

The query retrieves infant toys ordered in quantities of 2 or sports toys ordered in any quantity.

Creating Queries with Comparison and Logical Operators

You can use the Expression Builder to create more complicated queries. For example, you can use *comparison operators*, such as >, <, or =, to compare field values to constants and other field values. For example, you can use the greater-than operator (>) to create a query that retrieves records in which more than 1 toy is ordered.

You can also use *logical operators* to create criteria combining several expressions. For example, you can use the AND operator to retrieve records in which the number of toys ordered is greater than 1 AND less than 5. You can also use logical operators to negate expressions. For example, you could run a query that retrieves toy records that are NOT infant toys.

Use a Comparison Operator

1. Display the query in Design View, and then click the Criteria box for the field.

2. Click the Build button on the Query Design toolbar.

3. Click the appropriate comparison operator button.

   To see additional comparison operators, click the Operators folder, click Comparison, and then choose the comparison operator you want from the list on the right.

4. Enter a value or click a field whose value you want to compare.

5. Click OK.

6. Click the Run button on the Query Design toolbar.

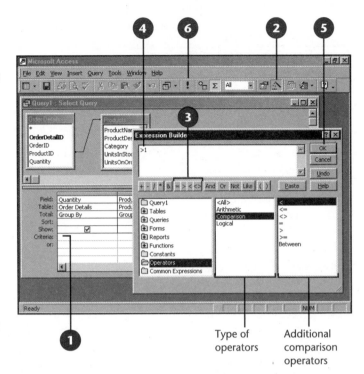

Type of operators

Additional comparison operators

Access retrieves only those records whose quantity is greater than 1.

Use a Logical Operator

1 Display the query in Design view, and then click the Criteria box.

2 Click the Build button on the Query Design toolbar.

3 Click the appropriate logical operator button.

To see additional comparison operators, click the Operators folder, click Logical, and then choose the logical operator you want from the list on the right.

4 Enter any values needed to complete the expression.

5 Click OK.

6 Click the Run button on the Query Design toolbar.

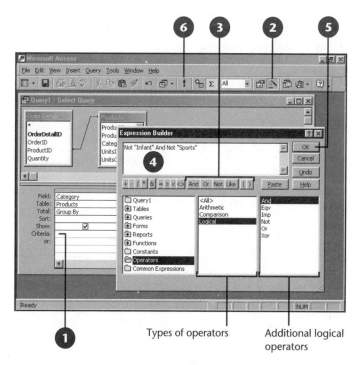

Types of operators

Additional logical operators

Access retrieves only those records in which the toy category is not Infant and not Sports.

Performing Calculations in Queries

In addition to the built-in functions you can use to compare values in a query, you can use the *Expression Builder* to create your own calculations using arithmetic operators.

By clicking the operator buttons you want to use and entering constant values as needed, you can use the Expression Builder to include expressions in a query. For example, to determine fees based on a contract amount, you can create an arithmetic expression in your query to compute the results. When you run the query, Access performs the required calculations and displays the results.

Create a Calculated Field

1 Within Query Design view, position the insertion point in the Field row of a blank column in the design grid.

2 Click the Build button on the Query Design toolbar.

3 Double-click the field (or fields) you want to use in the calculation.

4 Click the button corresponding to the calculation you want; or click the Operators folder, click the Arithmetic folder, and then click the operator you want to use.

5 Type any other values (constants) you want to include in the expression.

6 Click OK.

7 Click the Run button on the Query Design toolbar.

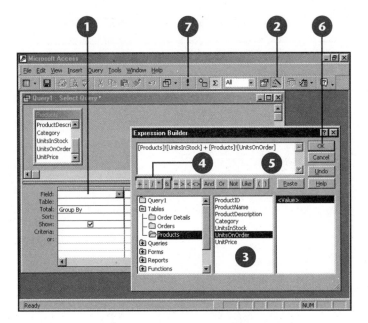

Access assigns the column name automatically; you can change it using the Caption property.

This column is equal to the number of items in stock plus the number of items on order.

Creating a Parameter Query

When you need to change the criterion value for a query, you either must edit the old query or create a new one. However, if the change involves simply altering a value, you might consider using a parameter query. A *parameter query* prompts the user for the value of a particular query field, rather than having the value built into the query itself. For example, if you want to display the records for particular toy types, a parameter query can prompt you for the type, saving you from creating a separate query for each type.

Rename a field. *Access assigns a name to a calculated field. If you want a different name, click the field in the design grid, and then click the Properties button on the Query Design toolbar. Enter a new name in the Caption box, and then click OK.*

Create a Parameter Query

1 Within Query Design view, click the Criteria box.

2 Enter the text of the prompt surrounded by square brackets.

3 Click the Run button on the Query Design toolbar.

4 Enter a criteria value in response to the prompt.

5 Click OK.

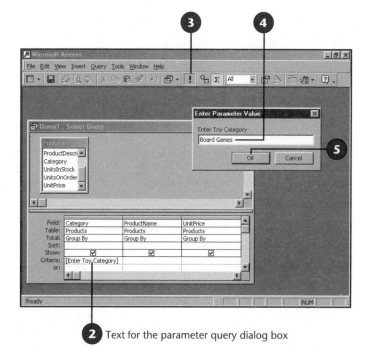

2 Text for the parameter query dialog box

Overall total

Totals broken down by category and whether or not the product is on special

Finding Duplicate Fields

In some tables, you need to find records that have duplicate values in particular fields. For example, in a table of purchase orders, you might want to discover which customers have more than one order. You can create a query that retrieves all the records from the Orders table that have duplicate values for the CustomerID field. Access provides a wizard to help you create the appropriate query.

Find Duplicate Records

1 In the Database window, click Queries on the Objects bar, click New, and then double-click Find Duplicates Query Wizard.

2 Choose the table or query that you want to search for duplicate records.

3 Click Next to continue.

4 Select the field or fields that might contain duplicate information.

5 Click Next to continue.

6 Select any other fields that you want displayed in the query.

7 Click Next to continue.

8 Enter a name for the new query.

9 Specify whether you want to view the query results or further modify the query design.

10 Click Finish.

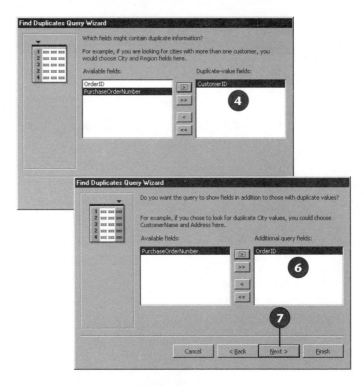

Access retrieves only those records with duplicate CustomerID values.

Finding Unmatched Records

When you have related tables, you might want to find which records in one table have no match in the other table. For example, if you have a table of products and a table of customer orders, you might need to know whether there are products that have no match in the Orders table. In other words, are there some products that no customer has yet purchased? Access provides a query wizard to help you answer questions of this type.

Find Unmatched Records

1. In the Database window, click Queries on the Objects bar, click New, and then double-click Find Unmatched Query Wizard.

2. Choose the table or query that whose values you want displayed in the query. Click Next to continue.

3. Choose the related table or query. Click Next to continue.

4. Specify the field that matches records in the first table to records in the second. Click Next to continue.

5. Choose which fields from the first table to display in the query results. Click Next to continue.

6. Enter a name for the new query.

7. Specify whether you want to view the query results or further modify the query design.

8. Click Finish.

Table displayed in the query results

Related table

Matching field

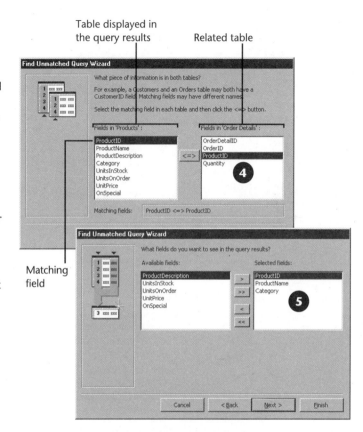

Access retrieves only those records that are not matched in the related Order Details table.

Creating New Tables with a Query

The data that appears after you run a query appears in table form and Access allows you to work with those results like tables. However, query results are not tables. If you want to place the results of a query into a separate table, you can use the *make-table query*. This query directs Access to save the results of your query to a new table in either the current database or a different database.

Create a New Table with a Query

1. In Query Design view, create a select query, including any combination of fields, calculated fields, or criteria.

2. Click the Query Type button drop-down arrow on the Query Design toolbar, and then click Make-Table Query.

3. Type the name of the table you want to create, or click the drop-down arrow, and then select a table from the list if you want to replace the existing one.

4. Click the Current Database option button if the table is in the currently open database, or click Another Database and type the name of another database (including the path, if necessary).

5. Click OK.

6. Click the Run button on the Query Design toolbar.

7. Click Yes when Access asks if you're sure you want to create the new table.

8. Open the new table to view the records resulting from the query.

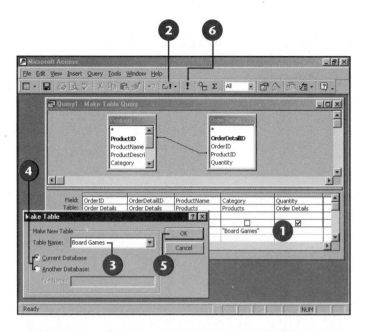

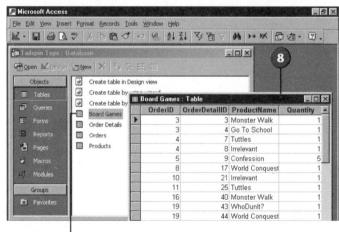

Access adds a new table to the database.

Adding Records with a Query

You can use a query to add records to a table by creating an *append query*. If the fields you've selected have the same name in both tables, Access automatically fills the matching name in the Append To row in the design grid. If the fields in the two tables don't have the same name, enter the names of the fields in the Append To row in the design grid.

TIP

Append records with a primary key. *If the table you are appending records to includes a primary key field, the records you are appending must have the same field or an equivalent field of the same data type. Access won't append any of the records if either duplicate or empty values would appear in the primary key field.*

Add Records with a Query

1 In Query Design view, create a select query.

2 Click the Query Type button drop-down arrow on the Query Design toolbar, and then click Append Query.

3 Type the name of the table to which you want to append the records, or choose one from the drop-down list.

4 Click the Current Database option button, or click Another Database and type the name of another database (including the path, if necessary).

5 Click OK.

6 Specify which fields will contain the appended values by entering the field names in the Append To row of the design grid.

7 Click the Run button on the Query Design toolbar.

8 Click Yes when Access asks if you're sure you want to append records to the table.

9 Open the table to view the appended records.

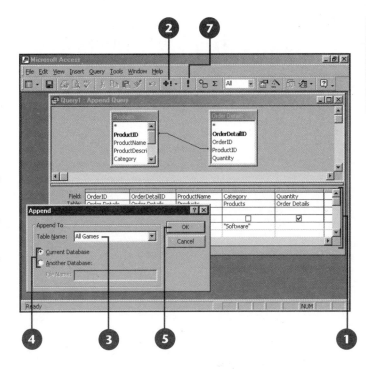

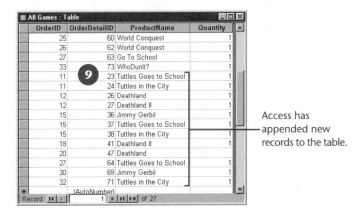

Access has appended new records to the table.

Deleting Records with a Query

If you want to remove records from a table based on a criterion or criteria, you can do so with a *delete query*. The delete query searches the table you specify and removes all records that match your criteria.

Because Access permanently deletes these records, use caution before you run a delete query. You can preview the results before you actually run the query. By clicking the Datasheet View button, you can see which records will be deleted before you actually run the query.

Create a Query to Delete Records

1. In Query Design view, create a select query.

2. Click the Query Type button drop-down arrow on the Query Design toolbar, and then click Delete Query.

3. Click the Datasheet View button on the Query Design toolbar to preview the list of deleted records.

4. If you're satisfied that the appropriate records would be deleted, click the Design View button to return to Query Design view.

5. Click the Run button on the Query Design toolbar.

6. Click Yes when Access asks if you're sure you want to delete records from the table.

7. Open the table to view the remaining records.

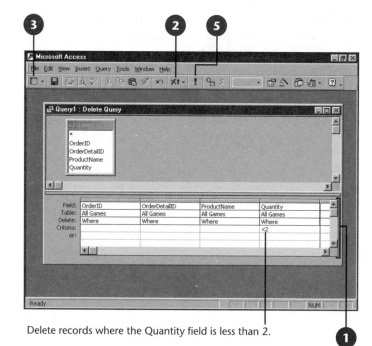

Delete records where the Quantity field is less than 2.

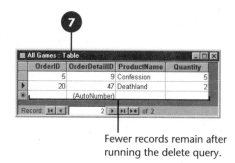

Fewer records remain after running the delete query.

Updating Records with a Query

An *update query* allows you to make changes to a set of records that match your query's criteria. For example, if you want to increase the unit price of board games in a toy product table by $3, you can construct a query that will locate those records and update them to the new value. Make sure you preview the changes to the records before you run the query, because once the records are changed you can't easily change them back.

Create a Query to Update Records

1. Display a new query in Query Design view. Add the fields or fields you intend to update and any fields that you want to use for the selection criteria.

2. Click the Query Type button drop-down arrow on the Query Design toolbar, and then click Update Query.

3. Enter an expression to update the selected field.

4. Enter a criterion, if needed, to indicate which records should be updated.

5. Click the Datasheet View button on the Query Design toolbar.

6. If you're satisfied that the appropriate records would be updated, click the Design View button to return to Query Design view.

7. Click the Run button on the Query Design toolbar.

8. Click Yes when Access asks if you're sure you want to update the records.

9. Open the table to view the remaining records.

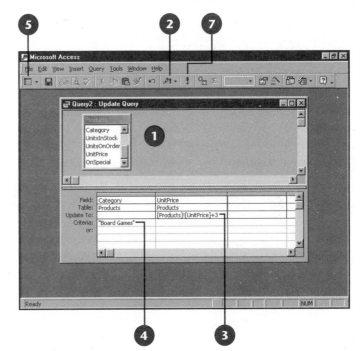

Access updates the Unit Price value by $3 for each of the board games.

Summarizing Values with a Crosstab Query

A *crosstab query* allows you to summarize the contents of fields that contain numeric values, such as Date fields or Number fields. In this type of query, the results of the summary calculations are shown at the intersection of rows and columns. For example, you can use a crosstab query to calculate the total number of toy products on sale, broken down by toy type. Crosstab queries can also involve other functions such as the average, sum, maximum, and minimum.

Create a Crosstab Query

1. In the Database window, click Queries on the Objects bar, click New, click Crosstab Query Wizard, and then click OK.

2. From the list at the top of the dialog box, select the table or query that contains the records you want to retrieve.

3. Click Next to continue.

4. Select the fields for the rows in the crosstab query.

5. Click Next to continue.

6. Select the field for the columns in the crosstab query.

7. Click Next to continue.

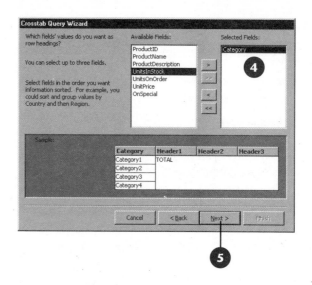

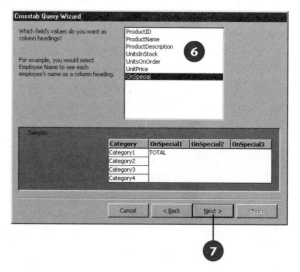

Use a PivotTable instead of crosstab query. *You can display crosstab data without creating a separate query in your database either by using the PivotTable Wizard in a form or by creating a PivotTable list in a data access page.*

Change column headings in a crosstab query. *If you want to change the column headings, open the query in Design view and open the Properties dialog box for the query. Enter the column headings you want to display in the Column Headings property box, separated by commas.*

Updating a crosstab query. *You cannot update crosstab queries. The value in a crosstab query cannot be changed in order to change the source data.*

(8) Click the field whose values you want to be calculated and displayed for each row and column intersection.

(9) Click the function you want for the calculation to be performed.

(10) Click to select the Yes, Include Row Sums check box if you want to see a total for each row, or clear the check box if you do not want to see a total for each row.

(11) Click Next to continue.

(12) Enter a name for your query.

(13) Indicate whether you want to immediately view the query or modify the design.

(14) Click Finish.

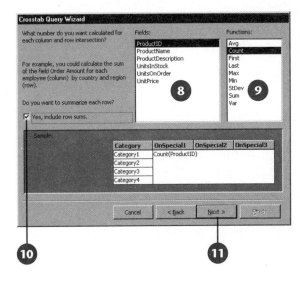

Overall total

Totals broken down by category and whether or not the product is on special

Creating SQL-Specific Queries

SQL (*Structured Query Language*) is a powerful database language used in querying, updating, and managing relational databases. For each query, Access automatically creates an equivalent SQL statement. If you know SQL, you can edit this statement, or write an entirely new one, to create new, more powerful, queries. Access supports three kinds of SQL-specific queries: union, pass-through, and data-definition. Each of these query types fulfills a different need.

TIP

View a query in SQL. *To see what your query looks like in SQL, click the View button and then click SQL View.*

Create a SQL-Specific Query

1. In Query Design view, click the Query menu, and then point to SQL Specific.

2. Click Union, Pass-Through, or Data Definition.

3. Enter SQL commands to create the query.

4. Save and view the query.

Click here to view the SQL commands used in constructing an Access query.

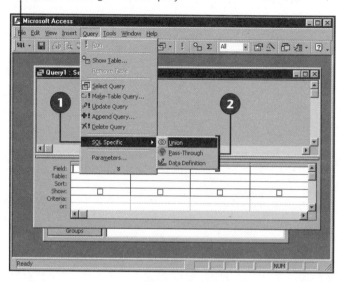

TYPES OF SQL-SPECIFIC QUERIES	
Type	**Definition**
Union	A query that combines related fields from multiple tables into one field, thus combining the data from several tables.
Pass-Through	A query that sends SQL commands directly to an SQL database server. This allows you to work with tables on the server instead of linking the tables to your Access database.
Data Definition	A query that deletes an index, or creates, alters, or deletes a table.

8

Creating Reports

To print a simple list of the records in your table, you can click the Print button. But if you want to include calculations, graphics, or a customized header or footer, you can create a report. A *report* is a summary of information in one or more Microsoft Access 2000 tables. Reports allow you to include enhancements that a simple printout of records in a table would not provide. In many cases a report answers important questions about the contents of your database. For example, a report might tell you how many movies in several different categories (such as drama, comedy, and western) have been rented each month or the amount of catalog sales made to customers in Canada in the last quarter. In addition to providing detailed and summary information that can include calculations, reports also provide these features:

- Attractive formatting to help make your report easier to read and understand

- Headers and footers that print identifying information at the top and bottom of every page

- Grouping and sorting that organize your information

- Graphics to enhance the appearance of a report with clip art, photos, or scanned images

Exploring Different Ways to Create a Report

As with most objects you create in a database, you have several ways to create a report—by using Access wizards or by creating it from scratch in Design view.

Click to create a report with the aid of the wizard.

Click to create a report from scratch in Design view.

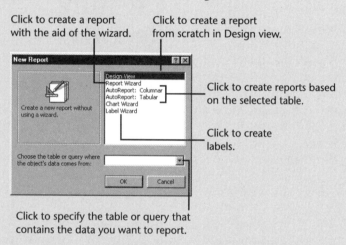

Click to create reports based on the selected table.

Click to create labels.

Click to specify the table or query that contains the data you want to report.

AutoReport Wizards

With the AutoReport Wizards, Access creates a simple report based on the data in the currently selected table or query. You can create a report using an AutoReport Wizard in two formats: *Columnar*, where each field appears on a separate line with a label to its left, or *Tabular*, where the fields in each record appear on one line with the labels at the top of the page.

Report Wizard

With the Report Wizard you can specify the kind of report you want to create, and the Report Wizard guides you through each step of the process. All you do is answer a series of questions about your report, and Access builds a report with your data, using your formatting preferences. Creating a report with the Report Wizard allows you to select the fields you want to include from available tables and queries.

Opens list of available tables and queries

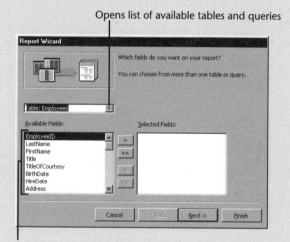

Fields from selected table or query; you can select fields from multiple tables and queries.

Design View

Once you have completed a report, you can further customize it in Design view. As always, you can also begin creating your report in Design view without using a wizard.

When you work with a report in Design view, Access displays not the report data but rather the individual parts, or controls, that make up the report, including titles, fields whose data appear in the report, labels that clarify the report contents, and objects such as headers and footers.

Previewing a Report

Once you have created your report and finalized its design, you can preview it using two views: Print Preview and Layout Preview. Print Preview displays the report as it will print, in a "what you see is what you get" format. Layout Preview displays a sample of the report as it will print, with just a few rows of data, so you can get a feel for the report's appearance without having to view all the data in the report.

8

Report in Design view

Same report in Print Preview

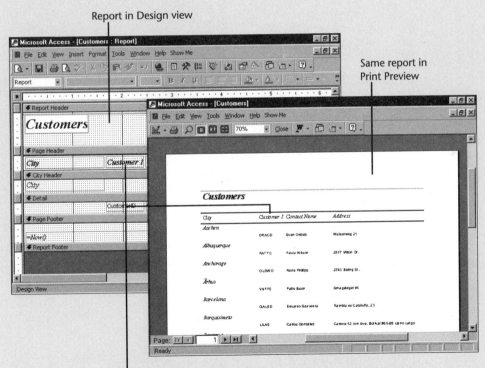

Objects in Design view correspond to objects in the printed report.

Creating Reports the Easy Way

One of the features you can use to create a simple report in Access is the AutoReport Wizard, which quickly arranges data in a selected table or query as an attractively formatted report.

The AutoReport: Columnar Wizard displays each record's data vertically, while the AutoReport: Tabular Wizard displays the data for each record horizontally. You can also create a report using the Report Wizard, which allows you to select the fields and information you want presented, and to choose from available formatting options that determine how the report will look. You can save and name reports created with either wizard.

Create and Save a Report Using the AutoReport Wizard

1. In the Database window, click Reports on the Objects bar, and then click New.

2. Click AutoReport: Columnar (to display records in a column) or click AutoReport: Tabular (to display records in rows).

3. Click the drop-down arrow, and then select the table or query you want to base the report on.

4. Click OK.

   Access displays the form in Print Preview, but you can switch to Design view, save, print, or close the report.

5. Click the Save button on the toolbar, and then type a name for your report. Click OK.

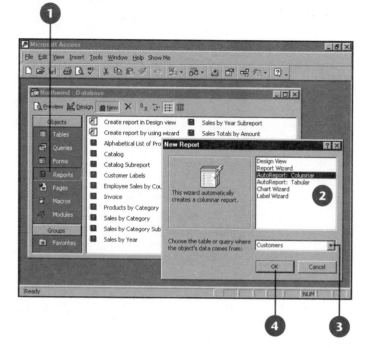

Create and Save a Report with the Report Wizard

1. In the Database window, click Reports on the Objects bar, click New, and then click Report Wizard.

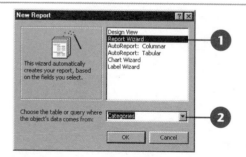

Create an instant report with the AutoReport command. *In the Database window, select the table or query that contains the data you want formatted as a report. Click the New Object drop-down arrow on the Database toolbar, and then click AutoReport. After a moment, Access generates a simple columnar report without headers or footers.*

Change the style of a report automatically. *After creating a report, change its style by using the AutoFormat command. Display your report in Design view, and then click the AutoFormat button. Choose one of the available styles for a report, and then click OK.*

Preview multiple pages. *If your report contains more than one page, click the Multiple Pages button on the Print Preview toolbar, and then move the pointer to select the number and arrangement of pages you want to see.*

2 Click the drop-down arrow for choosing a table or query to base the report on, click the table or query you want to use, and then click OK.

3 Select the fields you want to include, indicating the source of any fields you want to include from other tables or queries. Click Next to continue.

4 Specify any groupings of the records, choosing any or all of the selected fields (up to ten). Click Next to continue.

5 Specify the order of records within each group, sorting by up to four fields at a time, and specifying ascending or descending order. Click Next to continue.

6 Determine the layout and orientation of your report. Click Next to continue.

7 Specify the style of the report. Click Next to continue.

8 In the final wizard dialog box, name your report, and then indicate whether you want to preview or display it in Design view. Click Finish.

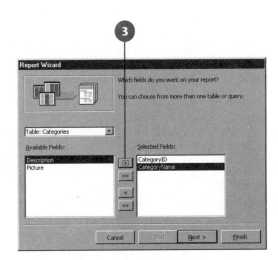

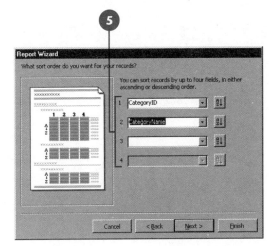

Using Sections in Design View

When Access displays a report or a form in Design view, it divides the report or form into *sections*, individual parts that control what elements appear and how they are formatted.

DESIGN VIEW SECTIONS

Section	Description
Report Header	Text that appears at the top of the first page of a report, such as a title, company logo, or introduction
Page Header	Text that appears at the top of each page of a report, such as page numbers or report date
Group Header	Text that appears before each group of records, such as a vendor name
Detail	Contains the main body of the report, the fields that display values
Group Footer	Text that appears at the end of a group of records, such as totals
Page Footer	Text that appears at the bottom of each page of a report, such as explanations of symbols or page numbers
Report Footer	Text that appears at the end of the report, such as for report totals or other summary information

Each section has a *selector*, a box to the left of its heading, that you can click to select the section. Any

formatting changes you make then affect just that section. Clicking the selector in the upper-left corner selects the entire report or form.

Header and footer sections come in pairs. *Headers* in a report display text at the top of each page or at the top of the report. *Footers* appear at the bottom of the page. Headers and footers can also appear at the start and end of records you have grouped together. As with other sections in a report, you can add controls to headers and footers that include text, expressions, page numbers, and date and time information.

Selector

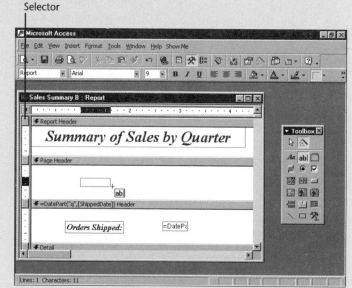

Working with Controls

Each item in a report or form—such as a field name, a field value, and the report title—is represented in Design view by a control. When you create a report or form with a wizard, the wizard arranges and sizes the controls to make the report according to the selections you provided. If you want to modify a report, you can do so in Design view by:

- ◆ Creating new controls
- ◆ Deleting controls
- ◆ Moving controls
- ◆ Sizing controls
- ◆ Changing control properties
- ◆ Changing the appearance of controls by formatting them, including applying borders and text effects such as bold type and italics
- ◆ Adding borders and shading

Types of Report Controls

There are three kinds of controls you can use in a report:

- ◆ *Bound controls* are fields of data from the table or query. You cannot create a calculation in a bound control.
- ◆ *Unbound controls* are controls that contain a label or a text box. You can create calculations in an unbound control.

- ◆ *Calculated controls* are any values calculated in the report, including totals, subtotals, averages, percentages, and so on.

Each type of control has specific characteristics you can change using the Properties feature. You can modify properties by right-clicking the control you want to, modify, and then clicking Properties. In the controls property sheet, you can specify the characteristics you want to change. Although there are menu commands and buttons you can use to change a specific characteristic, using the Properties button is a fast way to see all of the characteristics for a control and make several changes at once.

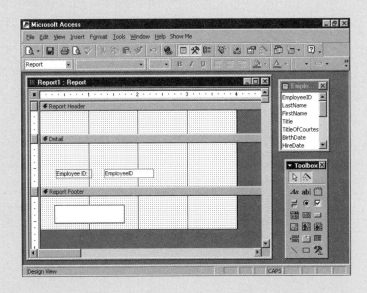

Creating a Report From Scratch

When you create a report from scratch in Design view, three sections appear: Page Header, Detail, and Page Footer. Once you create the report, you need to populate it with data. You can add one or more bound controls directly from the field list, or you can add other types of controls from the Toolbox.

When you work in Design view, you might want to display or hide the Ruler and the Grid, which provide guides to help you arrange your controls. Both are available on the View menu.

TIP

Toggle buttons. *When you create a report from scratch, three boxes might appear: the Field List box, the Toolbox, and the Sorting And Grouping box. You can hide or view these boxes by clicking their corresponding buttons on the Report Design toolbar.*

Create a New Report in Design View

1. In the Database window, click Reports on the Objects bar, and then click New.

2. Click Design View.

3. Click the drop-down arrow, and then select the table or query you want to base the report on.

4. Click OK.

5. To view or hide headers and footers, click View and then click Report Header/Footer or Page Header/Footer to view or hide that pair of headers and footers.

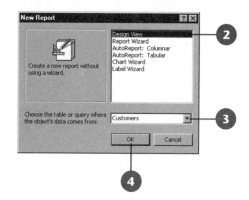

Add a Bound Control

1. Select the fields you want to include from the field list; press Shift or Ctrl while you click to select multiple fields.

2. Drag the selected field or fields to the section in which you want the field to appear. Two boxes appear for each field: one containing the label and one for the field values.

New report in Design view   Grid is hidden

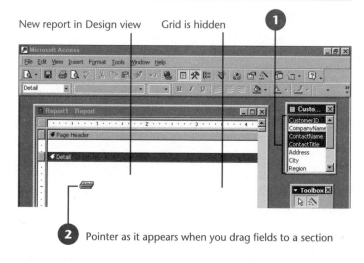

Pointer as it appears when you drag fields to a section

TIP

Insert information in headers and footers. *In Design view, use the Text Box button to add a text box control to a header or footer section. With the control still selected, click the Build button on the Report Design toolbar, and then click Expression Builder. Double-click the Common Expressions folder, and then double-click the expression you want to use, such as Page Number, Total Pages, Page N of M, Current Date/Time, and so on.*

TIP

Create an unbound report. *You can create a report without choosing a table or query on which it is based. Such reports are called* unbound reports. *A dialog box is an example of an unbound report.*

SEE ALSO

See "Setting Properties" on page 131 for information on using property sheets.

Add an Unbound Control

1. Click the Toolbox button corresponding to the control you want to add, such as a text box, a horizontal line, or a shape.

2. Drag the pointer over the area where you want the control to appear.

Ruler shows size of control as you drag

Grid provides dots that help you align controls

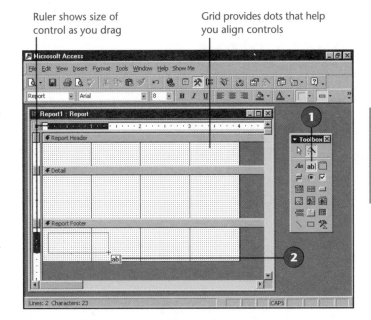

8

Modify Properties

1. Double-click the object (control, section, or form) you want to modify to open the object's property sheet.

   You can also right-click the object, and then click Properties.

2. Enter the property information you want to change and then close the property sheet.

Report selector   Section selector   Property sheet for a text box control

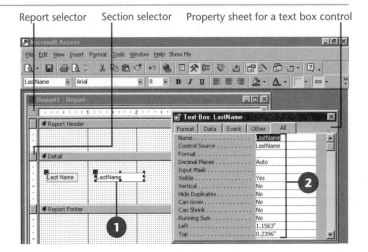

Using Toolbox Buttons and Controls

	TOOLBOX BUTTONS	
Button	**Name**	**Description**
	Select Objects	Click this button and then click the control you want to select. To select multiple controls that are grouped together, click this button and then drag a rectangle shape around all the controls you want to select.
	Control Wizards	Click to use control wizards when they are available.
	Text Box	This button creates a text box in which the user can enter text (or numbers) for the selected field in the record. Use this control for fields assigned a text or number data type.
	Label	This button creates a text label. Because the other controls already include a corresponding label, use this button to create labels that are independent of other controls, such as text needed for user instructions or the name of the form in a heading.
	Option Group	This button creates a box around a group of option buttons. The user is only allowed to make one selection from the buttons enclosed by a group box.
	Toggle Button	This button creates a button that allows the user to make a yes or no selection by clicking the toggle button. Use this control for fields assigned the yes/no data type.
	Option Button	This button creates an option button (also known as a radio button) that allows the user to make a single selection from at least two choices. Use this control for fields assigned the yes/no data type.
	Check Box	This button creates a check box that allows a user to make multiple yes or no selections. Use this control for fields assigned the yes/no data type.
	List Box	This button creates a list box that allows a user to select from a list of options. You can enter your own options in the list, or you can have another table provide a list of options.

	TOOLBOX BUTTONS	
Button	**Name**	**Description**
	Combo Box	This button creates a combo box in which the user has the option to enter text or select from a list of options. You can enter your own options in the list, or you can display options stored in another table.
	Command Button	This button creates a button that runs a macro or Microsoft Visual Basic function when the user clicks the button in the form.
	Image	This button inserts a frame, in which you can insert a graphic in your form. Use this control when you want to insert a graphic that remains the same in all the records displayed in a form, such as clip art or a logo.
	Unbound Object Frame	This button inserts an OLE object from another source. Use this button to insert an object that is linked to another program and needs to be updated to reflect recent changes.
	Bound Object Frame	This button inserts an OLE object from another source within the same database. Use this button to insert an object that is linked to another source in the database and needs to be updated to reflect recent changes.
	Page Break	This button forces the fields that start at the insertion point to appear on the next screen.
	Tab Control	This button creates a tab in your form. Creating tabs in a form gives your form the appearance of a dialog box in a program so that related controls can appear together on their own tab.
	Subform/Subreport	This button inserts another form within the current form at the insertion point.
	Line	This creates a line that you draw on the form.
	Rectangle	This button creates a rectangle or border that you draw on the form.
	More Controls	Click to display other toolboxes.

8

Arranging Information

The information in a form or report is arranged according to the arrangement of the sections and controls in Design view. You can modify that arrangement by changing section heights and by moving and resizing controls.

When you select a control on a form, *sizing handles* appear on the sides and at the corners of the control. You can drag the sizing handles to adjust the size of the control. You can also drag inside a selected control to move the control to a new location.

TIP

Change the size in two directions at once. *You can change the height and width of a control at the same time by dragging a corner sizing handle.*

Change the Size of a Control

1 In Design view, click the control you want to resize.

2 Position the pointer over a sizing handle until the pointer shape changes to a two-headed arrow.

3 With the sizing pointer, drag to resize the control.

For example, to make the control wider, drag the sizing handle on the center- right area of the control further to the right.

Sizing handles indicate control is selected

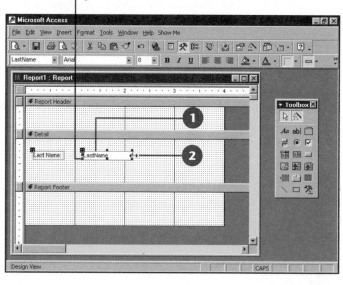

WORKING WITH CONTROLS	
To	**Do This**
Change control font	Select a control, click the Font drop-down arrow on the Formatting toolbar, and then click the font name you want, or click the Bold, Italic, or Underline button on the Formatting toolbar.
Remove formatting from a control	Select the control and click the button that corresponds to the formatting you want to remove.
Change the position of text within a control	Select the control and click the Align Left, Center, or Align Right button on the Formatting toolbar. If the control is in a header or footer, the control is aligned within the page margins.
Keep labels aligned with controls in the Detail section	When you adjust bound controls in the Detail section, be sure to make the same adjustments in the Header sections so that the headings appear directly over the data.

Move a Control

1. In Design view, click the control you want to move.

2. Position the pointer over an edge of a control until the pointer shape changes to a hand. This pointer is the move pointer.

3. With the move pointer, drag the control in the direction you want to go. Its label moves with it.

4. Release the mouse button when the control is located where you want.

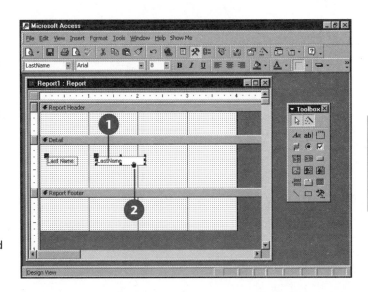

Change the Spacing Between Parts of a Report

1. In Design view, point to the bottom of the section whose height you want to change so that the pointer changes to a two-headed arrow with a horizontal line through it.

2. Drag the border up or down in the appropriate direction to change the spacing. You can drag the border all the way to the previous or next section to hide that section.

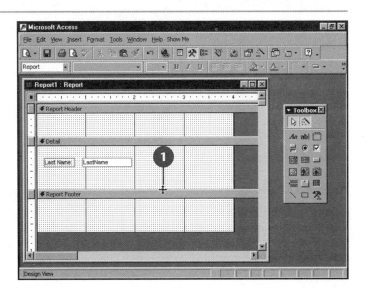

Creating Mailing Labels

Access provides a Label Wizard to help you create mailing labels quickly. The Wizard supports a large variety of label brands and sizes. You can also create customized labels for brands and sizes not listed by the wizard, provided you know the dimensions of your labels and label sheets.

You can create labels by drawing data from any of your tables or queries. In addition to data values, labels can also include customized text that you specify.

TIP

Create mailing labels for dot-matrix printers. *If you are creating mailing labels for a dot-matrix printer, you might have to make some adjustments to the page size settings. See Access's online Help for special instructions regarding working with dot-matrix printers.*

Create Mailing Labels

1. In the Database window, click Reports on the Objects bar, and then click the New button.

2. Click Label Wizard in the New Report dialog box, and select the table or query that will be used in the mailing labels. Click OK.

3. Select the type of mailing label you're using, and then click Next.

4. Specify the font style and color for the label text, and then click Next.

5. Double-click the field names in the Available Fields list to place them on your mailing labels. Type any text that you want to accompany the field values. Click Next.

6. Select a field to sort your labels by, if necessary, and then click Next.

7. Enter a name for your mailing labels report. Choose whether to preview the printout or modify the label design.

8. Click Finish to close the wizard.

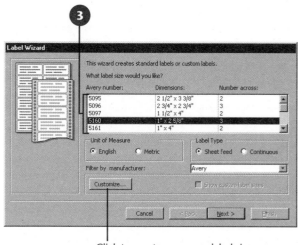

Click to create your own label size.

Type additional text here.

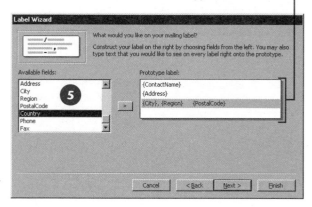

Setting Properties

Every object has *properties*, or settings, that control its appearance and function. A form or report has properties; each section in a form or report has properties, and each control in a section has properties. When you work with a control in a form or report, you can open a property sheet that displays all the settings for that control.

Properties button

TIP

Enter long settings. *When you are entering long information in a property box, right-click the box, and then click Zoom to open a Zoom box that allows you to see the entire setting you are modifying.*

SEE ALSO

See "Viewing Field Properties" on page 57 for information on opening property sheets for objects.

Modify Properties

1. In Design view, select the control, section, form, or report whose properties you want to modify, and then click the Properties button on the toolbar.

2. Click the tab that contains the property you want to modify.

3. Click the property box for the property you want to modify, and then do one of the following.

   ◆ Type the information or expression you want to use.

   ◆ If the property box contains an arrow, click the arrow and then click a value in the list.

   ◆ If a Build button appears to the right of the property box, click it to display a builder or a dialog box giving you a choice of builders.

4. When you're done, click the Close button.

1 Control whose property sheet is open

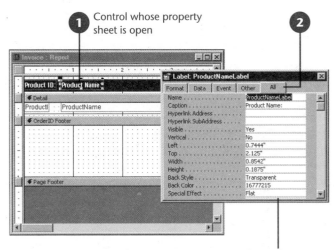

Property boxes appear on property sheet tabs.

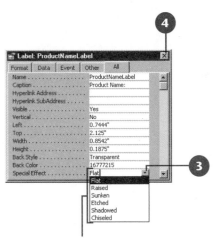

Possible values for the selected property box, which controls special effects for the selected control.

Performing Calculations in Reports

When you create a report, you might want to include summary information or other calculations. The wizards often include built-in functions, but you can use the Expression Builder to create your own by clicking buttons for the arithmetic operators you want to use and including constant values as needed.

For example, if you want to determine bonuses based on a percentage of sales, you can create an arithmetic expression to compute the results. When you generate the report, Access will perform the required calculations and display the results in the report. To display the calculations in the appropriate format, you can also use the Properties feature to specify formats for dates, currency, and other numeric data.

Choose Fields to Use in a Calculation

① In Design view, create a text box control and position it where you want the calculated field to appear, or select an existing unbound control.

② Click the Properties button on the Report Design toolbar.

③ Click the Control Source property box, which specifies what data appears in a control, and then click the Expression Builder button.

④ Click the equal sign (=) button.

⑤ Enter the values and operators you want to use.

◆ Click operator buttons to supply the most common operations.

◆ Double-click folders in the left pane to open lists of objects you can use in your expression, including existing fields, constants, operators, and common expressions.

◆ You can also manually type an expression.

⑥ Click OK to insert the calculation in the field, and then click the Close button.

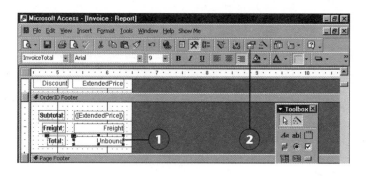

Folders you can open to display objects that can make up your expression

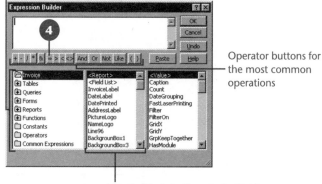

Operator buttons for the most common operations

List of objects in the selected folder

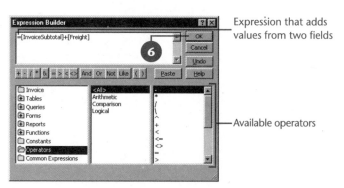

Expression that adds values from two fields

Available operators

TIP

Use a builder. *Access makes it easy to change many types of settings by providing* builders, *or tools that simplify tasks. The Expression Builder is just one of many builders in Access. You know a builder is available for a task when you click a property box and a Build button appears.*

SEE ALSO

See "Performing Calculations in Queries" on page 106 for information on using the Expression Builder.

Format Values in a Report

1 In Design view, position the insertion point in the field whose format you want to change, and then click the Properties button on the Report Design toolbar.

2 On either the All tab or the Format tab of the property sheet, click the Format property box, click the drop-down arrow that appears, and then click the format you want to use.

The names of the formats appear on the left side of the drop-down list and examples of the corresponding formats appear on the right side.

3 If you are formatting a number (rather than a date), and you do not want to accept the default, "Auto," click the Decimal Places property box, click the drop-down arrow, and then click the number of decimal places you want.

4 Click the Close button.

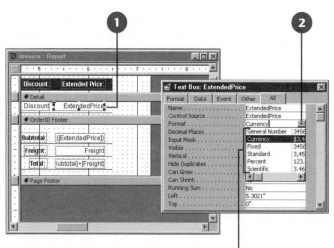

List of available number formats

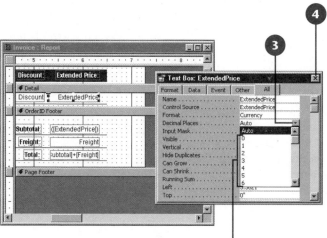

Possible number of decimal places for Currency format

8

Grouping Records

When you create a report with the Report Wizard, you can choose to group like records together to obtain subtotals and other calculations for each group. For example, in a report of sales representative sales figures for a year, you might group the representatives' sales by month. In this way, you can easily determine who was the top achiever each month.

In another report, you could group all the sales representatives' results together to see trends for the representatives' performance over a whole year. Even if you create your report from scratch or decide to group records later, you can use the Sorting And Grouping feature to further organize information in your report.

Sorting And Grouping button

Group Records

1. In Design view, click the Sorting And Grouping button on the Report Design toolbar.

2. Click the first Field/Expression box, and then click the drop-down arrow that appears. Choose a field for grouping records, or type an expression.

3. Click the corresponding Sort Order box, click the drop-down arrow that appears, and then click Ascending or Descending, depending on what sort order you want to use.

4. Select the Group Properties settings you want to use.

5. Repeat steps 2 through 4 for each Field/Expression you want to create to group and sort your data.

6. When you're done, click the Close button.

When you group data you can insert a group header for each group; in this case, a label for "Quarter" and a label for "Year."

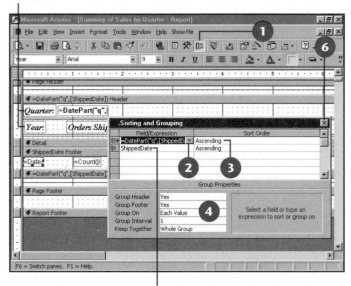

This report will show sales grouped by quarter and then sorted by shipping date.

Data is grouped by quarter.   Preview of grouped report

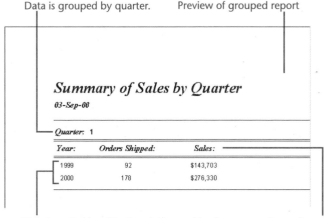

Summary of Sales by Quarter
03-Sep-00

Quarter: 1

Year:	Orders Shipped:	Sales:
1999	92	$143,703
2000	178	$276,330

Data is sorted by shipping date.   Header appears for each group.

Use a second field to further sort the records within each group. *Click the right side of the first blank field in the Field/Expression column, and then choose a second field for sorting records. You can also click the right side of the Sort Order column, and then choose either ascending or descending order for sorting records in each group.*

Select Group Properties

If you want to change the default Group Properties settings, you can do so from within the Group Properties dialog box.

1. Click the Group Header property box, and then choose Yes if you want to include a header that will separate the start of each group of records.

2. Click the Group Footer property box, and then choose Yes if you want to include a footer that will separate the end of each group of records. Choose this option if you want to include a subtotal or summary calculation for each group of records.

3. Click the Group On property box, and indicate whether you want to start a different group with each value or in a different manner.

4. Click the Group Interval property box and indicate the number of characters to group on.

5. Click the Keep Together property box and indicate whether you want to keep each group together on one page.

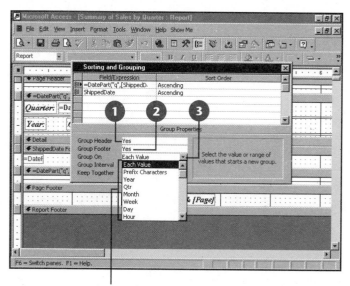

Options that appear in the Group On property box depend on data type; in this case, you can start a new group based on units of time.

Changing the Page Setup

Once you have created a report or form, you can change the page setup, which includes the margin, paper size and orientation, and grid and column settings.

SEE ALSO

See "Printing a Report" on page 138 for information on changing other printer-specific properties.

Change Page Setup Options

1. Click the File menu, and then click Page Setup.

2. To change margin settings, click the Margins tab, and then change the top, bottom, left, or right margins you want.

3. To change paper settings, click the Paper tab, and then select the orientation (portrait or landscape), paper size and source, and printer for customer labels you want.

4. To change column settings, click the Columns tab, and then change or select the column and row grid settings, column size, and column layout (Down, Then Across or Across, Then Down) you want.

5. Click OK.

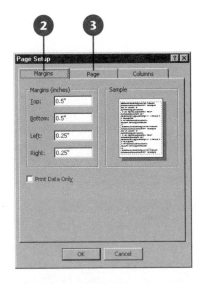

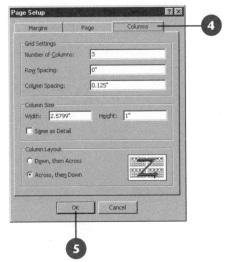

Previewing a Report

To get the complete picture of what a report will look like when you print it, you can display the report in Print Preview by clicking the Print Preview button in Design view or clicking the View drop-down arrow and then clicking Layout View. Layout view displays just a few records to give you an idea of the report's appearance without displaying all the data.

After completing the Report Wizard, you have the option of displaying the report in Print Preview. And after you create a report using AutoReport, the view changes to Print Preview, already in the magnified view, in which you see a close-up view of the report.

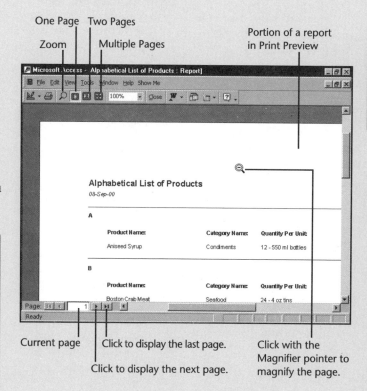

One Page   Two Pages

Zoom   Multiple Pages

Portion of a report in Print Preview

Current page   Click to display the last page.   Click with the Magnifier pointer to magnify the page.

Click to display the next page.

CHANGING THE PRINT PREVIEW MAGNIFICATION

To	Do This
Increase or decrease the magnification	Click the Zoom button on the Print Preview toolbar.
Return to the previous magnification	Click the Zoom button on the Print Preview toolbar.
Display the entire page in the Print Preview window	Click the One Page button on the Print Preview toolbar.
Display two pages side-by-side	Click the Two Pages button on the Print Preview toolbar.
Display multiple pages of a report	Click the Multiple Pages button on the Print Preview toolbar, and drag the pointer to select the number and arrangement of pages you want to see.

Printing a Report

Printing a report is as simple as clicking a button. Clicking the Print button on the Report Design toolbar prints one copy of all pages of the report. If you want to print only selected pages or if you want to specify other printing options, use the Print command on the File menu.

Print button

SEE ALSO

See "Previewing a Report" on page 137 for information about previewing a report before printing it.

TIP

Create a report snapshot.
In the Database window, click the report you want to use, click the File menu, click Export, click the Save As Type drop-down arrow, select Snapshot Format, enter a filename, and then click Save.

Print a Report

1. Click the File menu, and then click Print.

2. If necessary, click the Printer Name drop-down arrow, and then select the printer you want to use.

3. To print all the pages in a report, make sure the All option button is selected; or to specify certain pages in the report to print, click the Pages option button, and then type the page numbers in the From and To boxes.

4. Click OK.

Select Additional Printer Properties

1. Click the File menu, click Print, and then click Properties.

2. If your printer has additional print settings, choose the options you want.

   ◆ Printing to different sizes of paper

   ◆ Portrait or Landscape

   ◆ Multiple pages on a single sheet of paper

3. Click OK

Click to set printer properties for your printer; options available will depend on printer capabilities.

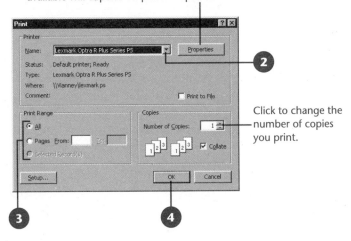

Click to change the number of copies you print.

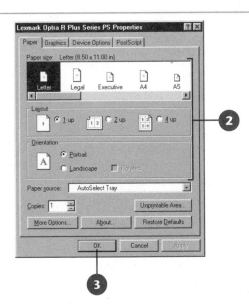

9

Creating Forms

Forms allow a database designer to create a user-friendly method of data entry. Instead of entering records in the grid of rows and columns in Datasheet view, you can use a form that can represent a paper form. Such a form can minimize data-entry errors because it closely resembles the paper-based form containing the information you want to enter in your table. A form can include fields from multiple tables, so you don't have to switch from one table to another when entering data.

If your table contains fields that include graphics, documents, or objects from other programs, you can see the actual objects in Form view. (In Datasheet view, the object is identified with text or with an icon.) To make it even easier to enter and maintain data, you can also include instructions and guidance on the form so that a user of the form knows how to complete it. You can add borders and graphics to the form to enhance its appearance.

Creating Forms

As with most objects you create in a database, you have several choices when creating a form.

♦ You can use the *AutoForm* command to create a simple form that contains all the fields in the currently selected table or query.

♦ With the *AutoForm Wizards,* Access creates a simple form (columnar, tabular, or datasheet) based on the table or query you specify.

♦ With the *Form Wizard,* you can specify the kind of form you want to create and the wizard guides you through each step of the process. You answer a series of questions about your form, and Access creates a form using your formatting preferences.

Of course, once you have completed a form, you can further customize it in Design view. As always, you can begin creating your form in Design view without using the wizard at all.

Click to create a form with the aid of the wizard.

Click to create a form in Design view.

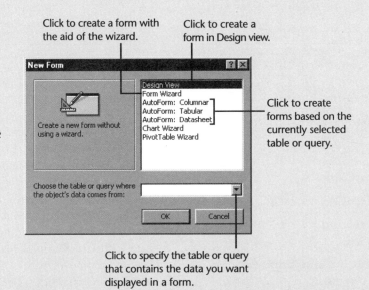

Click to create forms based on the currently selected table or query.

Click to specify the table or query that contains the data you want displayed in a form.

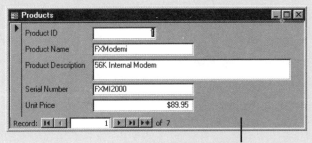

Sample Access form

Working with Form Controls

Each item on a form, such as a field name, a field value, and the form title, is called a *control*. When you create a form with a wizard, the wizard takes care of arranging and sizing the controls to make a form according to the selections you provided to the wizard. If you want to modify a form, you can do so in Design view by:

- Moving and sizing controls.

- Changing control properties.

- Changing the appearance of controls with borders, shading, and text effects such as bold and italics.

- Inserting new controls.

- Organizing controls using group boxes.

Types of Form Controls

There are three kinds of controls you can use in a form.

- *Bound controls* are fields of data from a table or query. A form must contain a bound control for each field that you want to appear on the form. You cannot create a calculation in a bound control.

- *Unbound controls* are controls that contain a label or a text box. Typically, you use unbound controls to identify other controls or areas on the form. You can create calculations from an unbound control.

- *Calculated controls* are any values calculated in the form, including totals, subtotals, averages, percentages, and so on.

To create a control, you click the control button for the kind of control you want to create and then drag the pointer over the area where you want the control to appear. The control buttons are available on the Toolbox in Design view.

In Design view, you see two parts for every control: the control itself and its corresponding label. When you drag a control to position it, its corresponding label moves with it (and vice versa). You cannot separate a label from its control.

If you are unsure of how to create controls, you can click the Control Wizard button on the toolbox to activate the Control Wizards. With the Control Wizards active, a wizard guides you through the process of creating certain types of controls. For example, if you create a list box control with the Control Wizards button active, the wizard appears, providing information about this type of control. It also prompts you to enter a name for the control label. To turn off the Control Wizards, click the Control Wizards button again (so that it is no longer indented).

Each type of form control has specific characteristics you can change using the Properties feature. You simply select the control you want to modify and then click the Properties button on the Form Design toolbar. In the control property sheet, you can specify the characteristics you want to change.

9

Creating a Form the Easy Way

To create a simple form in Access, you can use one of the AutoForm Wizards. These wizards quickly arrange the fields from the selected table or query as an attractive form. In a form created with the AutoForm: Columnar Wizard, you see each record's data displayed vertically, and with the AutoForm: Tabular Wizard, you see each record's data horizontally. With the AutoForm: Datasheet Wizard the form displays the records in Datasheet view. After you create a form, you can save and name it so that you can use it again. Any form you save is listed on the Forms tab of the Database window.

Create a Simple Form Using the AutoForm Wizard

1 In the Database window, click Forms on the Objects bar, and then click New.

2 Click AutoForm: Columnar (to display records in a column), AutoForm: Tabular (to display records in rows), or AutoForm: Datasheet (to display records in Datasheet view).

3 Click the drop-down arrow for choosing a table or query on which to base the form, and then select the name of the table or query you want.

4 Click OK.

After a moment, Access creates a form and displays it in Form view.

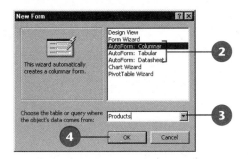

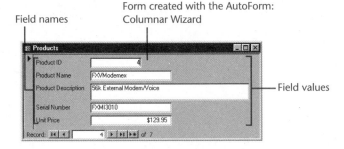

Field names

Form created with the AutoForm: Columnar Wizard

Field values

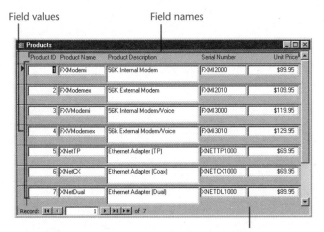

Field values

Field names

Form created with the AutoForm: Tabular Wizard

Field values   Field names

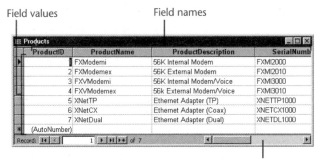

Form created with the AutoForm: Datasheet Wizard

Create a form instantly with the AutoForm command. *In the Database window, open the table or query that contains the data you want to display in a form. Click the New Object drop-down arrow on the Database toolbar, and then click AutoForm. After a moment, Access generates a simple (but unformatted) columnar form.*

Save a New Form

1 Display the new form in Form view, and then click the Save button on the Form View toolbar.

2 Type the name of your form.

3 Click OK.

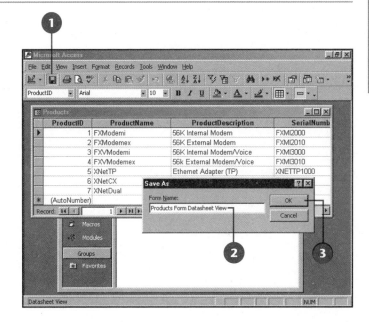

Creating a Custom Form

The *Form Wizard* lets you select the information you want to include in your form and choose from a variety of formatting options to determine how you want the form to look. You can choose the specific fields (including fields from multiple tables or queries) you want to see in the form. When you enter information in a form, the new data will be stored in the correct tables.

Create a Custom Form Using the Form Wizard

1. In the Database window, click Forms on the Objects bar, click New, and then double-click Form Wizard.

2. Click the drop-down arrow for choosing a table or query on which to base the form, and then click the name of the table or query you want.

3. Specify the fields that you want included in the form by double-clicking the fields.

4. Click Next to continue.

5. Determine the arrangement and position of the information on the form (columnar, tabular, datasheet, or justified). In the preview area of the dialog box, you can see a preview of your layout choice. Click Next to continue.

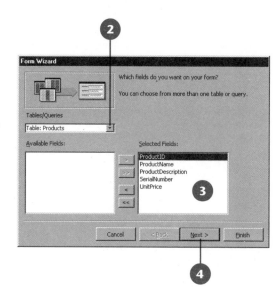

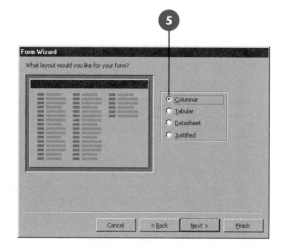

Create consistent layout styles. *The Form Wizard remembers your previous layout and style preferences. Once you have established a style you like, then you will be able to move quickly through the wizard dialog boxes, accepting the default selections as you go.*

6 Specify the style of the form, which affects its formatting and final appearance. In the preview area of the dialog box, you can see a preview of the selected style.

7 Click Next to continue.

8 Enter a name for your form.

9 Indicate whether you want to open the form or display it in Design view.

10 Click Finish.

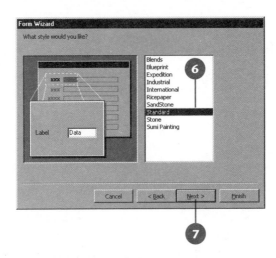

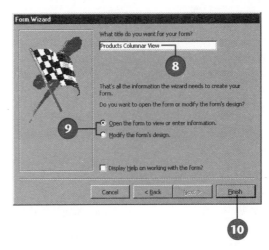

Creating a Form in Design View

Although a wizard can be a big help when you are first learning to create a form, you can create a form without the help of a wizard if you have a good idea of how you want it to look. Instead of answering questions in a series of dialog boxes, you can start working in Design view right away. You can create and modify controls, and move and format the controls, to create the exact form you want.

SEE ALSO

See "Adding and Removing Controls" on page 147 to learn how to insert new controls on a form and delete existing controls.

Create a Form in Design View

1. In the Database window, click Forms on the Objects bar, and then click the New button.

2. Click Design View, select the table or query from which the data will come, and then click OK.

3. If necessary, click the Field List button on the Form Design toolbar to add a bound control.

4. Select the field you want to add to the form.

5. Drag the field to the location in the form where you want the field to appear, and then release the mouse button to position the field.

6. Create new controls as needed by clicking the appropriate toolbox button.

7. Format the text in the form, as needed.

8. Click the Save button on the Form Design toolbar to name the form and save it in the database.

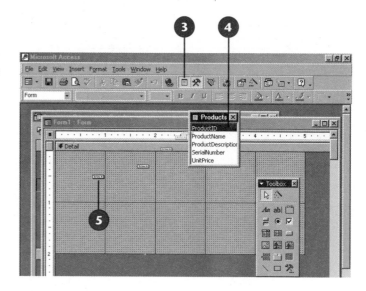

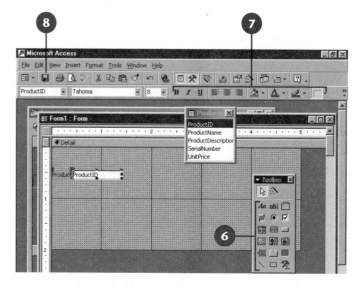

Adding and Removing Controls

Controls can make a form easier to use and improve its appearance. Controls also allow you to display additional information on your forms. To create a control on a form, you click the appropriate control button on the Toolbox. The Toolbox appears by default in Design view; however, if the Toolbox was closed for some reason, you need to redisplay it when you want to create new controls on a form. With the control pointer, drag in the form where you want the control to appear. You can also delete controls that you no longer want on the form.

SEE ALSO

See "Modifying a Form in Design View" on page 149 for more information on using this feature.

Add Controls to a Form

1 Click the Toolbox button on the Form Design toolbar, if necessary.

2 Click the button on the Toolbox for the type of control you want to create.

3 In the Form window, drag the pointer to draw a box in the location where you want the control to appear.

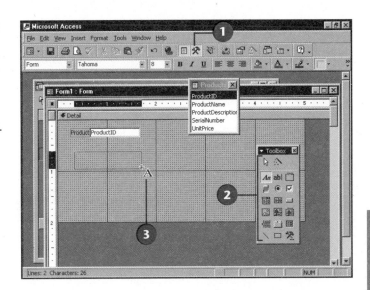

Remove Controls from a Form

1 Click the Toolbox button on the Form Design toolbar, if necessary.

2 Click to select the control you want to delete.

Small black boxes, called *handles,* appear around the control to indicate it is selected.

3 Press Delete.

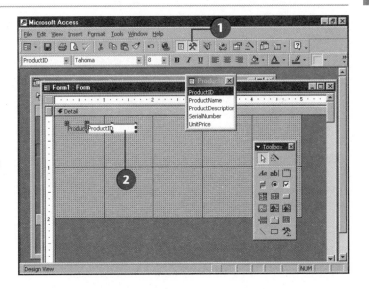

9

Editing an Existing Form

After you create a form, you might decide to modify certain features to make the form easier to use. For example, you might want more descriptive labels to identify each field. Or you might create a box around a group of fields to help the user identify and complete related fields.

To modify a form, you display the form in Design view, which you can do from the Forms option on the Objects bar in the Database window or from Form view. The View button lets you switch between Form view and Design view so that you can easily modify a form and view the results.

SEE ALSO

See "Using Toolbox Buttons and Controls" on page 126 for more information on controls.

Edit a Form

① In the Database window, click Forms on the Objects bar.

② Click the form you want to use.

③ Click the Design button, and make the modifications you want.

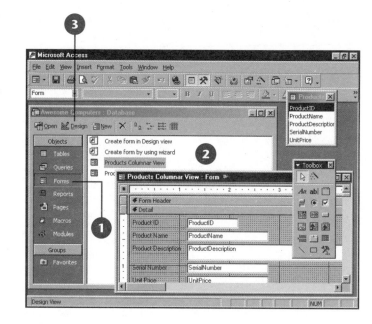

Switch Between Views

① In Design or Form view, click the View button drop-down arrow.

The View button changes according to the view you are in.

② Click the view name (Form View or Design View) of the view to which you want to switch.

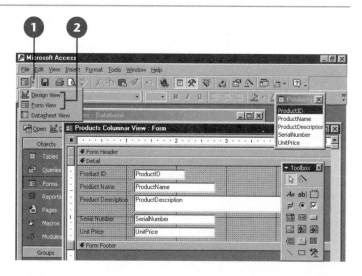

Modifying a Form
in Design View

Field List button
Click to display or
hide the Field List.

Toolbox button
Click to display or
hide the Toolbox.

AutoFormat button
Click to apply a
predefined style to
the form.

Properties button
Click to display properties
for the selected object.

Form header
Appears at the top
of the form

Field List
Click to place new
fields on the form.

Detail divider
Drag down to create
the form header.

Detail section
Appears for each record

Toolbox
Click to create new
controls on the form.

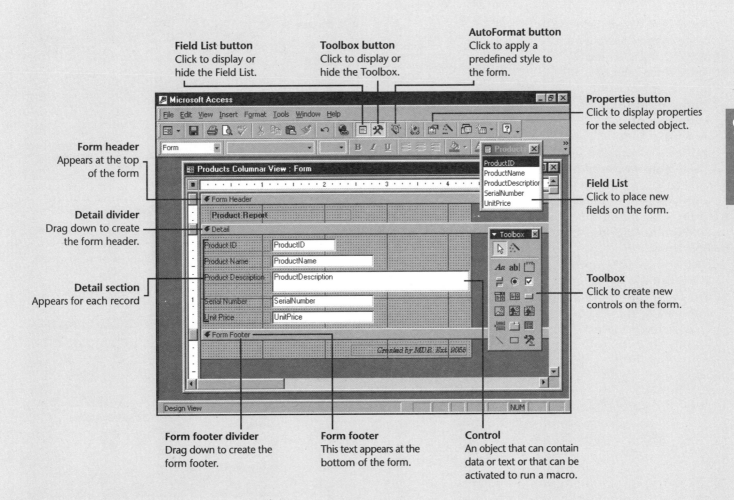

Form footer divider
Drag down to create the
form footer.

Form footer
This text appears at the
bottom of the form.

Control
An object that can contain
data or text or that can be
activated to run a macro.

9

Using the Control Wizards

The *Control Wizards* help you create controls on your form. Although there are many controls you can create, the procedures for creating each control are quite similar, with minor variations depending on the type of control. For example, when you want to include a list of valid options for a field on a form, you can create either a *combo box* or *list box* control. Both controls provide a list from which a user can choose when entering data. The easiest way to create either of these controls is with the Control Wizard. Each control has its own wizard.

Create a List Box or Combo Box

1 Display the form in Design view. Make sure the Toolbox is displayed and the Control Wizard button is selected.

2 Click the Combo Box or List Box button on the Toolbox.

3 In the Form window, drag a rectangle in the location where you want the control to appear. When you release the mouse button, the wizard dialog box for the selected control appears.

4 Specify whether you want the control to get its values from a table or query, from what you type in the box, or from what value is selected in the list or combo box. Click Next to continue.

5 If applicable, select the table that contains the values you want displayed in the list or combo box. Click Next to continue.

6 Select the field that contains the values you want displayed in control. Click Next to continue.

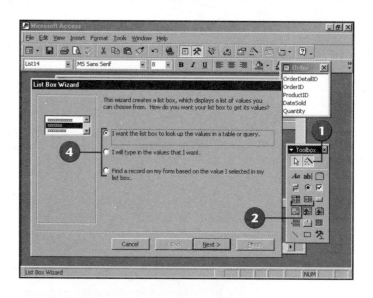

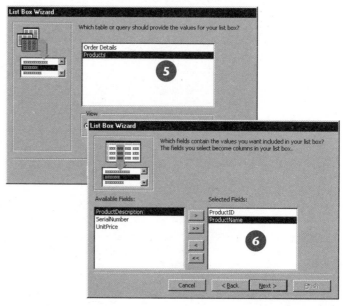

TIP

Create a list box with custom values. *If you want specific values (rather than values from a table) to populate the list box, click the I Will Type In The Values That I Want option button in the wizard's first step, and then enter the values manually when you are prompted by the wizard.*

TIP

Create a list box to display a specific record. *If you want your list box to cause Access to retrieve records, click the Find A Record On My Form Based On The Value I Selected In My List Box option button in the wizard's first step. The wizard then prompts you for the field from which the list box will receive its values. When the list box is added to the form, choosing a specific value causes Access to retrieve the matching record.*

TIP

Display Help on customizing the combo box. *To display Help on customizing the combo box, click to select the check box at the bottom of the wizard dialog box, where you label your list or combo box.*

7 Adjust the width of the columns for the list box as necessary. Click Next to continue.

8 If necessary, specify which column contains the value that will be stored in the list box control. Click Next to continue.

9 Specify whether you want Access merely to display the column value (for later use to perform a task) or to store the value in a field in a table.

10 If you choose to store the value in a field, specify the field.

11 Click Next to continue.

12 Enter a label for the new control, and then click Finish.

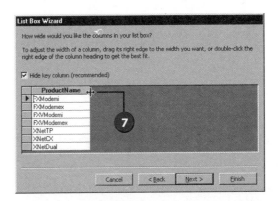

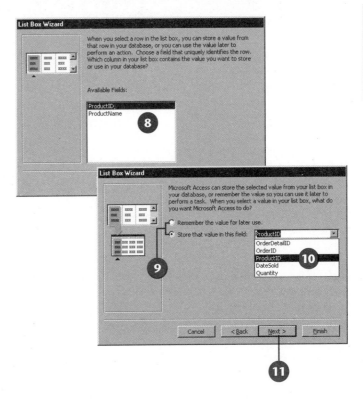

Creating a Subform

Some forms use fields from multiple tables. One of the most common involves a one-to-many relationship between two tables. For example, an order form would include a single order date and customer, but the order might involve several different products. Thus there are two tables involved: an orders table with information about the order and a detailed orders table with data about the products purchased.

The user should not have to enter the order date for each product. This can be avoided with a *subform*, a form embedded within a *main form*. The user enters the order date and other general information in the main form, and the individual products are listed in the subform. Access then stores the appropriate data in each table without the user being aware that multiple tables are involved.

Create a Subform

1. In the Database window, click Forms on the Objects bar, and then the double-click the Create Form By Using Wizard icon.

2. Click the Tables/Queries drop-down arrow and select the table that will appear in the main form.

3. Select the fields from the table that will appear in the main form. Make sure you include the common field that links the one table to the many table.

4. Click the Tables/Queries drop down arrow and select the table that will appear in the subform.

5. Select the fields from the table that will appear in the subform. Do not include the common field you entered in the previous step, since this will appear in the main form.

6. Click Next to continue.

Table containing general information (the *one* table)

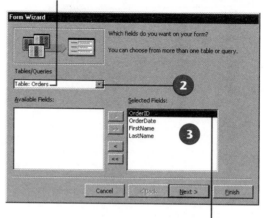

Common field between tables

Table containing detailed information (the *many* table)

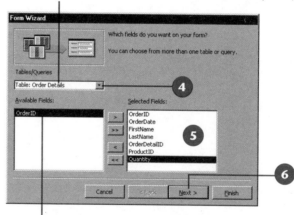

Do not include the common field twice.

Create a form with tables in a one-to-one relationship. *If the tables have a one-to-one relationship, use the Form Wizard to create the form, including the common field only once in the field list. The wizard will create a single form, combining the fields from both tables.*

Create a linked form. *If you want a linked form instead of a subform (so that the form appears in response to the user clicking a button,) click the Linked forms option button when the Form Wizard asks you how you want to view your data.*

See "Planning Tables and Table Relationships" on page 38 for more information on one-to-one, one-to-many, and many-to-many relationships between tables.

(7) Click the option to view the data by the *one* table

(8) Click the Form With Subforms option button.

(9) Click Next to continue.

(10) Specify whether you want the subform to be laid out in tabular or datasheet format. Click Next to continue.

(11) Specify a style for the form. Click Next to continue.

(12) Enter a name for the form and subform. Specify whether to open the form for viewing or to modify the form's design in Design view.

(13) Click Finish.

The form and subform are ready for data entry or further editing.

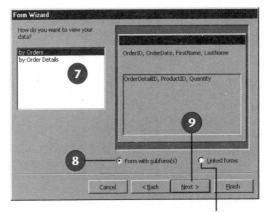

Click to create a linked form.

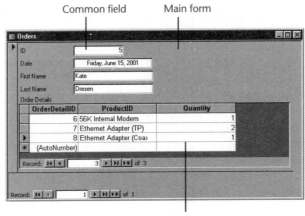

Common field   Main form

Subform

Editing in Form View

Access allows you to bypass Design view for certain editing operations. For example, you can edit form controls in Form view. You can open each form object's property sheet and make changes in the same way you would in Design view. You cannot, however, move, copy, or delete control objects. Nor can you modify form text or the form background. To do these things, you must be in Design view. You can, however, modify input boxes, buttons, list boxes, and other objects into which users will enter data.

TIP

Format input boxes in Form view. *You can format the text in an input box using the buttons on the Formatting toolbar. For example you can change the color, alignment, or style of the text within each input box.*

Edit a Form in Form View

1. Display the form in Form view.

2. Right-click a control object.

3. Click Properties on the shortcut menu.

4. Edit the object's properties in the property sheet.

5. Click the Close button.

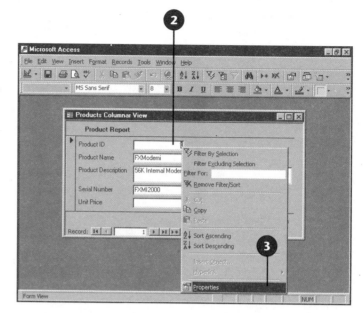

You can format control objects using buttons on the Formatting toolbar.

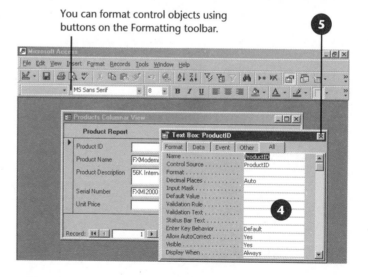

Improving the Appearance of Forms and Reports

The objects in a database most "on display" are the forms and reports designed for those individuals responsible for data entry and those who receive reports from the database. For this reason, database designers often give extra attention to the visual appearance and clarity of those objects.

Microsoft Access 2000 offers database designers many aids in creating attractive data entry and display objects. The wizards that create databases, forms, and reports format those objects attractively, but if you want to go beyond the design provided by a wizard, Access provides numerous formatting, layout, and style options. You can enhance the appearance of your forms and reports with different fonts and font styles, borders and lines, and judicious use of color. You can also add special effects to certain objects, giving them an embossed or 3-D effect. Access formatting features help you give your customized reports and forms the exact look you want.

Although most design changes take place within Design view, you can make color, line, and special effect formatting changes from within a form or report without having to switch to Design view.

Changing the Appearance of Text

You can change the appearance of the text in a report or form to make it easier to read or to create greater visual impact. For example, you can increase the size of the text or change its font type. You can also change the align-ment, which is the position of the text within its control. Just select the control whose formatting you want to change, and then click the appropriate button on the Formatting toolbar.

Click to change the font, font size, style attributes, or alignment

Click to change the color of background, text, lines, and borders.

Click to change the thickness of lines or borders.

Click to apply a special effect to buttons and other controls.

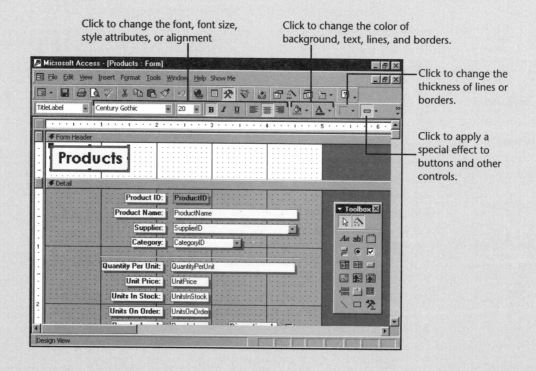

Formatting a Form or Report the Easy Way

A fast way to format a form or report is with the *AutoFormat* button, available in Design view. When you click this button on the Form Design toolbar or report Design toolbar, you can select and preview a variety of layouts and styles. After you make selections, Access formats the entire report or form consistently for you. After using AutoFormat, you can always make additional changes to the formatting.

AutoFormat button

Format a Form with AutoFormat

1. Display the form you want to format in Design view.

2. Click the AutoFormat button on the Form Design toolbar.

3. Click the style option you prefer.

4. Click OK.

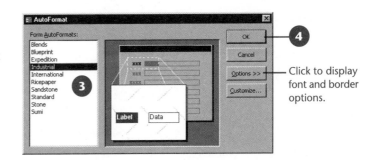

Click to display font and border options.

Format a Report with AutoFormat

1. Display the report you want to format in Design view.

2. Click the AutoFormat button on the Report Design toolbar.

3. Click the style option you prefer.

4. Click OK.

Click to display font and border options.

10

Adding Lines and Rectangles

You can make forms and reports that contain a lot of information easier to read by adding lines between sections or by adding rectangles around groups of controls. Lines and rectangles help organize the information so that reports are easier to read and forms are easier to fill out.

Add a Line to a Form or Report

1. Display the form or report in Design view.

2. Click the Line button on the Toolbox.

3. With the Line pointer, drag a line where you want the line to appear.

   Sizing handles appear.

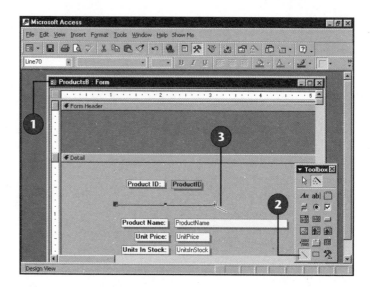

Add a Rectangle to a Form or Report

1. Display the form or report in Design view.

2. Click the Rectangle button on the Toolbox.

3. With the Rectangle pointer, drag a rectangle where you want the border to appear.

   Sizing handles appear at each corner and on each side of the border.

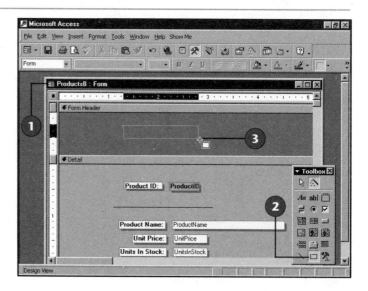

Changing Line or Border Thickness

You can adjust the thickness of any line, shape, or field border with the Line/Border Width button. You can modify field border thickness from Form or Report view, but to modify lines or rectangles, you must work in Design view.

After you choose one of the many Formatting toolbar buttons, such as Line/Border Width, any similar objects you subsequently create will be formatted with the currently selected formatting, as indicated on the toolbar button.

TIP

Set control defaults. *When you create a control, you can set the initial formatting. Create a control, format the control the way you want, click the Format menu, and then click Set Control Defaults.*

Change the Thickness of a Line or Border

1. Display the form or report in Design view, or, if you are modifying a field border, display the form or report in Form or Report view.

2. Select the line or border whose line thickness you want to adjust.

3. Click the Line/Border Width drop-down arrow on the Formatting toolbar, and then select the thickness you want.

If you want to format an existing object with the currently selected formatting, you can simply select the object, and then click the appropriate button on the Formatting toolbar— you don't need to click the button's drop-down arrow and repeat your selection from the menu.

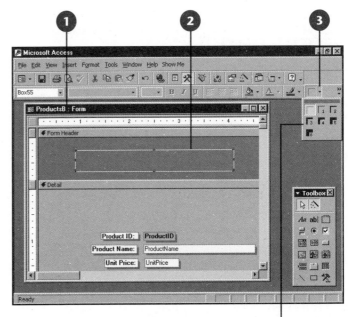

The greater the number, the thicker the line

10

Applying Conditional Formatting

Conditional formatting allows you to format a field based on values the user enters. For example, you can use a conditional format to make negative values appear in red and positive values appear in black.

TIP

Use conditional formatting in Form view. *To apply conditional formatting in Form view, select the input field, click the Format menu, and then click Conditional Formatting.*

TIP

Use expressions in a conditional format. *For more complicated conditional formats, select the input field, click the Format menu, and then click Conditional Formatting. Click the Condition 1 drop-down arrow, select Expression Is, type the conditional formatting expression in the box to the right, and then click OK.*

Apply Conditional Formatting to a Field

1 Display the form or report in Design view, and then click the field to which you want to apply conditional formatting.

2 Click the Format menu, and then click Conditional Formatting.

3 Specify the default format for the field.

4 Click the Condition 1 drop-down arrow, and then select Field Value Is.

5 Click the second drop-down arrow, and then select a condition type.

6 Enter values for the condition.

7 Specify the format when this condition is true.

8 Click Add to add a second formatting condition.

9 Click OK to apply the conditional formatting.

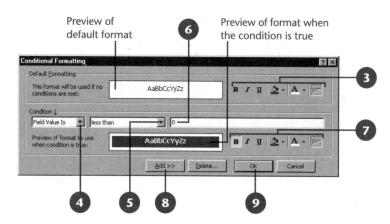

Preview of default format

Preview of format when the condition is true

Changing Colors

Choosing appropriate colors for your form or report is an important formatting decision. For example, colors on forms can be used to assist users in correctly filling them out. Also, if you have a color printer available, you can significantly enhance the appearance of a report or form by adding color to lines or text. Other elements you can add color to include rectangles, backgrounds, headers, footers, or detail areas of a report or form.

TIP

Change text color. *Display the form or report in Design view, select the box containing the text whose color you want to change, click the Font/Fore Color button drop-down arrow on the Formatting toolbar, and then select the color you want.*

Change Line or Border Color

1. Display the form or report in Design view, or, for a field border, in Form or Report view.

2. Select the line or border whose color you want to change.

3. Click the Line/Border Color drop-down arrow on the Formatting toolbar, and then select the color you want. You can also select Transparent to make the border around a colored object disappear.

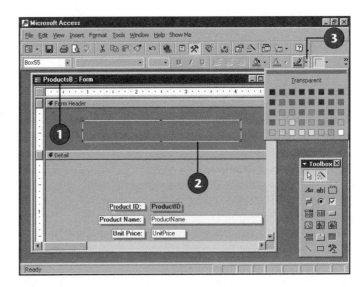

Change Fill Color

1. Select the object whose color you want to change.

2. Click the Fill/Back Color drop-down arrow on the Formatting toolbar.

3. Select the color you want.

Colors you've worked with recently appear at the bottom of the palette.

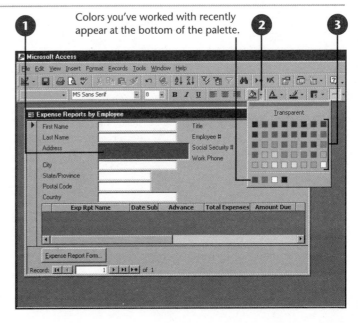

10

Aligning and Grouping Controls

Often when you work with multiple controls and objects, they look best when aligned with each other. For example, you can align three controls with the leftmost control in the selection so that the left sides of all three controls allign along an invisible line. You can also change the horizontal and vertical spacing between controls and objects. Access also lets you resize controls and objects relative to each other and group them together.

TIP

Rearrange layers of objects. *If filling a rectangle with color obscures the text, you can make the rectangle appear behind the text so that it doesn't block the text. Simply select the rectangle, click the Format menu, and then click Send To Back. You can also click the Format menu and then click Bring To Front to bring the text to the front.*

Align Objects and Controls to Each Other

1. Display the form or report in Design view, or, for a field border, in Form or Report view.

2. Select the controls and objects you want to align.

3. Click the Format menu, point to Align, and then click the alignment option you want.

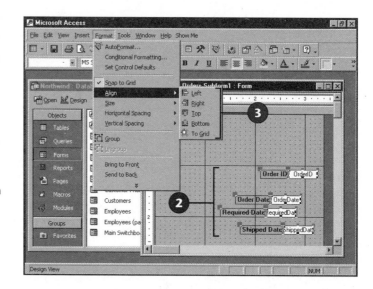

Change Horizontal or Vertical Spacing

1. Display the form or report in Design view, or, for a field border, in Form or Report view.

2. Select the controls and objects whose spacing you want to change.

3. Click the Format menu, point to Horizontal Spacing or Vertical Spacing, and then click the spacing option you want.

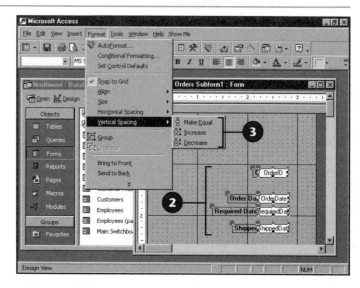

Change the Size of Controls and Objects

1. Display the form or report in Design view, or, for a field border, in Form or Report view.

2. Select the controls and objects you want to resize.

3. Click the Format menu, point to Size, and then click the sizing option To Fit, To Grid, To Tallest, To Shortest, To Widest, or To Narrowest you want.

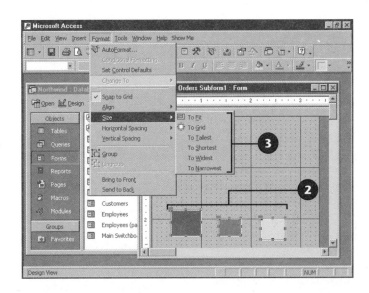

Group or Ungroup Controls and Objects

1. Display the form or report in Design view, or, for a field border, in Form or Report view.

2. Select the controls and objects you want to group or the object you want to ungroup.

3. Click the Format menu, and then click Group or Ungroup.

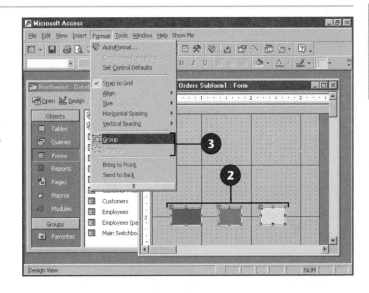

Applying Special Effects to Controls

You can apply special effects to one or more controls in a form or report to enhance the appearance of the form or report. For example, you can create three-dimensional effects, including flat (the default effect), raised, sunken, etched, shadowed, and chiseled. Use the effect that seems most appropriate for the tone of the form or report. For example, in a more formal financial report, you might choose the simple flat effect. In a report outlining future technology needs, consider using a high-tech shadowed effect.

SEE ALSO

See "Inserting a Picture" on page 170 for information on adding graphics to your reports, forms, and tables.

Apply a Special Effect to a Control

1 Display the form or report in Design view.

2 Select the control to which you want to apply a special effect.

3 Click the Special Effect drop-down arrow on the Formatting toolbar, and then select the effect you want to use.

Note that only the control's line or border is affected. Any text in the control is not affected by applying a special effect.

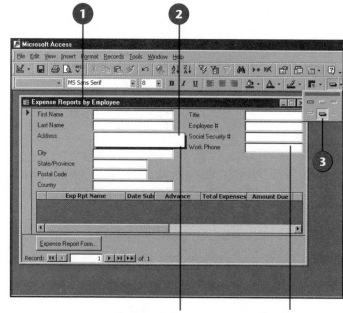

Shadowed effect

Sunken effect

Inserting Information from Other Sources

Microsoft Access 2000 allows you to incorporate information from a variety of sources into a database. For example, you can insert graphics to enhance the appearance of database forms and reports. You can insert Microsoft Excel charts and objects such as maps and graphs created with other software programs that display data from database tables or queries.

When you insert an object created in one program into a document created in another program, you are using a program-integration technology known as *object linking and embedding* (OLE). OLE is an important feature for many Access users because with it you can create a form or report that draws on information from any program that uses this popular technology. When you share objects using OLE, the menus and toolbars from the program that created the object are available to you from within your form or report. You can edit inserted information without having to leave Access.

You can also use the Access export and import features to easily move data between your database and other databases and programs.

Finally, Microsoft Office 2000's data-sharing techniques allow you to use other Office tools to work with your data. For example, you can merge your Access data with Microsoft Word to create form letters, or you can use Microsoft Excel's analysis tools on your Access data.

Sharing Information Among Documents

The ability to insert an object created in one program into a document created in another program allows you to create documents that meet a variety of needs. The table below includes terms that you'll find useful in understanding how you can share objects among documents.

TERM	DEFINITION
Source program	The program that created the original object
Source file	The file that contains the original object
Destination program	The program that created the document into which you are inserting the object
Destination file	The file into which you are inserting the object

To better understand how these objects and terms work together, consider this example: If you place an Excel chart in an Access database, Excel is the source program and Access is the destination program. The chart is the source file; the database is the destination file.

There are three ways to share information in Windows programs: pasting, embedding, and linking.

Pasting

You can cut or copy an object from one document and then paste it into another using the Cut, Copy, and Paste buttons on the source and destination program toolbars.

Embedding

When you *embed* an object, you place a copy of the object in the destination file. When you activate the embedded object, the tools from the source program become available in the destination file. For example, if you insert an Excel chart into an Access database, the Excel menus and toolbars become available, replacing the Access menus and toolbars, so you can edit the chart if necessary. With embedding, any changes you make to the chart in the database do not affect the original file.

Linking

When you *link* an object, you insert a representation of the object itself into the destination file. The tools of the source program are available, and when you use them to edit the object you've inserted, you are actually editing the source file. Moreover, any changes you make to the source file are reflected in the destination file.

Copying and Pasting Objects

When you copy or cut an object, Windows temporarily stores the object in an area in your computer's active memory called the *Windows Clipboard.* You can paste the object into the destination file using the Paste button or the Paste Special command, which gives you more control over how the object will appear in the destination file.

TIP

Watch file size when pasting objects. *When you click Paste, you are sometimes actually embedding. Because embedding can greatly increase file size, you might want to use Paste Special. You can select a format that requires minimal disk space and paste the object as a simple picture or text.*

SEE ALSO

See "Editing Text" on page 78 for information on using the Office Clipboard to copy and paste multiple items.

Paste an Object

1. Select the object in the source program.

2. Click the Copy button on the source program's toolbar.

3. Switch to Access and display the area where you want to paste the copied object.

4. Click the Paste button on the toolbar and position the object.

Paste Information in a Specified Format

1. Select the object in the source program.

2. Click the Copy button on the source program's toolbar.

3. Switch to Access and display the area where you want to paste the copied object.

4. Click the Edit menu, and then click Paste Special.

5. Click the object type you want.

6. Click OK.

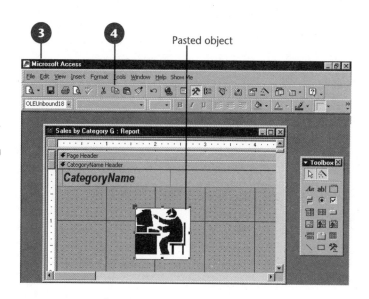

Pasted object

The object types that appear depend on what type of object is on the Clipboard.

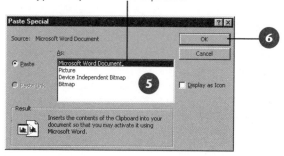

Inserting a New Object

You can create objects from scratch without leaving the Access program. After you drag to create a new unbound object frame control, the Insert Object dialog box appears, and you select the program in which you want to create the graphic. The programs that appear correspond to the software installed on your computer.

For example, if you want to create a picture in Microsoft Paint, a graphics accessory that accompanies the Microsoft Windows operating system, you can choose the Bitmap Image option.

TIP

Edit the original graphic.
Double-click the graphic object you created to redisplay the program in which you created the object, and then modify the graphic as necessary. When you close the program, the modified graphic will be inserted in the form or report.

Insert a New Object

1 In Design view, click the Unbound Object Frame button on the Toolbox.

2 With the Unbound Object pointer, drag a rectangle where you want the picture to appear. Make the rectangle approximately the same size as the picture you will insert.

3 Click the Create New option button.

4 Double-click the program in which you want to create an object.

5 Create the new object using the tools that appear in the program you selected.

6 Click outside the window in which you created the unbound object.

The program with which you created the object closes, and the new object is inserted in the form or report.

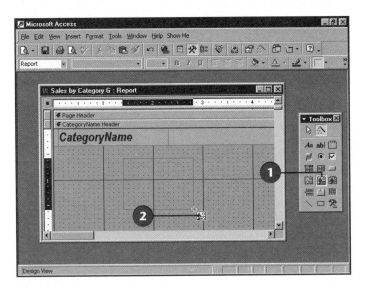

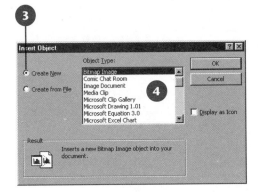

Inserting an Object from a File

There are several ways to embed or link an object from a file. If you want to embed a new object that you create from scratch, you can use the Insert Object command. If you want to insert an existing file, you can also use Insert Object and you can specify whether or not you want to link the object. If your object is already open in the program that created it, you can copy it, and in some cases, paste it into a form or report, automatically embedding it. Finally, you can use the Paste Special command to paste link a copied object—pasting and linking it at the same time.

TIP

Work with embedded objects. *If you click an embedded object once, you simply select it. You can then resize it. If you double-click an embedded object, you activate it, and the source toolbars and menus appear.*

Insert a File

1. Click the Insert menu and then click Object.

2. Click the Create From File option button, click the Browse button, select the file you want to insert, and then click Open.

3. To embed the object, make sure the Link check box is not checked. To link it, click the Link check box to select it.

4. Click OK.

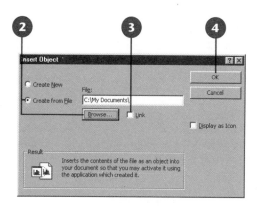

Paste Link an Object

1. In the source program, select the object you want to paste link.

2. Click the Cut or Copy button on the toolbar in the source program.

3. Switch to your database form or report.

4. Click the Edit menu, click Paste Special, and then click the Paste Link option button.

5. Click the format you want, and then click OK.

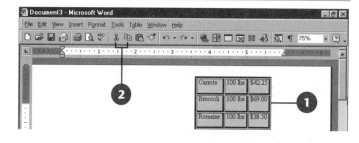

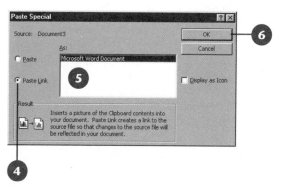

11

Inserting a Picture

You can insert interesting visuals, such as pictures or fancy text from the WordArt feature, into your forms and reports or even fields. For example, in an employee table a field could contain employee photos. Or a field might contain a Word document that is a recent performance review. When you run a report that includes this field, the report will display the contents of the field. In Datasheet view, you can double-click the field to display the field's contents.

TIP

Crop parts of a graphic that you want to hide.
Press and hold Shift and then drag a sizing handle over the area you want to crop. To create more space around the graphic, drag the handle away (while holding down Shift) from the center of the graphic.

Insert a Graphic File

1 Display the form or report in Design view.

2 Click the Image button on the Toolbox.

3 Drag a rectangle where you want the picture to appear. Make the rectangle approximately the same size as the picture you will insert.

4 Click the Look In drop-down arrow, and then locate the drive and folder containing the picture you want to insert.

For example, if you want to insert a picture from the clip art collection provided with Office, open the Clip Art folder in the Office folder.

5 Click the file you want to insert, and then click OK.

6 If necessary, drag the sizing handles to resize the graphic as needed.

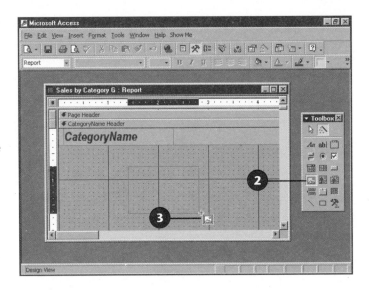

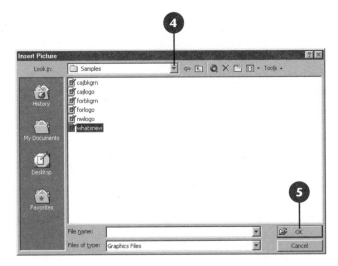

TIP

Insert sounds and motion clips. *In the Clip Gallery dialog box, click the Sounds or Motion Clips tab, click the sound or motion clip you want, and then click the Insert Clip button on the shortcut menu.*

TIP

Find more clip art on the Web. *In the Clip Gallery dialog box, click the Clips Online button to access clip art from a Microsoft Web site.*

TIP

Insert a picture. *In Design view, click the Insert menu, click Picture, click the Look In drop-down arrow, locate and select the picture you want to insert, and then click OK. You can also click the Image button on the Toolbox, drag a rectangle about the size of the image, and then select the picture.*

Make Forms Fun!

Insert a Clip Art Object

1 In Design view, click where you want to insert the object.

2 Click the Insert menu, and then click Object.

3 Click the Create New option button.

4 Click Microsoft Clip Gallery, and then click OK.

5 Click the Pictures tab, and then click a category.

6 Click the clip art graphic you want to insert.

7 Click the Insert Clip button on the shortcut menu.

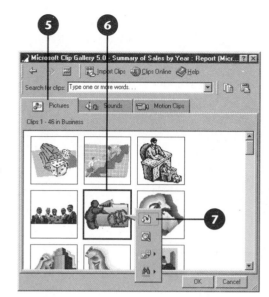

Insert a WordArt Object

1 In Design view, click where you want to insert the object.

2 Click the Insert menu, click Object, click Microsoft WordArt, and then click OK.

3 Enter and format the text, and then click Update Display.

4 Click the Close button.

WordArt Formatting toolbar

Enter text here.

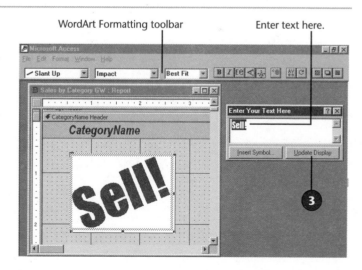

11

Moving and Resizing an Object

After you insert a graphic object, you can resize or move it with its selection *handles,* the little squares that appear on the edges of the object when you click the object to select it.

TIP

Resize objects proportionately. *To resize objects proportionately, drag one of the object's corner sizing handles until the object is the size you want.*

SEE ALSO

See "Touring a Table" on page 24 and "Changing the Size of Rows and Columns" on page 84 for more information on resizing windows.

Move an Object

1. In Design view, select an object you want to move.

2. Position the mouse pointer over the object, and then when the mouse pointer changes to a hand, drag it to move the outline of the object to a new location.

   Do not click a handle or else you will resize the object.

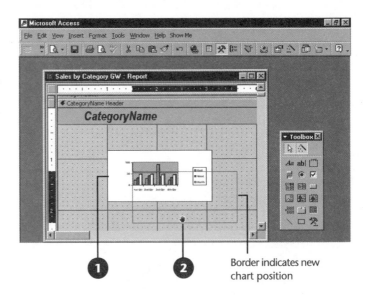

Border indicates new chart position

Resize an Object

1. In Design view, select the object you want to resize.

2. Position the mouse pointer over one of the handles.

3. When the pointer changes to a two-headed arrow, drag the handle until the object is the size you want.

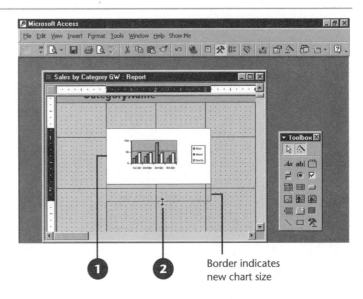

Border indicates new chart size

Inserting Excel Charts and Worksheets

There are several types of Excel objects that you can insert into your form or report. Two of the most common are worksheets and charts. You can insert a new Excel worksheet and then add data to it, or you can insert an existing Excel worksheet. You can also insert a chart from an Excel workbook.

TIP

Edit an inserted Excel worksheet. *If you want to modify the worksheet, double-click it, and then use the Excel tools to edit. When you're done, click the Close button, and then click Yes to save changes.*

TIP

Drag and drop to Excel. *You can drag objects from Excel right into Design view. Make sure that neither window is maximized and that both the object you want to drag and its destination are visible.*

Insert an Excel Chart

1. In Excel, click the chart you want to insert in the Access report or form.

2. In Excel, click the Copy button on the Standard toolbar.

3. Switch to Access, and, in Design view, display the form or report on which you want the chart.

4. Click the Paste button, and then click outside the chart to deselect it.

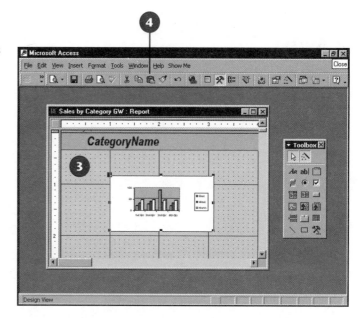

Insert an Excel Worksheet

1. Display the form or report into which you want to insert the Excel worksheet.

2. Click the Insert menu, and then click Object.

3. Click the Create From File option button.

4. Click the Browse button, locate and select the worksheet, and click OK.

5. Click OK.

Select to link the chart so it updates automatically if the chart changes.

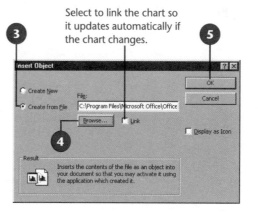

Inserting a Map

Microsoft Access allows you to chart data on a map so that you can display the relationship between data and geographic location.

The *Microsoft Map* feature helps you create and modify an existing map to reflect updated data. In addition, you can change the colors and patterns used to display the data within the map. You must update the geographic map when you change the data.

TIP

Install Map on the fly. *If Microsoft Map is not installed, you can install it without closing Excel. Follow the steps to create a map, and then insert the Microsoft Access 2000 or Office 2000 CD when it is requested.*

Create a Geographic Map

1. Display the form or report in Design view, click the Insert menu, and then click Object.

2. Click Microsoft Map, and then click OK.

   If you have Microsoft MapPoint 2000 installed on your computer, you can click Microsoft MapPoint.

3. Click the Insert menu, and then click External Data.

4. Click Microsoft Access, and then click OK.

5. In the Open Database dialog box, double-click the database you want to use.

6. Select the fields in the table to display in the map, and then click the Add button to include each field.

7. Click OK.

8. Select a map template, if necessary, and then click OK.

9. Click the File menu, and then click Exit & Return to [Form or Report].

TIP

Always refresh a map after changing database data.

Unlike chart data, Access does not automatically update map data whenever data changes.

SEE ALSO

See "Moving and Resizing a Object" on page 172 for information about moving and resizing a map.

Modify a Geographic Map

1. Display the form or report where the map is located.

2. Double-click the map.

3. If necessary, click the Map Refresh button on the Microsoft Map toolbar.

4. Change data and the way it is displayed in the map using buttons in the Microsoft Map Control dialog box. Press Esc to deselect the map.

5. Click the File menu, and then click Exit & Return to [Form or Report].

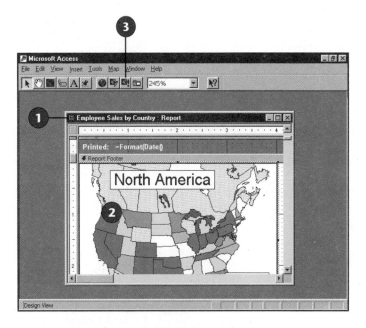

11

Inserting a Chart

You can create a chart from scratch using the graph program that comes with the Office 2000 suite, *Microsoft Graph.* Graph uses two views to display the information that makes up a graph: the *datasheet*, which is a spreadsheet-like grid of rows and columns that contains your data, and the *chart*, which is the graphical representation of the data.

A datasheet contains cells to hold your data. A *cell* is the intersection of a row and column. A group of data values from a row or column of data makes up a *data series*.

Graph automatically assigns a unique color or pattern to each data series, which you can customize by selecting one of the 18 chart types available in 2-D and 3-D formats. You can also save your customized settings as a format to use when you create other charts.

Create a Graph Chart

1. In Design view, click the Insert menu, and then click Chart.

2. Drag the pointer to create a rectangle the size of the chart you want to create.

3. When the Chart Wizard appears, click the Both option button, and then click the table or query you want to use to make the chart. Click Next to continue.

4. Click a field, and then click the Add button for each field you want to chart. Click Next to continue.

5. Click the chart type you want. Click Next to continue.

6. Make any layout modifications that are desired. Click Next to continue.

7. If you want the chart to change from record to record, select the fields that link the document and the chart. Click Next to continue.

8. Enter a chart name, click the No option button if you do not want to display the legend, and then click Finish.

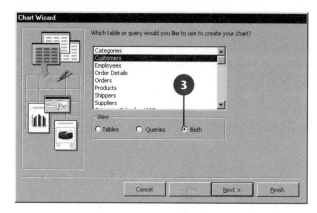

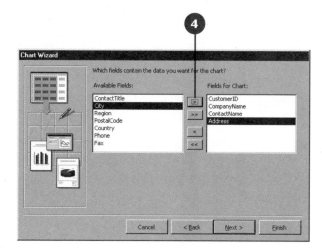

11

Open or edit the chart. *To open the chart, double-click it.*

Format a chart element. *Double-click the chart element (axis, chart, title, legend, and so on) you want to format, click the corresponding tab, enter or select the formatting you want, and then click OK.*

Change chart options. *Click the Chart menu, click Chart Options, click the tabs (Titles, Axes, Gridlines, Legend, Data Labels, Data Table) with the options you want to change, enter or select the options you want, and then click OK.*

Explode a pie slice. *Create a pie chart and then pull out one or more slices. Determine whether this adds to or detracts from the chart's effectiveness.*

Change a Chart Type

1. In Design view, double-click the chart on your form or report.

2. If necessary, click the More Buttons drop-down arrow to display the Chart Type button.

3. Click the Chart Type drop-down arrow.

4. Click the button for the chart type you want.

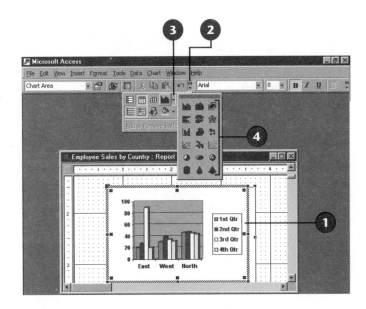

Save Chart Settings as a Custom Chart Type

1. In Design view, double-click the chart to select it.

2. Click the Chart menu, and then click Chart Type.

3. Click the Custom Types tab.

4. Click the User-defined option button.

5. Click Add.

6. Type a name and description for the chart, and then click OK.

7. Click OK.

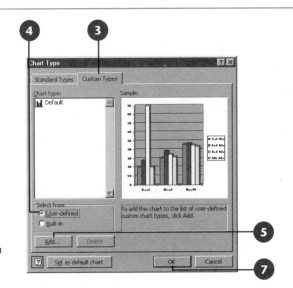

Getting Data from Other Programs

When you *import* data, you insert a copy of one file into another—in this case, Access. When you import data into Access, Access creates a new table to store the data, using labels from the first row of a worksheet or table for the new table. You use Access commands to edit the imported data.

"Do I have any control over the way Access imports my data?"

Import Data from Another Source

1 Open the database into which you want to import data, click the File menu, point to Get External Data, and then click Import.

2 Click the Files Of Type drop-down arrow, and then click the type of file you are importing.

3 If necessary, click the Look In drop-down arrow, and then select the drive and folder that contain the file you want to import.

4 Select the file you want to import.

5 Click the Import button.

6 If necessary, follow the instructions in the Import Spreadsheet Wizard to set up Excel data as an Access table.

7 Edit the imported information using Access commands and features, if necessary.

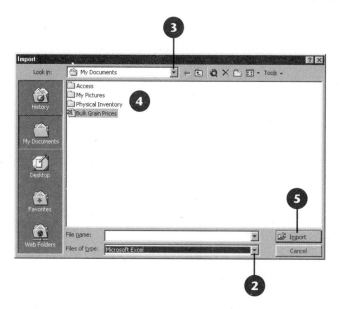

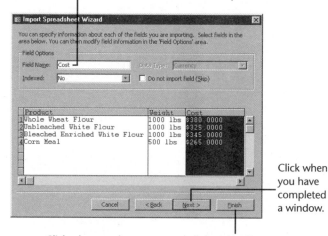

You can name fields and set other options.

Click when you have completed a window.

Click when you have answered all the wizard's questions and are ready to import the data.

Identify linked tables.
Right-click the table in the Object list in the Database window, and then click Properties on the shortcut menu. The property sheet shows that a table is linked to another data source and what that data source is.

"Can I edit data that I have linked from within the source and the destination programs?"

Link Data from Another Source

1 Open the database into which you want to link data, click the File menu, point to Get External Data, and then click Link Tables.

2 Click the Files Of Type drop-down arrow, and then click the type of file you are importing.

3 If necessary, click the Look In drop-down arrow, and then select the drive and folder that contain the file you want to link.

4 Select the file you want to link to.

5 Click Link.

6 If necessary, follow the instructions in the Link Spreadsheet Wizard dialog box to set up Excel data as an Access table.

7 From within the source or destination program, edit the linked information using the source program's commands.

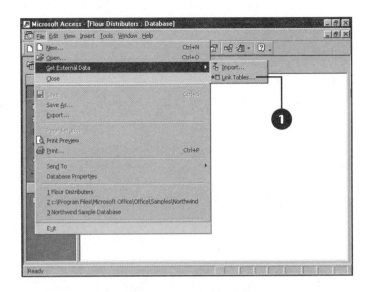

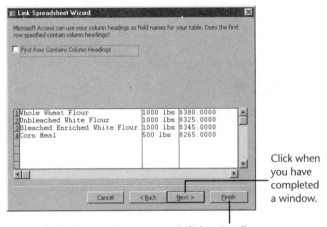

Click when you have completed a window.

Click when you have answered all the wizard's questions and are ready to link the data.

11

Exporting Data to Other Programs

When you *export* Access data, you save a database object in a new format so that it can be opened in a different program. For example, you might export a table to an Excel worksheet. Or you might want to save your database as an earlier version of Access so someone who hasn't yet upgraded to Access 2000 can edit, format, and print it. You can also attach any database object to an e-mail message as an Excel (.xls), Rich Text Format (.rtf), or Hypertext Markup Language (.html) file.

"Do I have any control over the way Access exports my data?"

Export an Object to Another Program

1 Open the database containing the object you want to export.

2 Click the File menu, and then click Export.

3 If necessary, click the Save In drop-down arrow, and then select the drive and folder where you want to save the file.

4 Click the Save As Type drop-down arrow, and then click the type of file you want to save the object as.

5 If necessary, type a new name for the file.

6 Click Save.

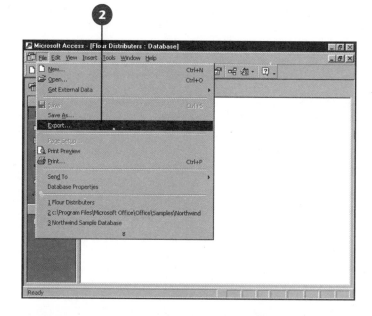

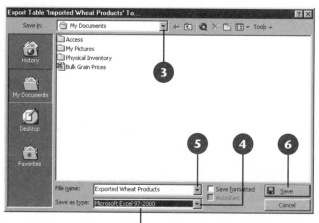

You might want to save an object in a different version of Access or as another database type so another user can edit, format, and print the file.

TIP

Copy and paste Access data. *If you want to place only part of an Access object in a file in another program, copy the information you want to insert, and then paste the information in the file where you want it to appear.*

TIP

Attach part of an object to an e-mail message. *Double-click the object in the Database window, select the portion you want to send, and then continue with step 2 of "Attach a Database Object to an E-Mail Message."*

Attach a Database Object to an E-Mail Message

1 In the Database window, click the object you want to attach to an e-mail message.

2 Click the File menu, point to Send To, and then click Mail Recipient (As Attachment).

3 Click the file format you want.

4 Click OK.

5 Log on to your e-mail system if necessary, and then type your message.

Access attaches the object to the message in the format you selected.

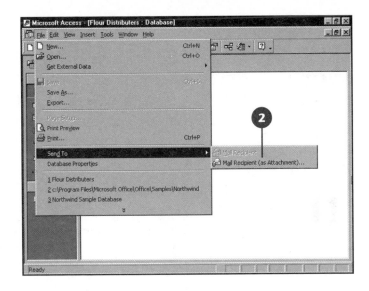

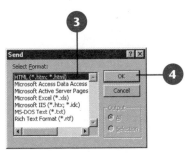

11

Merging Data with Word

Access is a powerful tool for storing and categorizing large amounts of information. You can combine, or *merge*, database records with Word documents to create tables or produce form letters and envelopes containing names, addresses, and other Access data. For example, you might create a form letter in Word and use an existing Access database with names and addresses to personalize the letters.

OfficeLinks button

Insert Access Data into a Word Document

1. In the Database window, click the table or query that you want to insert in a Word document.

2. Click the OfficeLinks drop-down arrow on the Database toolbar.

3. Click Merge It With MS Word.

4. Click the linking option button you want to use.

5. Click OK.

   If you selected the option for linking to an existing Word document, open the document.

6. In Word, click the Insert Merge Field drop-down arrow on the Mail Merge toolbar.

7. Click the field you want to insert. Repeat this step to insert as many fields as you need.

8. Click the Merge To New Document button on the toolbar.

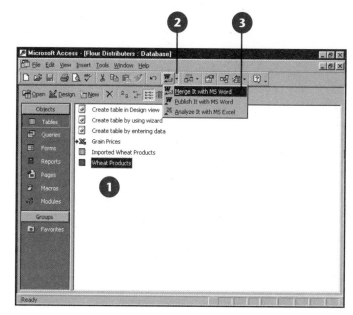

Jon

"1983"

15 yrs.

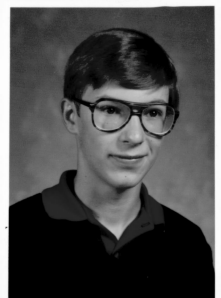

Create a Word Document from an Access Database

1 In the Database window, click the table, query, report, or form that you want to save as a Word document.

2 Click the OfficeLinks drop-down arrow on the Database toolbar.

3 Click Publish It With MS Word to save the data as a Rich Text Format file.

Word opens and displays the document.

4 Edit the document using Word commands and features.

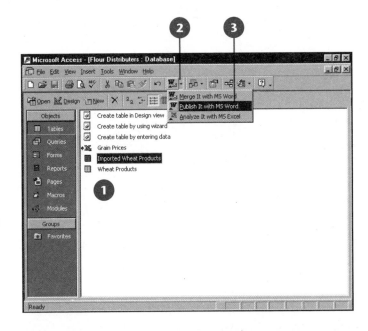

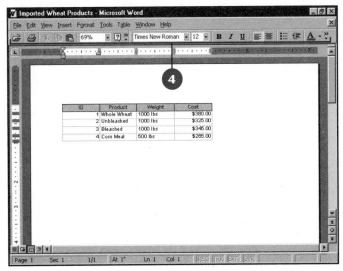

Analyzing Data in Excel

Before you can analyze Access data in a workbook, you must export the Access data to an Excel file. Exporting converts a copy of your open file into the file type of another program. In Excel, you can analyze the data using Excel's standard features and commands.

Insert an Access Table into Excel

1. In the Database window, click the table, query, report, or form that you want to analyze in Excel.

2. Click the OfficeLinks drop-down arrow on the Database toolbar.

3. Click Analyze It With MS Excel to save the table as an Excel file.

   Excel opens and displays the workbook.

4. Use Excel commands and features to edit and analyze the workbook.

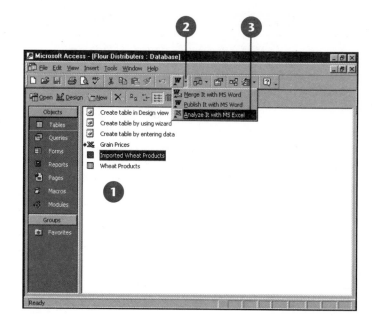

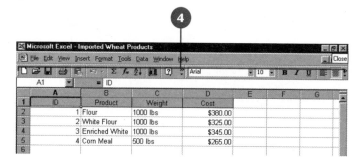

Working on the World Wide Web

The Internet and the World Wide Web have become an integral part of computing today. By providing quick and easy communication and data sharing to users around the world, the Internet has made it possible for data to have a global, rather than simply local, application. Microsoft Access 2000 provides support for the World Wide Web in four ways:

♦ By allowing database tables, queries, forms, and reports to contain links to objects on the Web

♦ With tools to navigate the Web from within the database

♦ Meeting with a remote audience over the Internet in "real time"

♦ With the ability to save tables, queries, forms, and reports as Web pages or to create Web pages based on data contained in the database

Each of these features makes it easier for you to include Web features in your database and makes your data available to the outside world.

Integrating Access and the Internet

One of the chief uses of computers today lies in accessing the *Internet*, a structure of millions of interconnected computers that allows users to communicate and to share data with one another. In its early years, the Internet was limited to a small community of university and government organizations. This was due, in part, to the sometimes difficult commands needed to navigate the Internet.

However, the introduction of the World Wide Web in the early 1990s led to an explosion in Internet use by businesses and the general public. The *World Wide Web* (or simply the Web) made Internet navigation easy by replacing arcane commands with a simple point-and-click interface within an application called a *Web browser*. The Web made data accessible to a wider audience than ever before. Companies could create Web sites containing product information, stock reports, and information about the company's structure and goals. Later innovations allowed business to accept and process orders online and to enter those orders into databases containing inventory and customer information.

Because of the importance of these developments, Microsoft has worked to integrate Access more tightly with the Internet and the Web. You can now navigate the Web from inside Access. Access databases can contain links to Internet resources, and you can save tables, forms, and reports as Web documents. These features make it possible for you to manage Access data locally and across the globe.

Creating Hypertext Links

The Web is a giant structure of documents connected together through hypertext links. *Hypertext links*, or *hyperlinks*, are elements on a Web page that you can activate, usually with a click of your mouse, to retrieve another Web document, which is called the *target* of the link. For example, a document about the national park system might contain a hypertext link whose target is a page devoted to Yosemite National Park. The great advantage of hypertext is that you don't have to know where or how the target is stored. You need only to click the hyperlink to retrieve the target. A target is identified by its *Uniform Resource Locator (URL)*, an address that uniquely identifies the location of the target on the Internet.

Access incorporates hypertext in two ways. First, through *hypertext fields*, fields in tables that contain hyperlinks, you can view and click a link and retrieve the link's target. Second, Access allows you to insert hyperlinks as elements within forms and reports. A footnote on a form, for example, could be a link to a Word document.

The targets of these links need not be pages on the Web. You can also direct the links to target other files on a hard disk drive, to an object within the current database, or to a different database altogether.

Navigating the Web

Once you activate a hyperlink, Access displays a toolbar, called the *Web toolbar*, which contains buttons that help you navigate the hyperlinks. As you progress through a series of links, the toolbar displays buttons that allow you to go forward and backward through the link sequence. The toolbar also includes a button to access a list of favorite Web pages or a *start page*, the Web page you initially see when you access the Web from your Web browser.

Creating Web Pages

Web pages are created in a special language called *HTML (Hypertext Markup Language)*, a cross-platform language which any operating system, including Microsoft Windows, Macintosh, and UNIX, can use to access a Web page. The crossplatform nature of HTML is one reason for the popularity of the Web.

Static Web Pages

Access allows you to export reports, forms, and tables to HTML format. Once you export these database objects, you can publish them as Web pages for others to view. These Web pages are *static Web pages* because their content is unchanged until you export the database object again. You have some control over the appearance of the Web page through the use of *HTML templates*, files that consist of HTML commands describing the page's layout. The templates can be used to insert company logos, graphics, and other elements. However, Access does not supply the templates for you, and you must have some working knowledge of HTML to create your own.

Active Server Pages

If you want your Web page to change whenever the source data changes, you need to create a *dynamic Web page*. Access provides two ways of exporting your reports,

forms, and tables to this dynamic Web page format. The more established method is with *Active Server Pages*, or more simply, *ASP*. Unlike files in HTML format, an ASP file causes the Web browser to automatically retrieve the most current data from the database. The data is then formatted according to the layout of the ASP file. An ASP file can also be used to save new data in the database, as would be the case with an online order form.

To create an ASP file, you need the name of the current database, a user name and password to connect to the database, and the URL of the Web server that will store the ASP file

In addition, the Web server must be running Microsoft Active Server 3.0 or later, have the ActiveX Server component installed, along with the Microsoft Access Desktop Driver, and have access privileges to the database. Because of these issues, creating an ASP file has to be done in cooperation with the administrator of the Web site.

Data Access Pages

Data access pages are Web pages bound directly to the data in the database. Data access pages can be used like Access forms, except that these pages are stored as external files, rather than within the database or database project. Although the pages can be used within Access, they are primarily designed to be viewed by a Web browser. Data access pages are written in *dynamic HTML* or *DHTML*, an extension of HTML that allows dynamic objects as part of the Web page.

Unlike ASP files, you can create a data access page within Access using a wizard or in Design view employing many of the same tools you use to create Access forms. However, a data access page requires that Internet Explorer 5.0 or later be installed.

12

Creating a Hyperlink Field

The Hyperlink data type allows you to create a *Hyperlink field*, a field that can store hyperlinks. The hyperlink can be a path to a file on your hard disk drive or network, or it can be a link to a page on the Web. When you click a Hyperlink field, Access jumps to the target specified by the link. For example, if you have a Clients table, and most of your clients have their own Web pages, you might want to create a Hyperlink field that contains links to each client Web page.

SEE ALSO

See "Viewing Field Properties" on page 57 for more information on working with data types.

Create a Hyperlink Field in a Table

1. Display the table in Design view.

2. Create a new field in which you want to store a hyperlink.

3. Click the Data Type drop-down arrow, and then click Hyperlink.

4. Click the Save button on the Table Design toolbar to save the changes to the table.

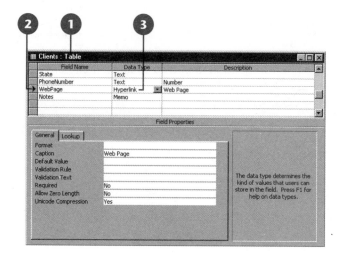

Inserting a Hyperlink to a File or Web Page

Use the Insert Hyperlink button to create a hyperlink within a Hyperlink field or as hypertext within a form or report. A hyperlink consists of the text that the user sees that describes the link, the URL of the link's target, and a ScreenTip that appears whenever the pointer passes over the link. If you have created a Hyperlink field for client Web pages, you use this method to add a URL for each client's Web page.

> **TIP**
>
> **Link to an e-mail address.** *To link to an e-mail address, click E-Mail Address in the Link To bar, and enter the e-mail address and subject.*

> **TIP**
>
> **Use ScreenTips.** *ScreenTips appear in the Web browser window if you're using Internet Explorer 4.0 or later.*

Insert a Hyperlink to a File or Web Page

1. Within a Hyperlink field or while editing a form or report in Design view, click the Insert Hyperlink button on the Design toolbar.

2. Click Existing File Or Web Page on the Link To bar.

3. Enter the hyperlink text.

4. Specify the linked document by either:
   - ◆ Entering the filename or URL of the linked document
   - ◆ Choosing the linked document from the Recent Files, Browsed Pages, or Inserted Links list

5. Click ScreenTip to create a ScreenTip that will be displayed whenever the mouse pointer moves over the hyperlink.

6. Click OK.

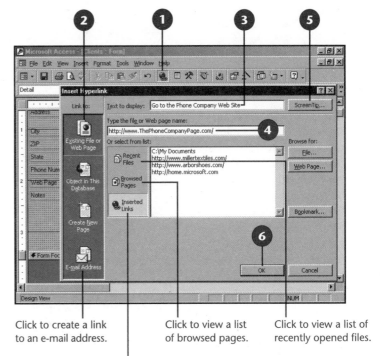

Click to create a link to an e-mail address.

Click to view a list of hyperlinks in the current document.

Click to view a list of browsed pages.

Click to view a list of recently opened files.

12

Linking to an Object in a Database

You can create hyperlinks that target forms, tables, and reports within the current database. You can also link to objects in other databases by specifying the database's filename and selecting the form, table, or report you want to target. You will have immediate access to those objects by clicking the hyperlink you insert.

TRY THIS

Use bookmarks in documents. *You can use a bookmark to link a database object to a specific location in a Word document or to a particular slide in a PowerPoint presentation.*

Link to a Database Object in the Database

1. Within a Hyperlink field or while editing a form or report in Design view, click the Insert Hyperlink button on the Design toolbar.

2. Click Object In This Database on the Link To bar.

3. Enter the hyperlink text.

4. Select the database object, and then click OK.

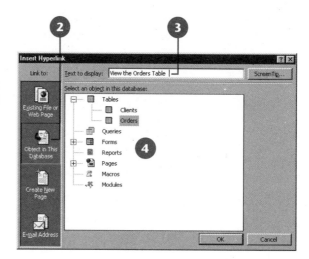

Link to an Object in Another Database

1. Within a Hyperlink field or while editing a form or report in Design view, click the Insert Hyperlink button on the Design toolbar.

2. Click Existing File Or Web Page on the Link To bar.

3. Enter the hyperlink text.

4. Enter the database filename.

5. Click Bookmark.

6. Select the database object, and click OK.

7. Click OK.

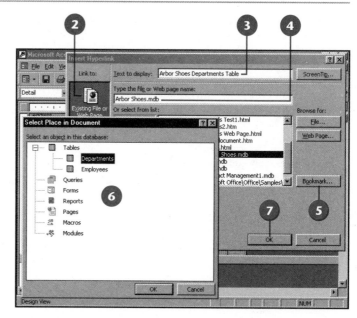

Linking to a New Document

You can create new documents at the same time you link to them. The documents can be Web pages, Office documents like Excel spreadsheets and PowerPoint presentations, or any other document type that is associated with an application on your computer. Once you create the new document, you have the choice of editing it immediately within the appropriate application, or editing it later.

TIP

Choose a document type.
Document types are determined by the file name extension. For example, Word documents are identified by the .doc extension.

Insert a Hyperlink to a New Document

1. Click Create New Page on the Link To bar.

2. Enter the hyperlink text.

3. Enter the name of the new document and the location in which you want it created.

4. Click one of the When To Edit option buttons to indicate whether you want to edit the document now or later.

5. Click OK.

   If you chose to edit the document immediately, the application for the document type opens.

6. Start editing your new document.

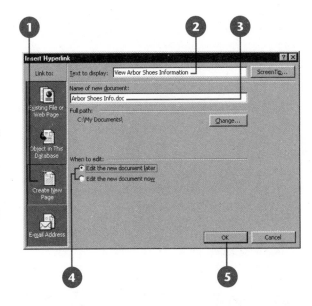

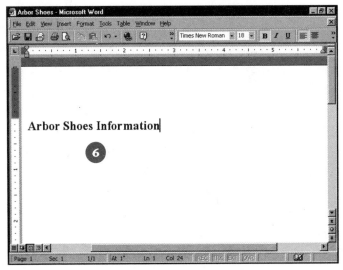

12

Navigating Hyperlinks

When you have added a hyperlink to a form, report, or table, you can activate the link by clicking it with the mouse. As the pointer moves over the hyperlink, the pointer changes to a hand, which indicates the presence of the link. If you have supplied a ScreenTip when you created the link, the tip appears, giving additional information about the link, and Access's Web toolbar also appears, allowing you to move forward and backward through a series of links. You can also jump to a specific page on the Web or to a file on your hard disk drive.

TIP

Remove or edit a hyperlink. *To remove or edit a Hyperlink field, right-click the link, point to Hyperlink, and then click Remove Hyperlink or Edit Hyperlink. To remove or edit a hypertext link from a form or report, right-click the link in Design view, and then click Remove or Edit.*

Navigate a Hyperlink

① Open a table, form, or report containing a hyperlink.

② Move the pointer over the hyperlink so that the pointer shape changes to a hand.

③ Click the hyperlink to display the linked document.

Hyperlink field   Web toolbar

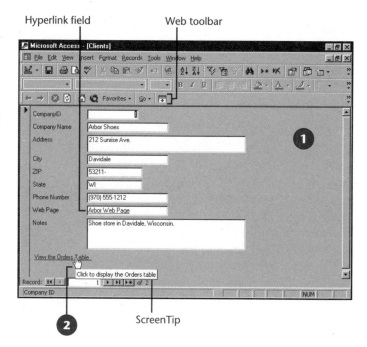

ScreenTip

Working with the Web Toolbar

The Web toolbar provides an easy way to navigate Web pages in any Office program. You can use the Web toolbar to go to your start page (also known as a home page), access a Web search page, or open a specific Web page. You can jump directly to a document on your computer or network, or to a Web page on your intranet or the Internet. In the Address box on the Web toolbar, type the address of the document (including its path; for example, *C:\My Documents\Memo\To Do List.doc*) or Web page (a URL; for example, *http://www.microsoft.com*) that you want to view and press Enter. While you're browsing, you can hide all the other toolbars to gain the greatest space available on your screen and improve readability.

When you have jumped to a document that you would like to return to in the future, you can add the document to a list of favorites. The Favorites button provides shortcuts to files you explore frequently so you won't need to retype long file locations. These shortcuts can open documents on your computer, network, intranet, and the Internet.

Web toolbar

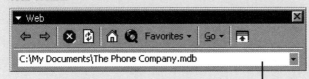

Enter the URL of the document you want to retrieve.

WEB TOOLBAR	
Button	**Description**
⇐	Click to move back in a series of hyperlinks.
⇒	Click to move forward in a series of hyperlinks.
⊗	Click to stop the current jump.
▣	Click to refresh the current page.
⌂	Click to go to the start page.
◉	Click to display a search page to search the Web.
Favorites ▾	Click to display a list of favorite Web pages and documents.
Go ▾	Click to go forward or backward, to the start page, or to define your start and search pages.
▣	Click to show only the Web toolbar.

12

Exporting Database Objects to HTML

Access's Export command lets you to save a table, query, form, or report as a Web page. If the page is saved in HTML format, it represents a snapshot of the data at the time you created the file. If your data changes, you must export it again if you want the Web page to be current.

> **TIP**
>
> **Use Export format.** *Tables, queries, and forms appear as HTML tables, but a report appears in HTML format with the same layout it had in Access.*

> **TIP**
>
> **Use HTML templates.**
> *Templates are usually stored in the \Program Files\Microsoft Office\Templates\Access folder. See online Help for more information on creating your own templates.*

Export to an HTML File

1 Open a table, query, form, or report.

2 Click the File menu, and then click Export.

3 Click the Save In drop-down arrow, and then select a location for the file.

4 Enter a filename for the Web page.

5 Click the Save As Type drop-down arrow, and then click HTML Documents.

6 Click Save All.

7 Enter the name of the HTML template you'll use for this Web page (if one exists).

8 Click OK.

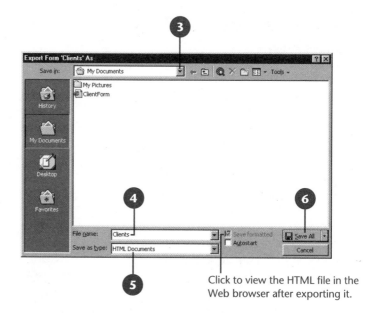

Click to view the HTML file in the Web browser after exporting it.

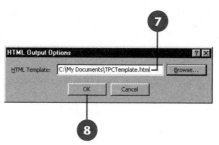

Exporting Database Objects to ASP Files

When you export a database object as an ASP file, you are giving Web users access to the information in your database. Unlike a static HTML file, an ASP file connects to the database and retrieves the most current information for the user to view.

SEE ALSO

See "Integrating Access and the Internet" on page 186 for a discussion of the technical issues surrounding the use of ASP files.

Export a Database Object to an ASP File

1. In the Database window, click the database object you want to export, click the File menu, and then click Export.

2. Click the Save As Type drop-down arrow, and then select Microsoft Active Server Pages.

3. Click the Save In drop-down arrow, and then select the location where you want to save the file.

4. Click Save.

5. Enter the name of the HTML template (if one exists).

6. Enter the name of the database file that contains the data you want the Web server to access.

7. Enter the user name you want the Web server to use to connect to the database.

8. Enter the password you want the Web server to use to log on to the database.

9. Enter the Web server URL.

10. Click OK.

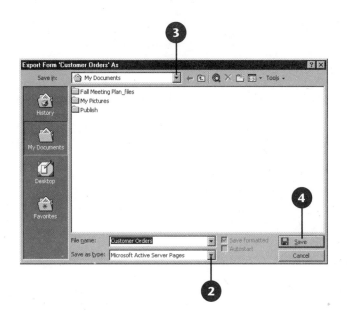

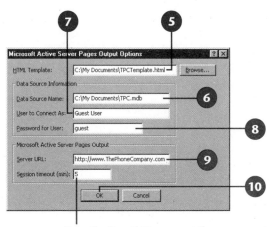

Enter the time that you want the Web server to remain inactive before disconnecting from the database.

Holding an Online Meeting

Microsoft NetMeeting is a program that comes with Access 2000. It allows you to host, participate, and collaborate in an online meeting over the Internet or an intranet. You can share and exchange information as if everyone were in the same room. As a host for an online meeting, you start the meeting and control the database. You can allow participants to make changes to the database. Each person in the online meeting can then take turns editing and controlling the database. As a participant and collaborator, you can share applications and documents, send text messages in Chat, transfer files, and work on the Whiteboard.

Start an Impromptu Online Meeting

1 Open the database you want to share.

2 Click the Tools menu, point to Online Collaboration, and then click Meet Now.

3 If this is the first time you've worked in an online meeting, the Microsoft NetMeeting dialog box appears. Fill out the information in the My Information and Directory boxes, and click OK.

4 In the Place A Call dialog box, do one of the following.

◆ Type or select the people you want to invite to the online meeting, and then click Call. To invite additional people, click Call Participant on the Online Meeting toolbar to display the Place A Call dialog box again.

◆ If you know the computer name or network Internet protocol address of the person you want to invite, click Advanced.

◆ Click Cancel to start NetMeeting so it runs in the background on your computer.

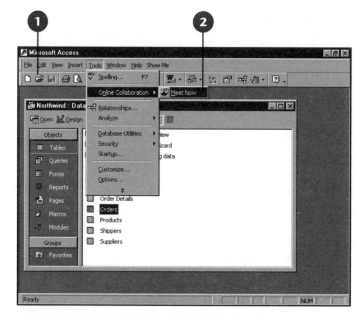

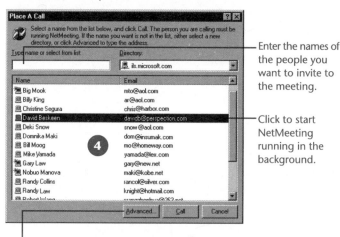

Enter the names of the people you want to invite to the meeting.

Click to start NetMeeting running in the background.

Click to enter the computer name or protocol address of the person you want to invite.

Receive an online meeting call. *You must have NetMeeting running on your computer to receive an online meeting call.*

Start NetMeeting using the Start menu. *Click Start on the taskbar, point to Programs, and then click NetMeeting.*

Join an online meeting. *If you receive an online meeting call, click Accept in the Join Meeting dialog box. If you receive an Outlook reminder for the meeting, click Start This NetMeeting (host) or Join This NetMeeting (participant). To receive an Outlook reminder to join a meeting, you need to have accepted the meeting from an e-mail message.*

Collaborate in an Online Meeting

1. As the host, click the Allow Others To Edit button on the Online Meeting toolbar.

2. When collaboration is turned on, click anywhere in the presentation to gain control. Double-click anywhere in the presentation to gain control if you are not the host.

3. Click the Allow Others To Edit button again to turn off collaboration, or press Esc if you don't have control of the presentation.

Participate in an Online Meeting

◆ Use the buttons on the Online Meeting toolbar to participate in an online meeting.

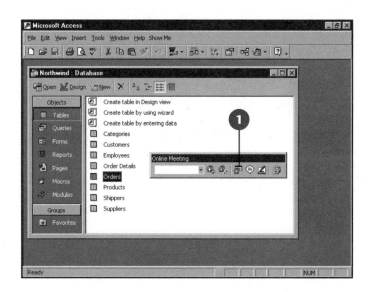

ONLINE MEETING TOOLBAR	
Button	**Description**
![button]	Allows the host to invite additional participants to the online meeting
![button]	Allows the host to remove a participant from the online meeting
![button]	Allows participants to edit and control the presentation during the online meeting
![button]	Allows participants to send messages in a Chat session during the online meeting
![button]	Allows participants to draw or type on the Whiteboard during the online meeting
![button]	Allows the host to end the online meeting for the entire group or allows a participant to disconnect

12

Creating Data Access Pages Using the Page Wizard

Data access pages allow you to create dynamic Web pages without the need of a Web server. Unlike an ASP file, you can also format data access pages, using many of the same tools you use when creating Access forms. Access organizes the data access pages in a separate object group in the Database window. Unlike other data objects, however, a data access page is stored in a file separate from the database file. One of the easiest ways to create a data access page is by using the Page Wizard.

TIP
Export to a data access page. *You can also create a data access page by using the Export command on the File menu and selecting Microsoft Access Data Access Page as the file type.*

Create a Data Access Page Using the Page Wizard

1. In the Database window, click Pages on the Objects bar.

2. Double-click the Create Data Access Page By Using Wizard icon.

3. Select the table and fields that you want to appear in the data access page. Click Next to continue.

4. Select any fields you want to act as group levels in the Web page. Click Next to continue.

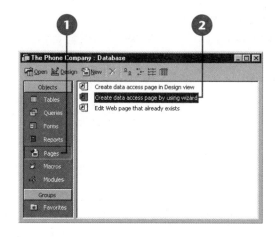

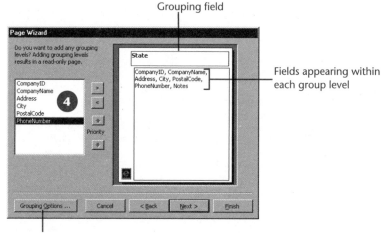

Grouping field

Fields appearing within each group level

Click to control how the group levels are determined.

SEE ALSO

See *"Grouping a Data Access Page" on page 202* for more information on grouped pages.

SEE ALSO

See *"Adding a Theme to a Page" on page 201* for more information on formatting your pages with predefined themes.

TIP

Name a data access page.
Access uses the title you enter as the page's filename, adding the .html file name extension.

TRY THIS

Delete a data access page.
You can delete a data access page from the Pages list by selecting the icon for the page and clicking the Delete button. When you do so, you'll be prompted to delete only the link to the page that appears in the Pages list, or both the link and the page itself.

⑤ Select the fields to sort the records in the page by. Click Next to continue.

⑥ Enter a title for the data access page.

⑦ Indicate whether you want to open the page in Access or to modify its design in Design view.

⑧ Click Finish.

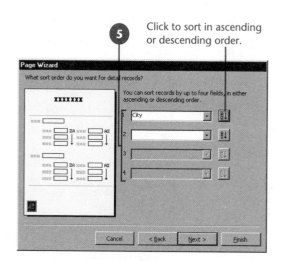

Click to sort in ascending or descending order.

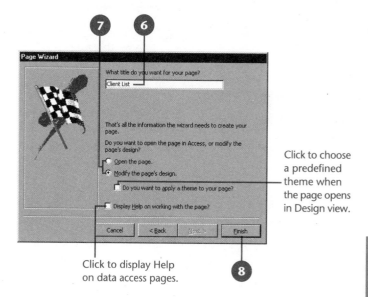

Click to choose a predefined theme when the page opens in Design view.

Click to display Help on data access pages.

12

Creating a Data Access Page in Design View

If you want to create a data access page without the Page Wizard, you can create it in Design view. Design view allows you to choose the tables, fields, and other objects that you want to appear on the Web page. You can format the appearance of the page using the same techniques you apply when you create Access forms.

> **TIP**
>
> **Work in HTML.** *If you know HTML, click the View menu, and then click HTML Source to display the page's underlying HTML code.*

> **TIP**
>
> **Create a data access page with the New button.** *You can create a data access page by clicking the New button on the Database Window toolbar, clicking Design View, and choosing the table or query you want placed in the data access page.*

Create a Data Access Page in Design View

1. In the Database window, click Pages on the Objects bar.

2. Double-click the Create Data Access Page In Design View icon.

3. If necessary, click the Field List button to display the list of tables and queries in the database.

4. Double-click the Tables or Queries folder, depending on what you want to base your page on.

5. Locate the table or query on which you want to base your page.

6. Drag a table or query icon from the field list to the Unbound section of the data access page.

7. Choose the layout of the fields in the page, and then click OK.

8. Click the Close button, click Yes when you are prompted to save your work, and then enter a filename for the resulting Web page.

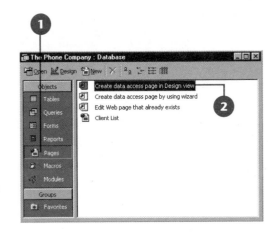

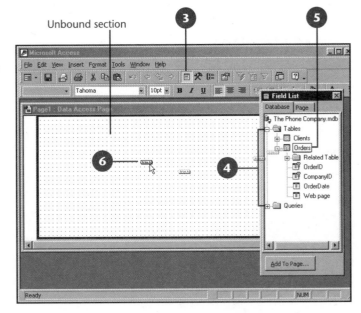

Unbound section

Adding a Theme to a Page

Access has a large collection of Web page *themes* that provide you with a variety of page designs. With the predefined themes you can format the background, fonts, and colors used in the Web page, or you can choose to format only one of these at a time. If you prefer a particular theme for your pages, you can set it as the default and all future pages will use that theme automatically.

TIP

Choose a theme with the Page Wizard. *You can choose a theme for your page with the Page Wizard. In the Page Wizard, choose to modify the page, and then click to select the Apply A Theme check box. When the page opens in Design view, you can choose the theme you want.*

Add a Theme to a Page

1. Display the data access page in Design view.

2. Click the Format menu, and then click Theme.

3. Select the theme you want to apply to your Web page.

4. Click to select the theme options you want.
   - ◆ Use the theme's vivid colors.
   - ◆ Apply the theme's active graphics.
   - ◆ Use the theme's background image.

5. Click OK.

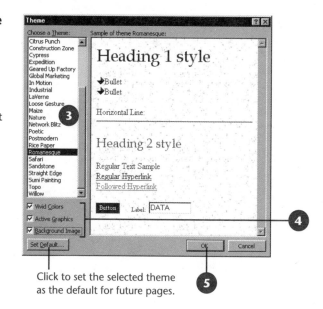

Click to set the selected theme as the default for future pages.

12

Grouping a Data Access Page

A *grouped data access page* is a hierarchical, interactive Web page in which records are grouped based on the values of a grouping field. When browsed, the page displays values of the grouping field, five records at a time. Each record will have a plus sign (+) button before it. Clicking this button will expand the page to show the complete record for that particular field value.

Group a Data Access Page

1. Display the data access page in Design view, and then select a field that will act as the grouping value.

2. Click the Promote button.

   Access creates a Group section that contains the group field and a plus sign that allows users to expand and collapse the record.

Click to display the detail section.

Group section

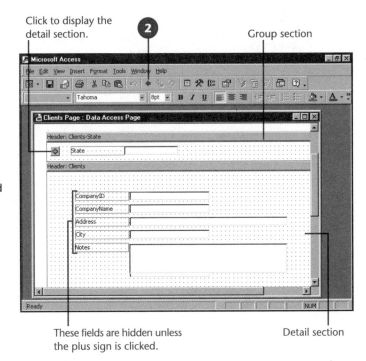

These fields are hidden unless the plus sign is clicked.

Detail section

TIP

Create a group with the Page Wizard. *You can also group your data access page with the Page Wizard. In the second step of the wizard, add a grouping level. You can also specify the grouping options that control how groups are selected.*

Remove a Group

1. Display the grouped data access page in Design view, and then select a grouping field.

2. Click the Demote button.

   Access removes the Group section, placing the grouping field in the Detail section.

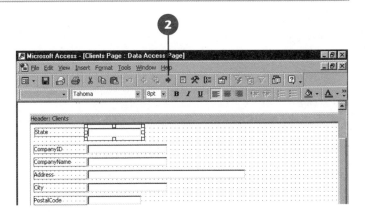

Use multiple groups. *You can add as many grouping fields as you want to a data access page. Access places each new grouping field within the hierarchy of the previous grouping fields.*

Specify Group Options

1 Display the grouped data access page in Design view, and then click the Sorting And Grouping button.

2 Change or modify any or all of the grouping properties.

3 Click the Close button.

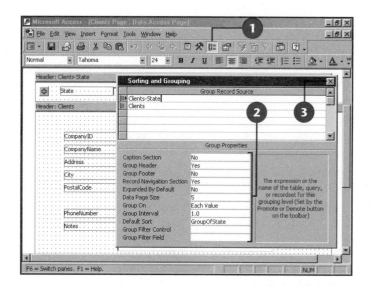

GROUP PROPERTIES	
Group Property	**Group Property Function**
Caption Section	Adds a caption to the Group section
Group Header	Adds a header to the Group section
Group Footer	Adds a footer to the Group section
Record Navigation Section	Displays a record navigation box
Expanded By Default	Expands the detail section when the browser opens the page
Data Page Size	Determines the number of records shown at one time
Group On	Determines the size of each group
Group Interval	Determines the interval of each group
Default Sort	Sorts fields by group
Group Filter Control	Specifies a combo or list box to filter the records in the group
Group Filter Field	Specifies which field to filter the records in the group

12

Viewing a Data Access Page

Once you create a data access page, you can open it from within the database or from your Web browser. If you choose to view the page in your browser, the browser will connect to the database and retrieve the information needed to display the page.

The data access page contains a navigation box to help you to retrieve the database records. The navigation box works in the browser the same way it works within Access. This tool allows you to move forward and backward through the database records, filter the data, sort it, or search for specific values.

TIP

Choose a Web browser for your data access page. *You must use Internet Explorer 5.0 or later to view a data access page.*

View a Data Access Page

1 In the Database window, click Pages on the Objects bar.

2 Double-click the data access page you want to view.

The page appears in a separate window.

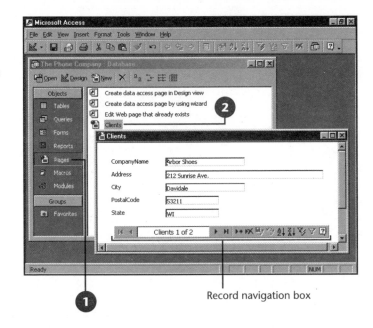

Record navigation box

Preview a Data Access Page in a Web Browser

1 In the Database window, open a data access page from the list of pages.

2 Click the File menu, and then click Web Page Preview.

Access starts your Web browser, loading the data access page.

3 Use the navigation box to review and modify the data.

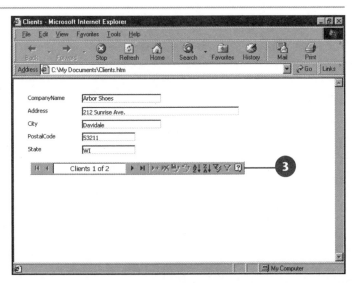

13

Managing a Database

Once you're familiar with the basics of creating and using a database, you're ready to work with some of the more advanced features of Microsoft Access 2000 that help you better manage your database. If you're working in a multi-user environment, where several people need access to the database, you need to explore ways of maintaining database security. Access provides several tools that help you control who can connect to your database and what a user can do once he or she is connected.

In addition to security issues, Access provides tools that help your database operate more efficiently. This includes the ability to compact your database file and to repair it if is damaged. You can also use Access to analyze the design of your database and tables in order to improve performance and reliability.

Finally, if you're interested in making your database easier to use, Access provides a Switchboard Manager that can put a user-friendly face on your database. With a switchboard, new users can access database reports and forms with a single click of a button, and you can control what parts of the database you want users to be able to access.

Securing a Database

As long as you are the only one working with a database, security issues are not usually a big concern. However, in a multi-user environment, you will probably need to consider how to secure the information your database contains. There are many threats to your data's integrity. It needs to be protected from users accidentally deleting important records or reports. Some parts of your database, such as a table containing employee salaries and social security numbers, will need to be restricted to a select group of users. You may even need to devise ways to protect your database from being hacked by someone using special programs designed to view your most sensitive data. Access security features help you ensure that your data will be secure under almost all circumstances.

Creating and Using Workgroups

A *workgroup* is a group of users in a multi-user environment who share data. A company's workgroup might consist of all of its employees, and to a certain extent, its customers and shareholders. Access stores workgroup information in a special file called the *workgroup information file*, also known as the *system database*. Access created a default workgroup information file during its initial setup. The information is typically stored in the System .mdw file located in the C:\Windows\System folder. You have been using this workgroup file since the first day you started Access, even if you weren't aware of it.

If you need to support several different workgroups, such as when there are several different multi-user environments (employees, customers, and shareholders, for example,) Office 2000 supplies a utility called the *Workgroup Administrator*, which allows you to create new workgroup information files. Even if you don't intend to support several workgroups, it is recommended that you replace the default workgroup information file with one of your own, because it is possible for unauthorized users to copy the default workgroup file and use it to gain access to your data.

If you do support several workgroups, you have to use the Workgroup Administrator to join the appropriate group *before* you start Access. As long as you're using only the default workgroup, you automatically joined the workgroup when you ran the Access Setup program and have remained joined to it since.

Working with User and Group Accounts

Access allows you to organize the users in a workgroup into *groups*. Each group might enjoy different privileges. Users in some groups might have the ability to add, edit and delete data; other user groups might be limited to viewing data. You can create workgroups and populate them with users. You can also specify the privileges for these groups or for individual users within a group. You can apply privileges to specific tables, queries, and reports or to whole databases. The list of users, groups and privileges also becomes part of the workgroup information file.

Using the Admins Group

Access, by default, creates the Admins group (short for Administrative), which is the group of users that have complete control over all database objects and the database itself. When you initially start Access, you are a member of the Admins group with the user name "Admin." As long as you are the sole user of your database, you are probably not even aware that you have such an account and are a member of such a group. Access keeps this feature hidden from you. However, if others will have access to your database, you may want to take steps to keep them from being given the same default privileges that you were given.

Activating Account Logons

To protect your data from other users acting as the Admin user, you have to specify a *password* for the Admin account. When you specify a password, you activate Access's logon procedure, requiring users to enter a user name and password before being able to start Access. You can then insert passwords for each individual account, requiring users to enter their own user name and password to start Access. User names and passwords are also stored in the workgroup information file.

You cannot assign a single user name and password to an entire group; each user must have a unique name and password. A user can create or change his or her own password; however, only the Admin user can clear a password if a user forgets it.

Assigning Ownership

Another Access security feature allows the *ownership* of the various tables, reports, forms, and databases. By default, the owner of an object is the account that created

the object (usually the Admin account). An account that owns a database object always has full privilege to edit or delete that object. An account that owns a database can always open the database. You can use the Admin account to assign ownership of these objects to various users and groups, even if they did not create the object themselves. In this way, you can prohibit certain users from accessing sensitive databases by assigning ownership to accounts not included their workgroup information file.

Using Database Passwords

Access prompts for the user password once, when the user starts Access. After that, Access does not query the user again, unless you assign a *database password* to a specific database. In this case, *all users* must enter a password before gaining access to that database. Adding a database password is an easy way to keep unauthorized users out of sensitive material; however, once the user gains access to the database, you will still need to use the other security features to control the user's privileges and behavior in that database.

Employing Encryption

A final area where the security of your data could be compromised is unauthorized data retrieval with applications other than Access. By using specialized utility programs, or even word processors, a user can bypass Access's security features to view your sensitive material. If this is a concern you can *encrypt* your data.

When you encrypt a database file, Access makes it indecipherable to unauthorized viewing, especially during electronic transmission or when it's stored on a disk or tape. The encryption does not affect Access, however, except that it can slow performance by 10 to 15 percent.

Creating a Workgroup Information File

When you install Access, the Setup program automatically creates a workgroup information file for you. The workgroup is identified by the workgroup ID (WID), a text string that the Setup program automatically creates based on your name and organization. Since this information can be determined by unauthorized users, you may want to create a new version of the workgroup information file, and with it a new WID, not so easily determined. Only someone who knows the WID will be able to create a copy of your workgroup information file and thus potentially gain access to Access's administrative accounts.

Create a Workgroup Information File

1. Exit Microsoft Access.

2. Start Windows Explorer, and then double-click MS Access Workgroup Administrator in the \Program Files\Microsoft Office\Office folder.

3. Click Create.

4. Type your name or the name of the Access database administrator.

5. Type the name of your organization.

6. Type any combination of up to 20 numbers and letters for the workgroup ID (keep this information in your records).

7. Click OK.

8. Type a new name and location for the new workgroup information file.

9. Click OK.

10. Click OK twice to confirm.

11. Click Exit.

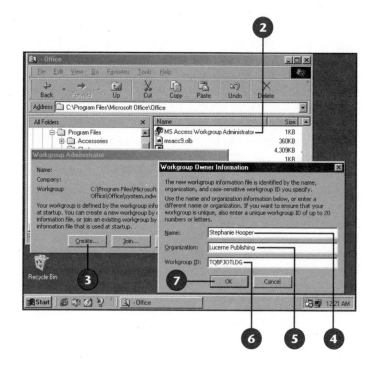

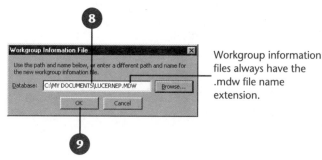

Workgroup information files always have the .mdw file name extension.

Joining a Workgroup

If you have several workgroup information files, you may have to choose which workgroup to join before starting Microsoft Access. You can do so with the same Workgroup Administrator program used to create new workgroup information files. Once you join a workgroup, Access uses that workgroup as the default group each time it starts—until you join a different group.

TIP

Locate the Workgroup Administrator. *If you cannot find the Workgroup Administrator, return to your Access Setup program and choose this option from the set of installation options.*

TIP

Use the Security Wizard. *You can also create and join a workgroup using the Security Wizard within Access. To start the wizard, click Security on the Tools menu and then click User-Level Security Wizard.*

Join a Workgroup

1. Exit Microsoft Access.

2. Start Windows Explorer, and then double-click MS Access Workgroup Administrator in the \Program Files\Microsoft Office\Office folder.

3. Click Join.

4. Enter the location and filename of the workgroup information file for the workgroup you want to join.

5. Click OK.

6. Click OK to confirm the change.

7. Click Exit to close the Workgroup Administrator.

Workgroup information file currently in use

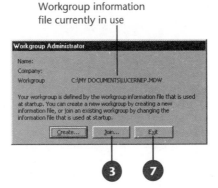

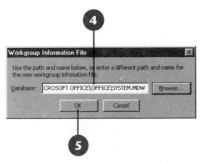

Creating User and Group Accounts

If many users work on the same database or a database contains confidential information, you might want to restrict access to specific information for certain users. You can do this by setting up individual accounts for each user. If users share a common characteristic or job description (such as those in charge of entering personnel data), you may want to place them in a common group. Members of the same group would share the same rights and privileges within Access.

Create a User Account

1. Click the Tools menu, point to Security, and then click User And Group Accounts.

2. Click the Users tab.

3. Click New.

4. Type a name for the new user.

5. Type a personal identifier.

6. Click OK.

7. Click OK.

Click to delete the selected user from the user list.

Groups of which the user is a member

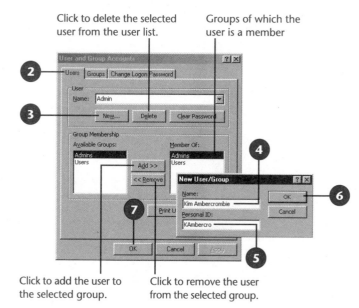

Click to add the user to the selected group.

Click to remove the user from the selected group.

Create a Group Account

1. Click the Tools menu, point to Security, and then click User And Group Accounts.

2. Click the Groups tab.

3. Click New.

4. Type a name for the new group.

5. Type a personal identifier.

6. Click OK.

7. Click OK.

Click to delete the selected group.

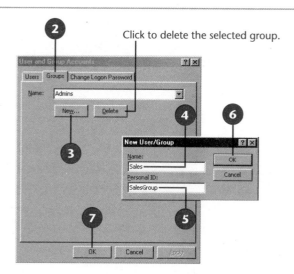

Activating User Logons

Until you activate the logon procedure for a workgroup, Access automatically logs on all users in the Admin account, giving them complete control over all databases. You can force users to log on to Access by creating a nonblank password in the Admin account.

Activate the Logon Procedure

1. Start Access as the Admin user (the initial setting for Access).

2. Click the Tools menu, point to Security, and then click User And Group Accounts.

3. Click the Change Logon Password tab.

4. Verify that the current user is Admin.

5. Type a password.

   You do not need to type a password in the Old Password box, because until this moment, no password should have been defined for the Admin account.

6. Verify the password by retyping it in the Verify box.

7. Click OK.

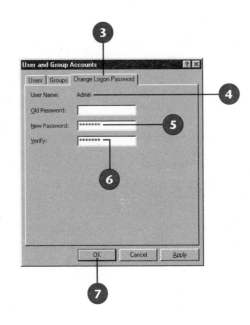

When you try to open a database, Access will prompt you for your name and password.

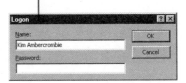

Setting User and Group Permissions

Once you have defined users and groups, you will want to define permissions for them. *Permissions* indicate the ability of each user or group to modify databases or database objects. Permissions also control a user's ability to create new objects. For example, you might want to limit the ability to view the Salaries table to a small group of users, and limit the ability to edit that table to an even smaller group.

Change Account Permissions

1. Start Access, type **Admin** as the user name, press Tab, and enter the password for the Admin account.

2. Click the Tools menu, point to Security, and then click User And Group Permissions.

3. Click the Permissions tab.

4. Click the Users option button or the Groups option button, depending on whether you want to modify the rights of individual users or entire groups.

5. Click the name of the person or group for whom you want to change permissions.

6. Click the Object Type drop-down arrow, and then select an object type.

7. Click the name of an existing object or click <New Object>.

8. Click to select the applicable check boxes to add or remove permissions for the selected object.

9. Click Apply.

10. Click OK.

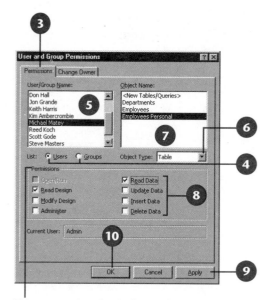

This user can view data in the Employees Personal table but cannot update, insert, or delete that data.

TIP

Set personal identifiers for user accounts. *Personal IDs contain between 4 and 20 letters (capitalization matters) or numbers or both. Along with the account name, a personal ID uniquely tags a user or group in a workgroup. Make sure you keep a copy of both the personal ID and account name in a secure location in case you need to retrieve an account that has been accidentally deleted or moved.*

TIP

Simplify user permissions. *Instead of assigning permissions to each user, assign permissions to groups and then add users to the appropriate groups.*

TIP

Print a list of permissions. *You can use the Documenter to print a report describing the permissions for each object in the database.*

SEE ALSO

See "Documenting a Database" on page 228 for information on using the Documenter utility.

DATABASE PERMISSIONS

Permission	Permits a User to	Applies to
Open/Run	Open a database, form, or report, or run a macro	Databases, forms, reports, and macros
Open Exclusive	Open a database with exclusive access	Databases
Read Design	View objects in Design view	Tables, queries, forms, reports, macros, and modules
Modify Design	View and change the design of objects, or delete them	Tables, queries, forms, reports, macros, and modules
Administer	Have full access to objects and data, including the ability to assign permissions	Tables, queries, forms, reports, macros, and modules
Read Data	View data	Tables and queries
Update Data	View and modify data	Tables and queries
Insert Data	View and insert data	Tables and queries
Delete Data	View and delete data	Tables and queries

Setting Object Ownership

By default, the Admin account owns all objects in a database (and the database itself). You can change the ownership of any object and assign the object to a specific user or group. The owner of an object has administrative-like powers. That individual can assign permissions for the object and thereby control who else can gain access to that object. However, the Admin account will also have full privileges to every object, regardless of ownership.

Set Ownership

1 Start Access, type **Admin** as the user name, press Tab, and enter the password for the Admin account.

2 Click the Tools menu, point to Security, and then click User And Group Permissions.

3 Click the Change Owner tab.

4 Click the Object Type drop-down arrow, and then select the type of object you want to own.

5 Click the specific object in the Object list.

6 Click whether you want to assign the object to a group or a specific user.

7 Click the New Owner drop-down arrow, and then select the user or group you want.

8 Click Change Owner.

9 Click OK.

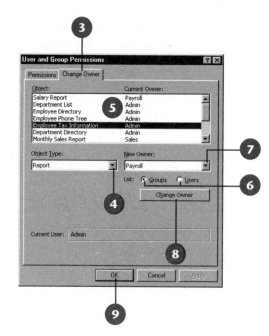

Securing a Database

If you want to provide extra security for a database, you can protect it by forcing users to enter a password before they can gain access to the database. This password is different from the account password used to log on to Access and applies to all users, even those with an Admin account.

TIP

Remember your password!
Don't lose or forget the password you assign to a database because it cannot be recovered. If you forget your password, you won't be able to open the database.

TIP

Remove a database password. *To remove a database password, open the database in exclusive mode under an administrative account, click the Tools menu, click Security, and then click Unset Database Password. Enter the current password, and then click OK.*

Set a Database Password

1. Make sure all users close the database, and then create a backup copy of the database.

2. Start Access, and then log on to an account with administrative permissions.

3. Click the File menu, and then click Open.

4. Select the database you want to use.

5. Click the Open drop-down arrow, and then click Open Exclusive to open the database exclusive of all other users.

6. Click the Tools menu, point to Security, and then click Set Database Password.

7. Type a password.

8. Retype the password.

9. Click OK.

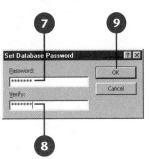

Encrypting a Database

An unauthorized user could access your data by bypassing Access entirely. Special utility programs exist that allow users to retrieve data without going through Access. You can guard yourself from this problem by encrypting your database. *Encryption* makes the database file indecipherable to these types of programs. Be aware, however, that encryption does not prohibit someone from using Access to open and read an encrypted database file.

TIP

Decrypt a database. *Open the encrypted database, click the Tools menu, point to Security, click Encrypt/Decrypt Database, and either replace the encrypted file or create a new, decrypted version.*

TIP

Encryption and performance loss. *An encrypted database will perform 10 to 15 percent slower.*

Encrypting a Database

1. Make sure all users close the database.

2. Click the Tools menu, point to Security, and then click Encrypt/Decrypt Database.

3. Locate and select the database file you want to encrypt.

4. Click OK.

5. Specify a name and location for the encrypted version of your database file.

   You can use the same name and location of the old database file if you want Access to replace the original file with the encrypted version.

6. Click Save.

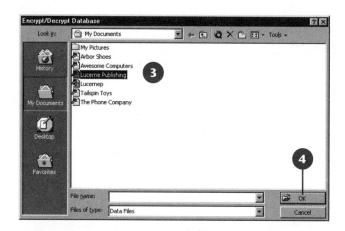

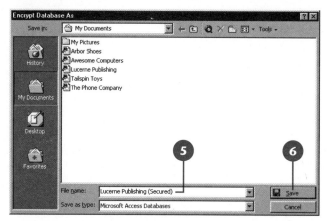

Locking Database Records

In a multi-user environment, several users could attempt to edit the same record simultaneously. Access prevents conflicts of this sort using *record locking*, ensuring that only one user at a time can edit data.

You can also prevent conflicts by opening the database in *exclusive mode*, preventing all other users from accessing the database while you're using it. This technique is useful for administrators who need sole access to the system while making changes to the database itself.

SEE ALSO

See "Securing a Database" on page 215 for an example of opening a database in exclusive mode.

Setting Record Locking

1. Click the Tools menu, and then click Options.

2. Click the Advanced tab.

3. Indicate whether the default strategy for opening the database is shared (allowing simultaneous access by other users) or exclusive (keeping out other users).

4. Click the Default Recording Locking strategy option button you want to use.

5. Verify that the Open Databases Using Record-Level Locking check box is selected.

6. Click OK.

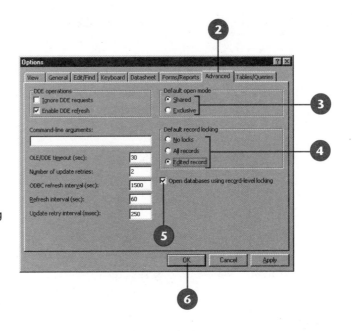

RECORD LOCKING STRATEGIES	
Locking Type	**Description**
No Locks	Access does not lock the record you're editing. When you save changes, Access gives you the option to overwrite another user's changes, copying your version to the clipboard, or to discard your changes.
All Records	Access locks all records in the table for the entire time you have it open, so no else can edit or lock the records.
Edited Record	Access locks the record you're currently editing and displays a locked record indicator to other users who may try to edit the record.

Replicating a Database

In some multi-user environments, users are scattered over a wide area, making it impossible for them to use the same database file. One method of providing access for these users is by *replicating* the database. The original database becomes the *Design Master*, and the other database files are *replicas*. You can add records to any of the database files, but you can only make structural changes (such as adding tables) to the Design Master.

Periodically, you should *synchronize* each replica with the Design Master. This ensures that each file has the most current data and database design. If a conflict arises between the values entered in the databases, you can choose which values are correct.

Create a Replica

1. If necessary, remove the database password from the database.

2. Open the database in exclusive mode.

3. Click the Tools menu, point to Replication, and then click Create Replica.

4. Click Yes to close the database.

5. If necessary, click Yes to make a backup copy of the database.

6. Enter the name and location of the replica.

7. Click OK.

8. Click OK to confirm the creation of the Design Master and the replica.

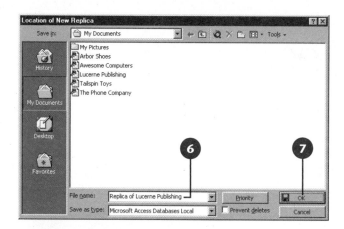

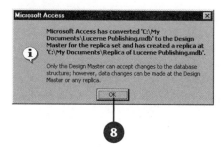

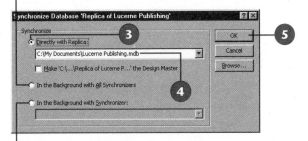

13

TIP

Replicate a database instead of sharing one copy over a network. *Replication helps to reduce network traffic because not everyone uses the same copy. You can also back up the Design Master while other users continue to work on their replicas.*

TIP

More about the Design Master. *The Design Master is a database to which system tables, fields, and replication properties are added. Only one Design Master exists per replica set.*

TIP

Synchronization and updates. *Synchronization exchanges updated records and objects between two replicas. The exchange can be one-way or two-way. If any replica is on the Internet, an additional dialog box appears when you synchronize, letting you choose whether you want to synchronize with someone on your network, intranet, or the Internet.*

Update a Replica

1 Open the replica you want to update.

2 Click the Tools menu, point to Replication, and then click Synchronize Now.

3 Click the Directly With Replica option button.

4 Enter the name and location of the Design Master, if necessary.

5 Click OK.

6 Click Yes to close and re-open the replica.

Resolve Replication Conflicts

1 Open the Design Master or the replica you want to check for conflicts.

2 Click the Tools menu, point to Replication, and then click Resolve Conflicts.

3 If there's a conflict, click View, resolve the conflict, and then click OK.

4 Click Close

Click to synchronize all replicated databases managed by a Synchronizer (as resources allow).

Click to have the Synchronizer that manages the open replica set perform the synchronization (as resources allow).

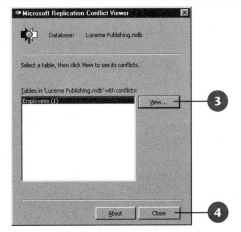

Compacting and Repairing a Database

What do you when your database starts acting erratically, or when even the simplest tasks cause Access to crash? Problems of this type can occur when a database gets corrupted or when the database file becomes so large as to be unwieldy.

A database can become corrupted when, for example, Access suffers a system crash. Access can repair many of the problems associated with a corrupted database.

The size of the database file may also be the trouble. When you delete objects like forms and reports, Access does not reclaim the space they occupied. To use this space you have to *compact* the database, allowing Access to rearrange the data, filling in the space left behind by the deleted objects.

Compact and Repair a Database

1 Make sure all users close the database.

2 Open the database with administrative privileges.

3 Click the Tools menu, and then point to Database Utilities.

4 Click Compact And Repair Database.

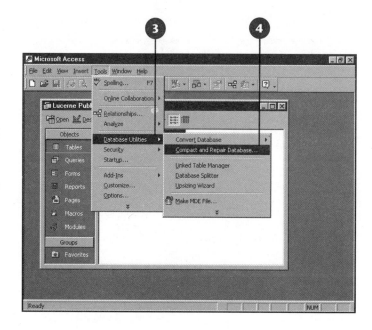

Splitting a Database

You can reduce the size of a database file by splitting the database. When Access *splits* a database, it places the tables in one file, called the *back-end database*, and the other database objects, like forms and reports, in the current database file. This technique stores all of the data in one location, while allowing each user to create his or her own forms and reports in his or her own database files.

TIP

Make a backup copy of your database. *It is a good idea to back up your database before compacting or splitting it. If an error occurs during either process and data is lost, you can retrieve data from your backup.*

Split a Database

1. Make sure all users close the database, and then close the switchboard, if necessary.

2. Open the database with administrative privileges.

3. Click the Tools menu, point to Database Utilities, and then click Database Splitter.

4. Click Split Database.

5. Enter the name and location of the back-end database that contains the database tables.

6. Click Split.

7. Click OK.

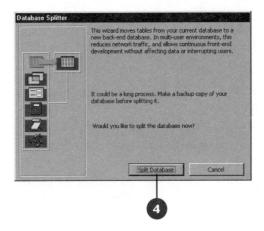

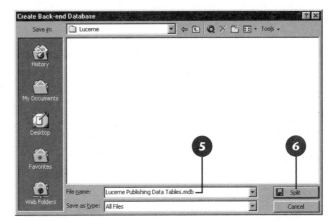

13

Analyzing a Database

From time to time, you should analyze your database to ensure that it works as efficiently as possible. Begin by running the *Performance Analyzer*, which provides ways to organize your database optimally and helps you make any necessary adjustments. Whenever you determine that several fields in a table store duplicate information, run the *Table Analyzer* to help you split the data into related tables (a process called *normalization*), but leave the original table intact.

"How can I make sure my database is performing at its best?"

Optimize Database Performance

1. Open the database you want to analyze.

2. Click the Tools menu, point to Analyze, and then click Performance.

3. Click the All Object Types tab.

4. Click to select any number of objects whose performance you want to analyze.

5. Click OK.

If the Performance Analyzer has suggestions for improving the selected object(s), it displays them in its analysis results.

6. Click each item and then review its analysis notes.

7. Press and hold Ctrl and click the suggested optimizations you want Access to perform.

8. Click Optimize.

9. Click Close.

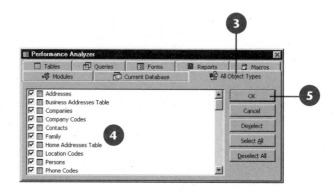

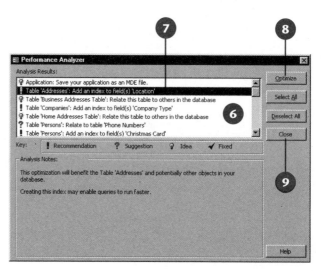

Performance Analyzer results. *The Performance Analyzer returns recommendations, suggestions, and ideas. You should have Access perform the recommended optimizations. Suggested optimizations have potential tradeoffs, and you should review the possible outcomes in the Analysis Notes box before having Access perform them. You perform idea optimizations manually by following the instructions in the Analysis Notes box.*

Analyze the Design of Your Tables

1. With your database open, click the Tools menu, point to Analyze, and then click Table.

2. If an explanation screen for the Table Analyzer Wizard opens, read it, click Next to continue, and then read the second explanation screen. Click Next to continue.

3. Click the table you want to analyze. Click Next to continue.

4. Click the option button for letting the wizard decide which fields to place in which tables. Click Next to continue.

5. Continue following the wizard instructions for naming the new tables, specifying the primary key for the new tables, and so on.

6. Click Finish or click Cancel if the wizard recommends not to split the table.

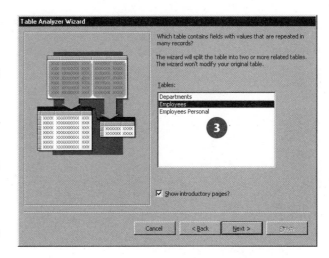

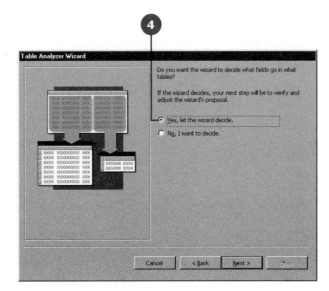

Converting Access Databases

In a multi-user environment, you may need to support users that run different versions of Access, or you may need to upgrade older databases to Access 2000. When you open a database from a previous Access version, Access 2000 prompts you to either upgrade the database file or open it without upgrading. You can also convert a database to the previous Access format.

TIP

Open a database instead of converting. *If you open a database instead of converting it, you won't be able to edit the design of any object.*

Converting an Old Database to Access 2000

1. Click the Open Database button on the Database toolbar.

2. Select the old database file, and then click Open.

3. Click the option button whether you want to convert the database to Access 2000 format or open the database without converting it.

4. Click OK.

Converting a New Database to the Previous Version of Access

1. Click the Tools menu, point to Database Utilities, and then point to Convert Database.

2. Click To Prior Access Database Version.

3. Enter the name and location for the converted database (use the name and location of the current database if you want to replace it with the new version).

4. Click Save.

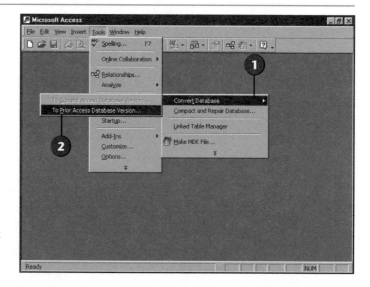

Using Add-Ins

Add-ins are additional programs, designed to run seamlessly within Access. Some add-ins are installed when you run the Access Setup program, while others can be purchased from third-party vendors. One of these add-ins is the Switchboard add-in, used to create and manage database switch-boards. Another add-in, the *Linked Table Manager*, helps users work with linked tables in their database. To work with add-ins, Access provides the *Add-In Manager*, a utility to install and remove your add-in files.

Install and Uninstall Add-Ins

1. Open a database.

2. Click the Tools menu, point to Add-Ins, and then click Add-In Manager.

3. Click Add New, and then locate and open the add-in you want to install.

4. Double-click the available add-in you want install.

5. Click any installed add-in you want to remove, and then click Uninstall.

6. Click Close.

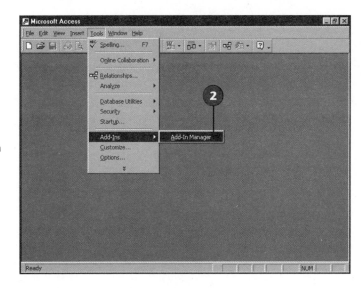

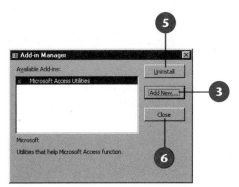

Creating a Database Switchboard

Switchboards are forms that provide easy access to many of your database's features. With a properly designed switchboard, your database users can display forms, print reports, and run macros with a single click of an action button. You can even hide all the other features of Access, making your switchboard the only thing the users see when interacting with your database.

To help you create a switchboard, Access provides the Switchboard Manager add-in. The Switchboard Manager makes it easier to create new switchboards or edit the content of existing switchboards.

TIP

Edit the switchboard design. *To edit your switchboard's design, open the switchboard form in Design view.*

Create a Switchboard

1. Click the Tools menu, point to Database Utilities, and then click Switchboard Manager.

2. Click Yes when you are asked to create a switchboard.

3. Click Edit to edit the content of the switchboard's main page.

4. Type a name for the main page.

5. Click New to add an action button to the page.

6. Enter text for the button.

7. Choose a command from the Command drop-down list box.

8. Choose a form, report, macro, switchboard or function name from the Report drop-down list box.

9. Click OK.

10. Repeat steps 5 through 9 to add additional action buttons to the switchboard.

11. Click Close.

12. Click Close.

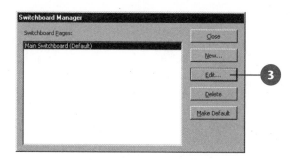

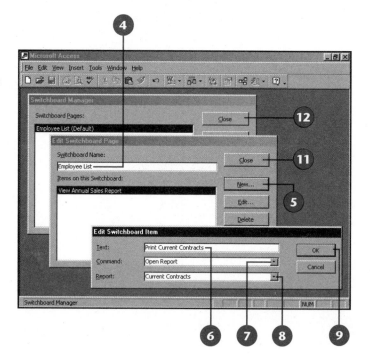

Managing a Switchboard

Once a switchboard is created, you can edit it using the same Switchboard Manager command you used to create it in the first place.

In your revisions, you may want to add extra pages to the switchboards or delete action buttons you've previously created. You can also edit action buttons so that they perform new tasks. The switchboard can thereby grow and change as your database changes.

TIP

Open a switchboard automatically. *To cause Access to open the switchboard automatically whenever the database is opened, click the Tools menu, click Startup, click the Display Form/Page drop-down arrow, and then select Switchboard.*

Add a Switchboard Page

1. Click the Tools menu, point to Database Utilities, and then click Switchboard Manager.

2. Click New.

3. Type a name for the new page.

4. Click OK.

5. Select the new page from the Switchboard Pages list, and then click Edit to edit the page's content.

6. Click Close to close the Switchboard Manager.

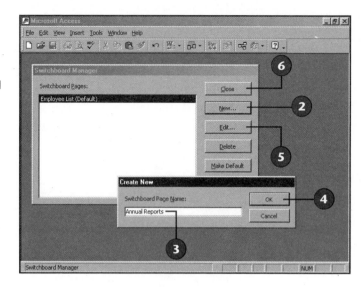

Define the Default Switchboard Page

1. Click the Tools menu, point to Database Utilities, and then click Switchboard Manager.

2. Select the page that you want to act as the default.

3. Click Make Default.

4. Click Close.

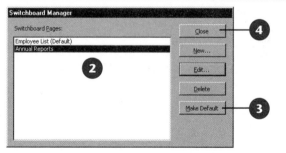

13

Documenting a Database

Complex databases can include many tables, forms, permissions, and user accounts. Access helps you keep tabs on all the elements in a database with the *Documenter* utility. You can use Documenter to print all the information about a database in a summary report.

TIP

Save Documenter output.
You can save the summary report created by the Documenter by clicking the File menu and then clicking Export. Access will then export the report to a Word file, Excel worksheet, or another format.

Document a Database

1 Click the Tools menu, point to Analyze, and then click Documenter.

2 Click the All Object Types tab.

3 Select the objects that you want to document.

4 Click Options.

5 Click the definitions you want to print for the selected object(s).

6 Click OK.

7 Click OK.

8 Check how many pages will print, and then click the Print button or the Print Preview button.

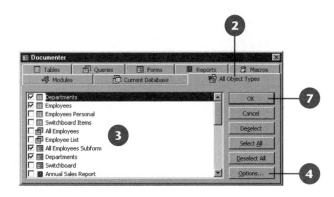

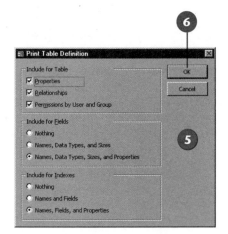

14

Customizing Access

There are several ways you can customize Microsoft Access to meet your needs and the needs of those who will use the databases you create. You can:

◆ Edit Access's menus and toolbars, adding new commands and subtracting unused ones

◆ Create new menus and toolbars

◆ Design a complete custom application with menu bars and toolbars tailored to a specific database

Access also allows you to create *macros*, stored collections of actions that perform a specific task. Macros allow you to create new commands designed to work with a particular database. You can attach macros to menus, toolbars, and form controls. You can write a macro so that it executes its actions only if a particular condition is met.

Adding and Removing Toolbar Buttons

You can modify Access's toolbars so that they display only the buttons you want. For example, you could add buttons to a toolbar for commands you frequently use, or you could remove buttons from toolbars that have too many. When monitors are set to low resolution, sometimes not all toolbar buttons are visible, and removing buttons can make the ones you need more readily visible.

TIP

Set options for toolbars and menus. *To set some general options for toolbars and menus, click the Tools menu, click Customize, click the Options tab, select the options you want, and then click OK.*

Add a Toolbar Button

1. Click the More Buttons drop-down arrow on the toolbar.

2. Point To Add Or Remove Buttons.

3. Click Customize.

4. Click the Commands tab.

5. Click the category containing the toolbar button you want to add.

6. Drag a command from the Commands tab to the toolbar.

7. Click Close.

A solid vertical line appears to the right of where the new button will be inserted.

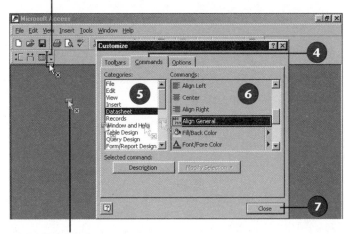

Drag-and-drop pointer

Remove a Toolbar Button

1. Click the More Buttons drop-down arrow on the toolbar.

2. Point to Add Or Remove Buttons.

3. Click to clear the check box next to the button you want to remove.

4. Click outside the toolbar to deselect it.

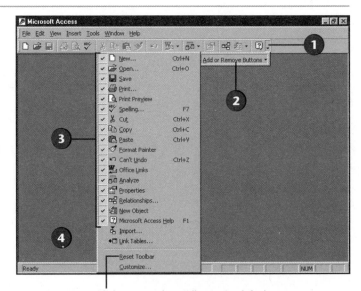

Click to reset the toolbar to its default state.

Customizing a Toolbar

You can create your own toolbars to increase your efficiency. You might, for example, create a toolbar that contains the features, including macros, that you use most often when you are performing a particular task, such as editing records in a table.

You can change the properties of an existing Access toolbar or one that you create using the Customize dialog box, which allows you to control, among other things, the toolbar's placement. A toolbar is said to be *docked* when it "snaps" into place on the border of a window.

Create a New Toolbar

1 Click the View menu, point to Toolbars, and then click Customize.

2 On the Toolbars tab, click New.

3 Type a name for the new toolbar.

4 Click OK.

5 Add buttons to the new toolbar by dragging commands found on the Commands tab.

6 Click Close.

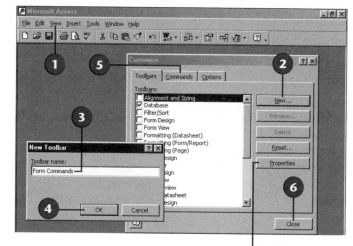

Click to modify the selected toolbar's properties.

Change a Toolbar's Properties

1 Click the View menu, point to Toolbars, click Customize, and then click the Toolbars tab.

2 Select the toolbar from the list and click the Properties button.

3 Modify the toolbar properties.

4 Click Close.

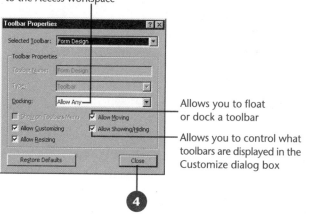

Controls how the toolbar adheres to the Access workspace

Allows you to float or dock a toolbar

Allows you to control what toolbars are displayed in the Customize dialog box

14

Customizing the Menu Bar

You can customize the existing Access menu bar by adding buttons, commands, and macros that you use frequently. Adding items to the menu bar is a great way to have easy access to features without adding more buttons or toolbars. The ability to drag features from different parts of the program window makes it easy to add items to the menu bar.

Add a Menu Command

1. Click the View menu, point to Toolbars, and then click Customize.

2. Click the Commands tab.

3. Select a category.

4. Drag the command to the appropriate place on the menu you want to modify. A solid horizontal line appears below the place where the new menu command will be placed.

5. Click Close.

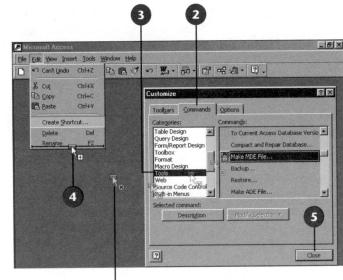

Drag-and-drop pointer

Remove a Menu Command

1. Click the View menu, point to Toolbars, and then click Customize.

2. Open the menu containing the command you want to remove.

3. Drag the menu command you want to remove to an empty area in the database workspace.

4. Click Close.

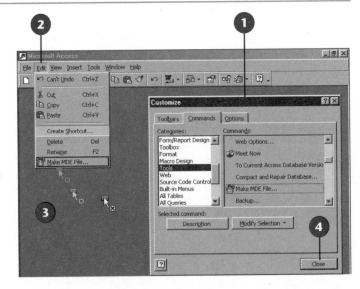

Create a New Menu

1. Click the View menu, point to Toolbars, click Customize, and then click the Commands tab.

2. Click New Menu in the Categories box.

3. Drag New Menu from the Commands list to an empty spot on the menu bar.

4. Click Close.

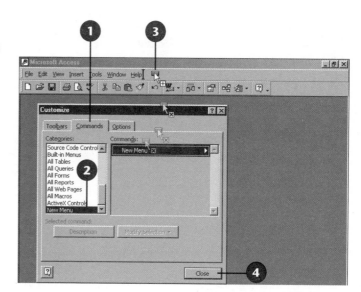

Name a New Menu

1. Click the View menu, point to Toolbars, click Customize, and then click New Menu on the menu bar.

2. Click Modify Selection.

3. Click the Name box and type a new name.

4. Press Enter.

5. Click Close.

Accelerator key

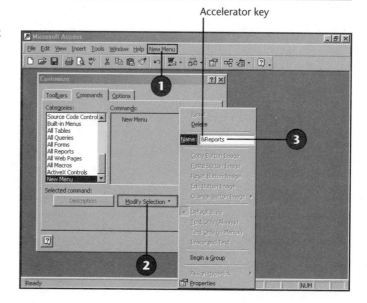

Editing Toolbar Buttons and Menu Entries

Access includes tools that allow you to edit toolbar buttons and menu entries. You can specify whether the button or menu item will display text, an image, or both text and an image. If you choose to display an image, you can edit the image, copy it from another button or use one of Access's predefined images.

TIP

Start a menu group. *You can organize a menu into groups of commands, separated by horizontal lines. To create a group, select the menu entry that will be the first item in the group, click Modify Selection in the Customize dialog box, and then click Begin Group.*

Edit a Button or Menu Entry

1 Click View, point to Toolbar, and then click Customize.

2 Select the button on the toolbar or comand on the menu you want to edit.

3 Click Modify Selection.

4 Choose the commands that will modify the selection in the way you prefer.

◆ Click Copy Button Image to copy the button image.

◆ Click Reset Button Image to reset the selected item to its default image.

◆ Click Edit Button Image to edit the button image.

◆ Click Change Button Image to select from a group of predefined images, as shown.

◆ Click Image And Text to paste a button image into the selected item.

◆ Click Begin A Group to begin a group of menu items.

5 Click Close.

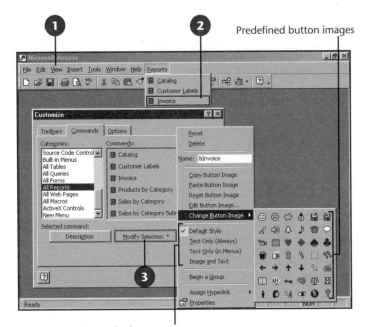

Predefined button images

Choose whether to display text, an image, or both text and image.

Customizing Access Startup

You can customize an Access database by specifying what happens when a user first opens it. For example, you can set startup options to choose which menus and commands are available and what title and icon appear in the program title bar. You can create a complete customized menu bar for Access to use, rather than the default menu bar.

TIP

Start with a switchboard.
If you create a database switchboard, you can have Access display the switchboard at startup by choosing the switchboard in the Display Form list of the Startup dialog box.

SEE ALSO

See "Creating a Database Switchboard" on page 226 for information on switchboards.

Set Startup Options

1. Click the Tools menu, and then click Startup.

2. Set the startup options you want to use for the database you are creating.

3. Click OK.

4. Open and close the database or restart Access to see the new startup.

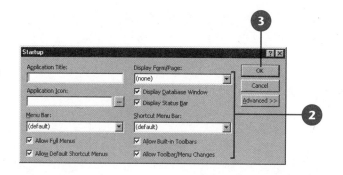

ACCESS CUSTOM STARTUP OPTIONS	
Term	**Definition**
Application Title	Type a title bar name.
Application Icon	Click to select a bitmap (.bmp) or icon (.ico) filename for the title bar.
Menu Bar	Click to choose a menu bar.
Allow Full Menus	Click to display all the built-in menus or to hide commands that change the database.
Allow Default Shortcut Menus	Select a custom shortcut menu bar for the open database.
Display Form/Page	Select the form or data access page that will appear when you open the database.
Display Database Window	Click to display the Database window when you open the database. Clear to prevent the window from appearing.
Display Status Bar	Click to display the status bar when you open the database.
Shortcut Menu Bar	Select a shortcut menu to set your own menu bar as the default shortcut menu bar for the forms and reports in the current database.
Allow Built-In Toolbars	Click to view and use the default toolbars.
Allow Toolbar Menu Changes	Click to allow toolbar changes.

Learning About Macros

A *macro* is a stored collection of actions that perform a particular task, such as opening a specific form and report at the same time or printing a group of reports. You can create macros to automate a repetitive or complex task or to automate a series of tasks. Using a macro to automate repetitive tasks guarantees consistency and minimizes errors caused when you forget a step. Using a macro can also protect you from unnecessary complexity. You can perform multiple tasks with a single button or keystroke. For whatever reason you create them, macros can dramatically increase your productivity when working with your database.

Macros consist of actions or commands that are needed to complete the operation you want to automate. Sorting, querying, and printing are examples of *actions*. *Arguments* are additional pieces of information required to carry out an individual action. For example, an Open Table macro action would require arguments that identify the name of the table you want to open, the view in which to display the table, and the kinds of changes a user would be able to make in this table. Because there are no wizards to help you make a macro, you create a macro by entering actions and arguments directly in Design view. After creating a macro, make sure you save your work and give the macro a meaningful name.

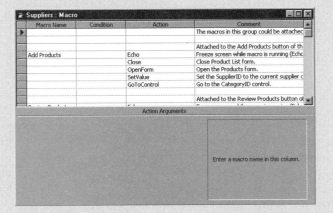

Creating a Macro

Before you begin creating a macro, you should plan the actions required to complete the tasks you want to automate. Practice the steps needed to carry out the operation and write them down as you go. Finally, test your written instructions by performing each of the steps yourself.

TIP

Edit an existing macro.
Open the macro in Macro Design view, change the necessary actions and arguments, and then save the changes. To insert a new action, click the Insert Rows button on the Macro Design toolbar; remove an action by selecting the action row and then clicking the Delete Rows button. To create a new macro based on an existing one, open the macro in Macro Design view, and then click the Save As command on the File menu. Give the macro a new name, and modify the new macro as needed.

Create and Save a Macro

1 In the Database window, click Macros on the Objects bar.

2 Click the New button.

3 Click the Action drop-down arrow, click the action you want to use, and then press Tab.

There are several dozen actions from which you can choose.

4 Type a comment if you want to explain the action.

5 Click the table name in the first Action Arguments box, and then select a value from the drop-down list.

6 To add more actions to the macro, click the right side of a new Action row, and repeat steps 2 through 5. The macro will carry out the actions in the order in which you list them.

7 Click the Save button on the toolbar.

8 Enter a descriptive macro name that helps identify the tasks the macro carries out.

9 Click OK.

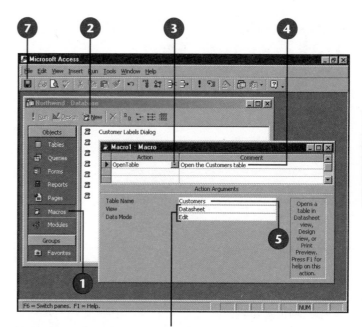

Depending on the action, you may need to provide additional arguments.

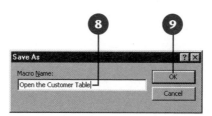

Running and Testing a Macro

To have a macro perform its actions, you must *run* it, or instruct it to execute its actions. There are two ways to run a macro. You can have the macro perform all the steps in a sequence at once, or you can test a macro by running it to perform one step at a time, allowing you to review the results of each step.

By testing your macro, you might discover that it did not perform all its tasks in the way you expected. If so, you can make changes and retest the macro as you continue to make adjustments in Macro Design view.

TIP

Run a macro from the Database window. *In the Database window, click the Macros tab, and then double-click the name of the macro you want to run.*

Run a Macro in a Sequence

1. Display the macro you want to run in Macro Design view.

   If your macro does not automatically switch you to the correct view, switch to the view in which you want to run the macro.

2. Click the Run button on the Macro Design toolbar.

   If the macro encounters an action it cannot perform, a message box appears stating the action it could not carry out.

3. If necessary, click OK to close the message box.

4. Click Halt to stop the macro.

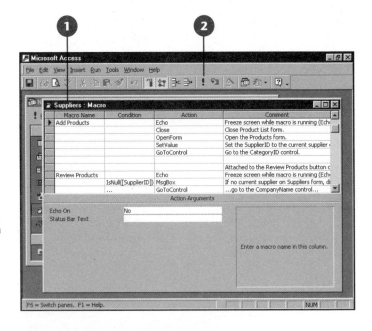

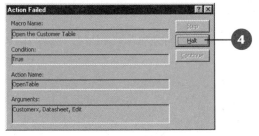

Run the macro in the correct view. *Keep in mind that a macro will perform only the actions that are appropriate in the currently active view, so be sure to display the correct view before you run the macro. You can also have the first action in the macro display the view in which you want to run the macro.*

Run all steps in a macro. *If the Single Step button on the Macro Design toolbar is active, you can still run all the steps in the macro without stepping. In the Macro Single Step dialog box, click Continue.*

Stop the macro before it finishes. *In the Macro Single Step dialog box, click Halt.*

Place a macro on a toolbar. *If you want to place a macro on the toolbar, click the Tools menu, click Customize, click the Commands tab, choose the All Macros category, drag the macro you want to the toolbar, and then click OK.*

Test a Macro Step-by-Step

1 Display the macro you want to run in Macro Design view.

2 Click the Single Step button on the Macro Design toolbar.

If necessary, switch to the view in which you want to run the macro.

3 Click the Run button on the toolbar.

If the Run button does not appear, click the Tools menu, click Run Macro, click the Macro drop-down arrow, and then double-click the macro you want to run.

4 Click Step to perform the first action in the macro.

5 Repeat step 4 until the macro finishes.

If the macro encounters an action it cannot perform, you see a message box stating the action it could not carry out.

6 Click OK to close the message box.

7 Click Halt to stop the macro.

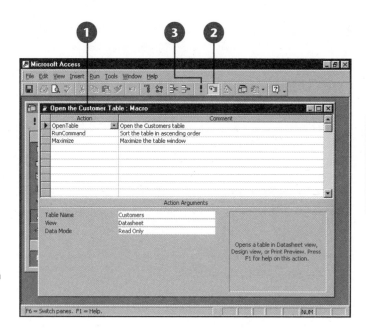

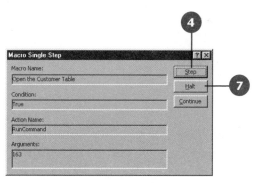

14

Creating Macro Groups

If you have numerous macros, grouping related macros in macro groups can help you to manage them more easily. When Access runs a macro group, the first macro in the group starts with the first action, continuing until it reaches a new macro name or the last action in the window.

To run a macro group, use the macro group name followed by the macro name. For example, you refer to a macro group named *Report1* in the *Employees* macro as *Report1.Employees*.

TIP

Display the Macro Name column. *You can display the Macro Name column by clicking Macro Names on the View menu.*

Create a Macro Group

1. Open a macro in the Macro window.

2. Click the Macro Names button.

3. Type a name for the macro group next to the first action in the Macro Name column.

4. Click the Close button.

5. Save your changes.

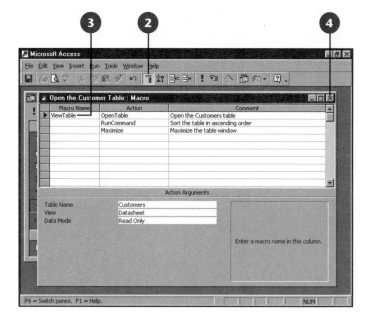

Creating Conditional Macros

Sometimes you may want a macro to run only if some prior condition is met. For example, you could create a macro that prints a report only if the number of records to print is greater than zero. You can do this by creating a *conditional expression*, an expression that Access evaluates as true or false. If the condition is true, Access carries out the actions in the macro or macro group.

SEE ALSO

See "Using Expression Builder" on page 69 for more information about the Expression Builder.

Create a Macro Condition

1. Open a macro in the Macro window.

2. Click the Conditions button on the Macro Design toolbar.

3. Click the Build button on the Macro Design toolbar to open the Expression Builder.

4. Enter an expression that Access could evaluate as either true or false.

5. Click OK.

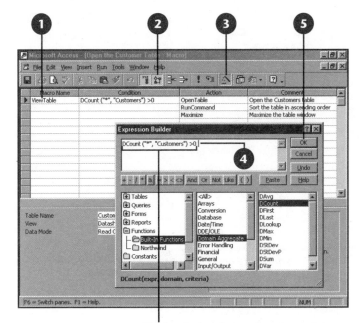

Checks whether the number of records in the Customers table is greater than zero.

Assigning a Macro to a Button

Database designers often attach macros to form controls, particularly buttons, so that when a user clicks the button, the macro is activated. If you create a button, you can use the Command Button Wizard to specify the action that will occur when the button is clicked. If you want to assign a macro to a button, you choose the action of running the macro.

TIP

Assigning a macro to a button. *If you don't use the Command Button Wizard to assign your macro to the button, you need to open the property sheet for the control and assign the macro to the Click event.*

Assign a Macro to a Button

1. In Design view for a form, click the Command Button tool on the Toolbox.

2. Drag the image onto the form, report, or page.

3. Click Miscellaneous.

4. Click Run Macro and then click Next.

5. Choose the macro you want to run, and then click Next.

6. Specify the text or image that will appear on the button, and then click Next.

7. Enter a name for the command button control, and then click Finish.

8. Save the form or report, and then test the button to verify that your macro runs when the button is clicked.

Select the Control Wizards button to display the Command Button Wizard.

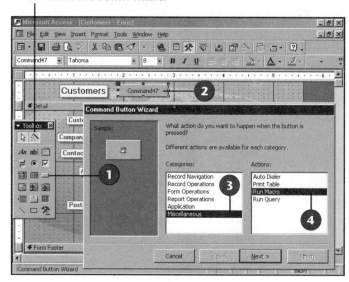

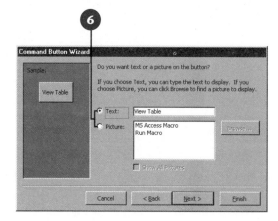

Assigning a Macro to an Event

An *event* is a specific action that occurs on or with a certain object. Clicking a button is an event, called the Click event. The Click event in this case occurs on the button object. Other events include the Dbl Click event (for double-clicking) and the On Enter event, which occurs, for example, when a user "enters" a field by clicking it.

If you want to run a macro in response to an event, you have to work in the object's property sheet. The property sheet lists all of the events applicable to the object. You can choose the event and then specify the macro that will run when it occurs or create a new macro in the Macro window.

Assign a Macro to an Event

1. In Design view, double-click the object in which the event will occur.

2. Click the Event tab.

3. Click the box for the event you want to use.

4. Click the drop-down arrow, and then click the macro you want to use.

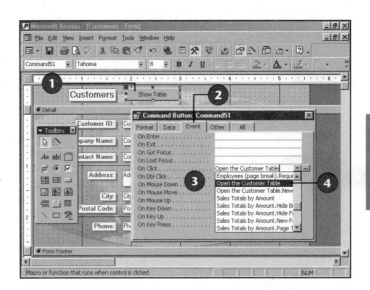

Create a New Macro for an Event

1. In Design view, double-click the object.

2. Click the Event tab.

3. Click the specific event to which you want to assign the macro.

4. Click the Build button.

5. Double-click Macro Builder.

6. Enter a name for the new macro, and then click OK.

7. Enter the actions for the new macro, and then close the Macro window.

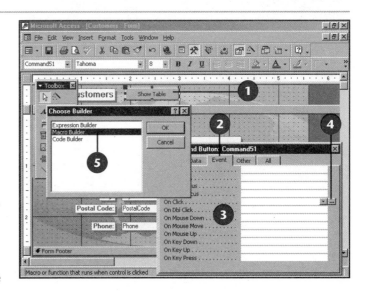

14

Creating a Message Box

When you create a macro, you may want to give database users information about how the macro works as it runs. You can create message boxes for your macros that, for example, ask the user if he or she wants to proceed. You do this with the MsgBox action. The MsgBox action allows you to specify the text of the message, whether or not a beep sounds when the box is displayed, the type of box that appears, and the box's title.

Access supports five different types of message boxes. Each one has a different icon. The icons convey the importance of the message box, ranging from merely being informative to indicating a serious error.

Create a Message Box

1. In the Database window, display the macro in Design view you want to add a message box.

2. Type **MsgBox**.

3. Specify the text you want contained in the message box.

4. Indicate whether a beep will accompany the message.

5. Specify the box type.

   Refer to the table for the message box type.

6. Enter the box title.

7. When you're done, click the Close button.

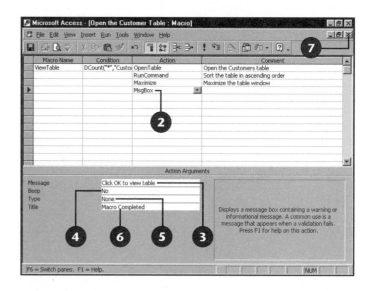

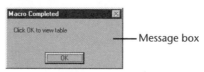

— Message box

MESSAGE BOX ICONS	
Icon	Type
✖	Critical
?	Warning?
⚠	Warning!
ⓘ	Information

Working with VBA

I f you want to create customized Microsoft Access 2000 applications, you'll need to learn how to work with the Microsoft Office 2000 programming language, *Microsoft Visual Basic for Applications*, or *VBA*. VBA is more powerful and more flexible than Access macros, and you can use it in all major Office applications.

To create a VBA application, you have to learn VBA conventions and syntax. Access provides extensive online Help available to assist you in this task. Office 2000 makes VBA more user-friendly by providing the Visual Basic Editor, an application that includes several tools to help you write error-free VBA applications.

With VBA you can create applications that run when the user initially opens a database, or you can link applications to buttons, text boxes, or other controls. You can even use VBA to create your own custom functions, supplementing Access's library of built-in functions.

VBA may be a difficult language for the new user, but its benefits make the effort of learning it worthwhile.

Enhancing a Database with VBA

Office 2000 applications like Access, Excel, and Word share a common programming language: VBA. With VBA, you can develop applications that combine tools from these Office 2000 products, as well as other programs that support VBA. Because of the language's power and flexibility, programmers often prefer to use VBA over Access macros to customize their Access applications.

Introducing the Structure of VBA

VBA is an *object-oriented* programming language because, when you develop a VBA application, you manipulate objects. An object can be anything within your database, such as a table, query, or a database. Even Access itself is considered an object. Objects can have properties that describe the object's characteristics. Text boxes, for example, have the Font property, which describes the font Access uses to display the text. A text box also has properties that indicate whether the text is bold or italic.

Objects also have *methods*, actions that can be done to the object. Deleting and inserting are examples of methods available with a record object. Closely related to methods are events. An *event* is a specific action that occurs on or with an object. Clicking a form button initiates the Click event for the button object. VBA also refers to an event associated with an object as an *event property*. The form button, for example, has the Click event property. You can use VBA to either respond to an event or to initiate an event.

Writing VBA Code

Unlike Access macros, which are created in the Macro Design window, the VBA programmer types the statements, or *code*, that make up the VBA program. Those statements follow a set of rules, called *syntax*, that govern how commands are formulated. For example, to change the property of a particular object, the command follows the general form:

```
Object.Property = Expression
```

where *Object* is the name of a VBA object, *Property* is the name of a property that object has, and *Expression* is a value that will be assigned to the property. The following statement sets the Caption property of the Departments form:

```
Forms!Departments.Caption="Department Form"
```

You can use Access's online Help to learn about specific object and property names. If you want to apply a method to an object, the syntax is:

```
Object.Method arg1, arg2, …
```

where *Object* is the name of a VBA object, *Method* is the name of method that can be applied to that object, and *arg1, arg2, …* are optional *arguments* that provide additional information for the method operation. For example, to move to page 2 of a multipage form, you could use the GoToPage method as follows:

```
Forms!Departments.GoToPage 2
```

Working with Procedures

You don't run VBA commands individually. Instead they are organized into groups of commands called *procedures*. A procedure either performs an action or calculates a value.

Procedures that perform actions are called *Sub procedures*. You can run a Sub procedure directly, or Access can run it for you in response to an event, such as clicking a button or opening a form. A Sub procedure initiated by an event is also called an *event procedure*. Access provides *event procedure templates* to help you easily create procedures for common events. Event procedures are displayed in each object's event properties list.

A procedure that calculates a value is called a *function procedure*. By creating function procedures you can create your own function library, supplementing the Access collection of built-in functions. You can access these functions from within the Expression Builder, making it easy for them to be used over and over again.

Working with Modules

Procedures are collected and organized within *modules*. Modules generally belong to two types: class modules and standard modules. A *class module* is associated with a specific object. For example, each form or report can have its own class module, called a *form module* or *report module*. In more advanced VBA programs, the class module can be associated with an object created by the user.

Standard modules are not associated with specific objects, and they can be run from anywhere within a database. This is usually not the case with class modules. Standard modules are listed in the Database window on the Modules Object list.

Building VBA Projects

A collection of modules is further organized into a *project*. Usually a project has the same name as a database. You can create projects that are not tied into any specific databases, saving them as Access add-ins that provide extra functionality to Access.

Using the Visual Basic Editor

You create VBA commands, procedures, and modules in Office's *Visual Basic Editor*. This is the same editor used by Excel, Word, and other Office applications. Thus, you can apply what you learn about creating programs in Access to these other applications.

The Project Explorer

One of the fundamental tools in the Visual Basic Editor is the Project Explorer. The *Project Explorer* presents a hierarchical view of all of the projects and modules currently open in Access, including both standard and class modules.

The Modules Window

You write all of your VBA code in the *Modules window*. The Modules window acts as a basic text editor, but it includes several tools to help you write error-free code. Access also provides hints as you write your code to help you avoid syntax errors.

The Object Browser

There are hundreds of objects available to you. Each object has a myriad of properties, methods, and events. Trying to keep track of all of them is daunting, but the Visual Basic Editor supplies the *Object Browser*, which helps you examine the complete collection of objects, properties, and methods available for a given object.

Creating a Standard Module

All standard modules in a database are listed in the Modules section of the database window. You can open a module for editing or create a new module. When you edit a module or design a new one, Access automatically starts the Visual Basic Editor.

SEE ALSO

See "Enhancing a Database with VBA" on page 246 for more information on standard modules.

TIP

Open the Visual Basic Editor. *You can open the Visual Basic Editor directly by pressing and holding Alt while you press F11. You can also toggle back and forth between Access and Visual Basic Editor by pressing and holding Alt whle you press F11.*

Create a New Standard Module

1 In the Database window, click Modules on the Objects bar.

2 Click the New button.

Access starts the Visual Basic Editor, opening a new module window.

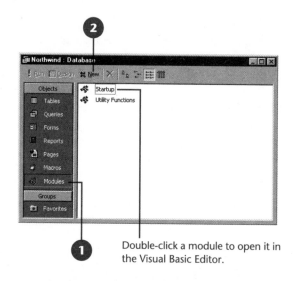

Double-click a module to open it in the Visual Basic Editor.

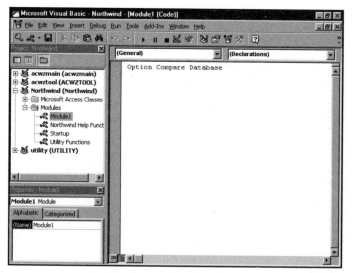

Understanding Parts
of the Visual Basic Editor

The Project Explorer displays a hierarchical list of all open projects and modules.

The Modules window allows you to enter VBA commands.

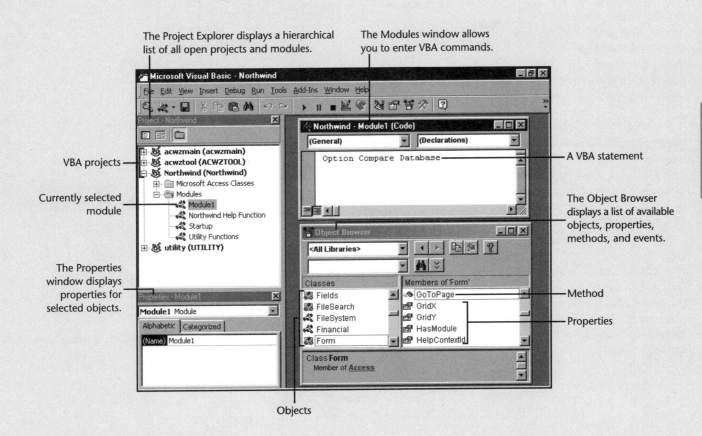

VBA projects

Currently selected module

The Properties window displays properties for selected objects.

A VBA statement

The Object Browser displays a list of available objects, properties, methods, and events.

Method

Properties

Objects

Creating a Sub Procedure

You can either type a Sub procedure directly into the Modules window, or the Visual Basic Editor can insert it for you. Sub procedures all begin with the line:

```
Sub ProcedureName( )
```

where *ProcedureName* is the name of the Sub procedure. If the Sub procedure includes arguments, enter them between the opening and closing parentheses. Not every Sub procedure requires arguments.

After entering the first line, which names the procedure, you insert the procedure's VBA commands. Each Sub procedure ends with the line:

```
End Sub
```

Create a Sub Procedure

① In the Visual Basic Editor, click the Modules window to select it.

② Click the Insert menu, and then click Procedure.

③ Enter the procedure's name.

④ Click the Sub option button, if necessary.

⑤ Click OK.

The Editor inserts the opening and closing lines of the new Sub procedure.

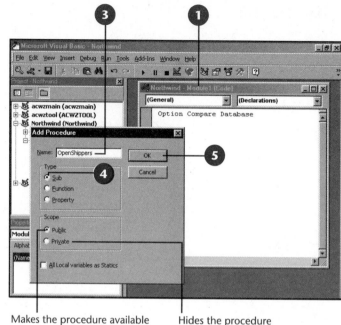

Makes the procedure available to other modules in the project

Hides the procedure from other modules

Indicates the Sub procedure is available to other modules

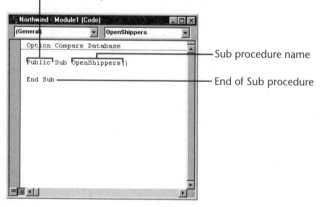

Sub procedure name

End of Sub procedure

Writing VBA Commands

You insert VBA commands by typing them into the appropriate place in the Module window. This, of course, requires some knowledge of VBA. Access provides online Help to assist you in writing VBA code.

The Visual Basic Editor also helps you with hints that help you complete a command accurately. If you have entered a command incorrectly, the Editor notifies you of the error and may suggest ways of correcting the problem.

One of the most useful VBA objects you'll encounter in writing VBA code is the *DoCmd* object, which represents Access commands. You can use DoCmd in your commands to perform basic operations, like opening tables, reports, and forms.

Write a VBA Command to Open a Table

1. Click the Modules window to activate it.

2. Click a blank line after the Sub *ProcedureName* command in the Modules window.

3. Type **DoCmd.** Make sure you include the period.

4. Double-click OpenTable in the list box that appears, and then press the Spacebar.

5. As indicated by the hints supplied by the Editor, type the name of a table from the current database. Make sure you enclose the name in quotation marks.

6. Type a comma.

7. Double-click acViewNormal to open the table in Normal view.

8. Type a comma.

9. Double-click acReadOnly to open the table in Read-only mode.

10. Press Enter to add a new blank line below the command.

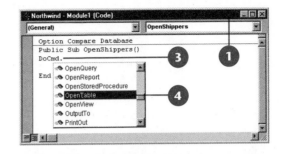

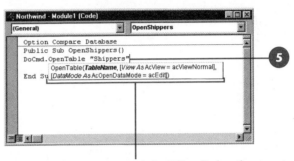

As you type the VBA command, the Editor displays the correct syntax. Optional arguments are enclosed in square brackets [ ].

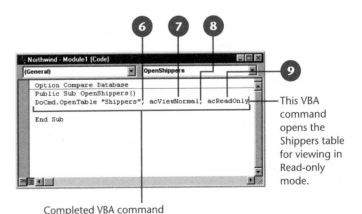

This VBA command opens the Shippers table for viewing in Read-only mode.

Completed VBA command

15

Running a Sub Procedure

After writing a Sub procedure, you may want to test it. You can run a Sub procedure from within the Visual Basic Editor, but you might have to return to Access to view the results. If the Sub procedure is a long one, you can also click buttons to pause it or to stop it altogether.

TIP

Run a procedure from the keyboard. *You can also run a Sub procedure by pressing F5. If you need to halt the procedure, press the Ctrl and the Break keys simultaneously.*

TIP

Rename a module. *If you want to rename a module, select the module from the Project Explorer and then enter a new name in the Name box, located in the Properties window.*

Run a Sub Procedure

1 Click the Save button on the Database toolbar to save changes to the VBA project.

2 Enter a name for your module if requested.

3 Click anywhere within the Sub procedure that you want to run.

4 Click the Run button on the Database toolbar.

If the Macros dialog box appears, select the macro you want to run and click run.

5 Return to Access, if necessary, to view the results of your Sub procedure.

Click to pause the procedure.

Click to stop the procedure.

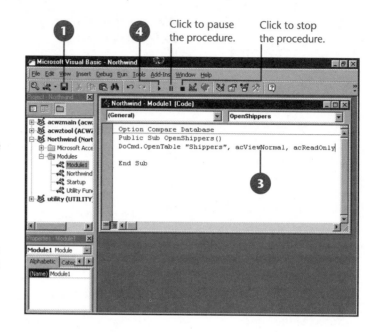

Copying Commands from the Object Browser

The Object Browser displays a hierarchical list of all of the objects, properties, methods, and events available to VBA procedures. The browser organizes these different objects into *libraries*. The list of libraries is not limited to those built into Access itself. It also includes libraries from other Access projects and add-ins. You can use the Object Browser as a reference tool, or you can copy and paste commands from the browser directly into your Sub procedures.

TIP

Search for objects. *The Object Browser contains a search tool that helps you locate an object's name.*

Insert an Object from the Object Browser

1. In the Visual Basic Editor, click the Object Browser button to display the Object Browser.

2. Click the Libraries drop-down arrow, and then select the library that contains your object.

3. Select the object you want to insert.

4. Click the Copy button.

5. Return to the Sub procedure in the Modules window.

6. Click the location in the Sub procedure where you want to paste the object name.

7. Click the Paste button on the toolbar.

Enter a search string for an object, property, method, or event.

Click to search for an object, property, method, or event.

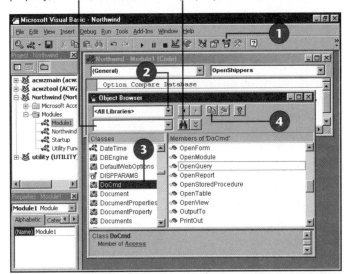

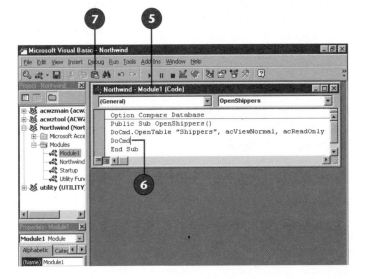

15

Creating a Custom Function

In addition to Sub procedures, you can also create function procedures that Access uses as custom functions. Each function procedure begins with the line:

`FunctionName( )`

where *FunctionName* is the name of the function procedure. Within the parentheses, place any variables needed for the calculation of the function. You can learn more about variables from Access's online Help.

After statement of the function's name and variables, add VBA commands to calculate the result of the function. The function concludes with the End Function line.

Create a Custom Function

1 In the Visual Basic Editor, open a Modules window, click the Insert menu, and then click Procedure.

2 Enter the function's name.

3 Click the Function option button.

4 Click OK.

The Editor inserts the opening and closing lines of your new custom function.

5 Enter variable names needed for the function, separated by commas.

6 Enter VBA commands required to calculate the function's value.

7 Insert a line assigning the calculated value to a variable with the same name as the function.

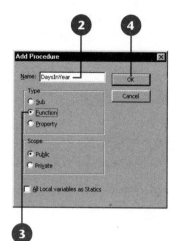

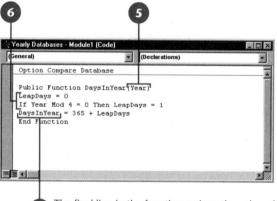

7 The final line in the function assigns the value of the number of days in the year to the DaysInYear function.

Running a Custom Function

Once you've completed a custom function, you can use it in any Access query, report, or form. The easiest way to access the function is through the Expression Builder.

TIP

Save a module. *Save changes to your module before using a customized function. Otherwise, the function will not appear in the Expression Builder.*

SEE ALSO

See "Enhancing a Database with VBA" on page 246 for more information on function procedures.

Run a Custom Function

1 Open Expression Builder from any query, report, or form.

2 Double-click the Functions folder.

3 Double-click the name of the project containing your custom function (usually the name of the current database).

4 Click the module containing the custom function.

5 Double-click the name of the custom function.

6 Edit the function, replacing the variable names within the parentheses with the appropriate field names or constants.

7 Click OK.

8 Test your query, form, or report to verify the values returned by the custom function.

The variable name is replaced with a reference to the Year field in the Years table.

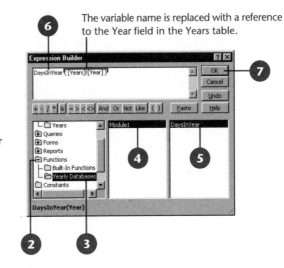

Values in this column are calculated using the custom function, DaysInYear.

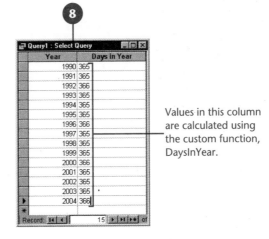

15

Creating a Class Module for a Form or Report

Similar to the standard modules that you create, you can also create class modules with the Visual Basic Editor. You usually begin a class module in Design view for a form or report. In most cases, class modules are associated with events such as clicking a form button or opening the form. Unlike standard modules, class modules do not appear in the Modules Object list in the Database window. Instead, you can access them from within the Project Explorer.

SEE ALSO

See "Enhancing a Database with VBA" on page 246 for more information on Class modules.

Create a Class Module for a Form or Report

1 Display a form or report in Design view.

2 Open the property sheet for a control or object within the form or report.

3 Click the Event tab.

4 Click the event box that you want to associate with a VBA procedure.

5 Click the Build button.

6 Click Code Builder.

7 Click OK.

The Visual Basic Editor opens a Modules window and automatically creates an Event procedure for the control and event you selected.

8 Enter the VBA commands you want.

The Command 1 button control

The property sheet for the Command 1 button control

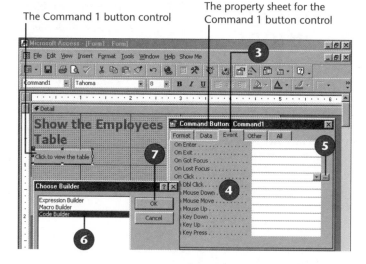

The Visual Basic Editor automatically creates an event procedure assigned to the Click event and the Command 1 button control.

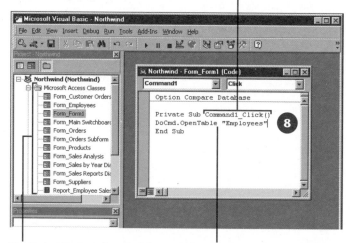

The Project Explorer lists all of the form and report modules, as well as other class modules.

When the user clicks the Command 1 button on the form, Access will open the Employees table.

Setting Project Properties

By default, Access assigns the same name to the project containing your VBA modules and procedures as your database's name. You can change the project's name to make it more descriptive. You can also password-protect your VBA project to keep other users from accessing and changing your procedures.

TIP

Remember your project password. *Save your password. If you lose it, you will not be able to open your code to edit it later.*

SEE ALSO

See "Optimizing Performance with an MDE File" on page 260 for information on protecting your VBA code by saving the database in the MDE file format.

Set Project Properties

1. Open the Visual Basic Editor by pressing and holding Alt while pressing F11.

2. Select your project from the list of projects in Project Explorer.

3. Click the Tools menu, and then click *ProjectName* Properties, where *ProjectName* is the current name of your project.

4. Click the General tab.

5. Enter a new name for your project, if necessary.

6. Enter a description of your VBA project.

7. Click the Protection tab.

8. Click the Lock Project for Viewing check box if you want to keep others from viewing your project's source code.

9. Enter a password to unlock the project for viewing.

10. Confirm the unlocking password.

11. Click OK.

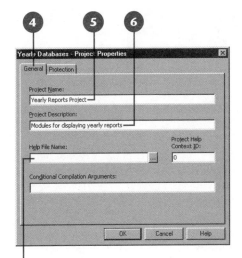

If you've created a Help file for your project, enter the name and location here.

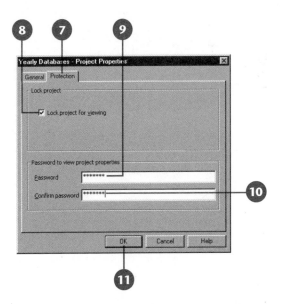

Debugging a Procedure

The Visual Basic Editor provides several tools to help you write error-free code. However, sometimes a procedure does not act the way you expect it to. To deal with this problem, you can use the Editor's debugging tools to help you locate the source of the trouble.

One the most common approaches to debug failed code is to "walk through" the procedure step by step, examining each thing the procedure does. In this way, you can try to locate the exact statement that is causing you trouble.

Stepping Through a Procedure

1. Click the View menu, point to Toolbars, and then click Debug.

2. Click the first line of the procedure you want to debug.

3. Click the Step Into button on the Debug toolbar to run the current statement and then to move to the next line in the procedure.

4. Continue clicking the Step Into button to move through the procedure one line at a time, examining the results of the procedure as you go.

5. Click the Stop button on the Debug toolbar to halt the procedure at a specific line.

The Editor highlights the line currently running in the program.

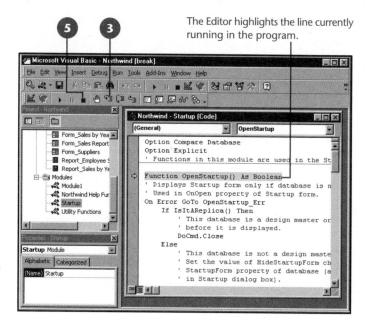

Identifying VBA
Debugging Tools

Click to open the Immediate window.

Click to open the Locals window.

Click to open the Watch window.

The Locals window shows the value and type of all variables used in your VBA procedure. You can use the Locals window to check the effect of your VBA procedure on all variables.

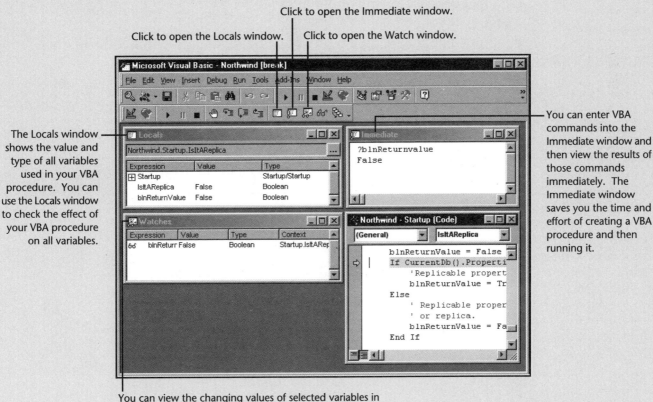

You can enter VBA commands into the Immediate window and then view the results of those commands immediately. The Immediate window saves you the time and effort of creating a VBA procedure and then running it.

You can view the changing values of selected variables in the Watch window. The Watch window helps you check the effect of your VBA procedure on these variable values.

Optimizing Performance with an MDE File

If you share your modules with others, you may want convert the database file to MDE format. In creating an MDE file, Access removes the editable source code and then compacts the database. Your VBA programs will continue to run, but others cannot view or edit them.

There are several advantages to converting a database to MDE format. In MDE format a database is smaller, and its performance will improve as it optimizes memory usage. Note, however, that you should create an MDE file only after the original database has been thoroughly tested.

Make an MDE File

1 Close your database.

2 In the Access program window, click the Tools menu, point to Database Utilities, and then click Make MDE File.

3 Locate and select the database you want to convert to MDE format.

4 Click Make MDE.

5 Specify a location

6 Enter a name for the MDE file.

7 Click Save.

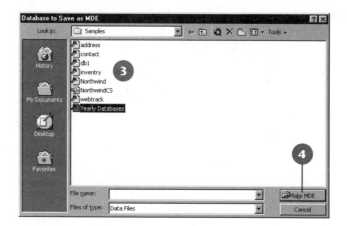

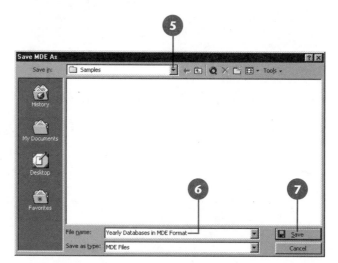

Index

Joan and Patrick Carey, a husband-and-wife team, have authored, developed, or managed over 40 books in the software industry, for both academic and trade audiences. Topics that the Careys have tackled include statistical analysis with Microsoft Excel, surfing the World Wide Web, and understanding operating systems and networks. When they're not staying up late writing, they keep busy with their four young children. When they're not writing and rearing, they sleep. Joan, Patrick, and the kiddies live in Madison, Wisconsin, but can also be found peak-bagging in Estes Park, Colorado, during the summer.

Acknowledgments

We would like to thank David Beskeen and Steve Johnson and all the staff at Perspection for their vision, hard work, and enthusiastic support for this project. We are especially grateful for their team spirit and active desire to make book production a positive, affirming experience. Copy editor Jane Pedicini deserves special mention for her high editorial standards. We dedicate this book to our four little sons, John Paul, Thomas, Peter, and Michael, who have so cheerfully accommodated the demands that go with such a project.

The manuscript for this book was prepared and submitted to Microsoft Press in electronic form. Text files were prepared using Microsoft Word 97 for Windows 95. Pages were composed in PageMaker for Windows, with text in Stone Sans and display type in Stone Serif. Composed pages were delivered to the printer as electronic files.

Cover Design
Tim Girvin Design

Graphic Layout
David Beskeen

Compositors
Gary Bellig
Tracy Teyler

Proofreader
Jane Pedicini

Indexer
Michael Brackney
Savage Indexing Service

Stay in the *running* for maximum *productivity.*

These are *the* answer books for business users of Microsoft® Office 2000. They are packed with everything from quick, clear instructions for new users to comprehensive answers for power users—the authoritative reference to keep by your computer and use every day. THE RUNNING SERIES—learning solutions made by Microsoft.

- RUNNING MICROSOFT EXCEL 2000
- RUNNING MICROSOFT OFFICE 2000 PREMIUM
- RUNNING MICROSOFT OFFICE 2000 PROFESSIONAL
- RUNNING MICROSOFT OFFICE 2000 SMALL BUSINESS
- RUNNING MICROSOFT WORD 2000
- RUNNING MICROSOFT POWERPOINT® 2000
- RUNNING MICROSOFT ACCESS 2000
- RUNNING MICROSOFT INTERNET EXPLORER 5
- RUNNING MICROSOFT FRONTPAGE® 2000
- RUNNING MICROSOFT OUTLOOK® 2000

mspress.microsoft.com